Praise for *Smart Client Deployment with ClickOnce*

"ClickOnce demos may look simple, but those techniques only work for simple applications. Brian Noyes gives us the information we need to use ClickOnce in the real world, and he does it with a comprehensive and organized presentation. If you expect your smart client application to move very far beyond 'Hello, World,' you'll want this book to help you deploy it."

—*Billy Hollis, president/owner, Elysian Consulting, Microsoft Regional Director*

"Once again Brian has outdone himself. As a writer, I tend to be very critical of all technical publications, including my own . . . and it is such a pleasure to read anything Brian writes because he studies his topics well, resulting in an accurate, thorough, yet concise piece of work. ClickOnce being a new technology that deals with the pains we all have with application deployment, versioning, and security, it is important to have a text that will guide you through the learning process, give you sound advice for adopting the technology, and explain why you should even care. Brian gives his readers all of that."

—*Michele Leroux Bustamante, chief architect, IDesign, Microsoft Regional Director*

"ClickOnce is the key to Windows and smart client deployment. Brian's book is the key to successfully using ClickOnce. This book walks you through using ClickOnce, from the basics to advanced scenarios. It is an excellent resource."

—*Rockford Lhotka, principal technology evangelist, Magenic Technologies, Microsoft Regional Director*

"Brian covers ClickOnce with a view to real-world deployment issues, which is obviously based on real-world experience. In and of itself, that is enough for me to buy the book. However, it is an even better investment by virtue of the fact that ClickOnce is a core part of the .NET Framework for Windows Forms 2.0 now, and Windows Presentation Foundation in the future."

—*Michael Weinhardt, SDK programmer/writer, Application Model, Windows Presentation Foundation, Microsoft*

"This book covers the most important ingredient needed for the success of a smart client application—deployment. The author's unassuming writing style, combined with his in-depth coverage of the topic, makes this book an invaluable resource for all serious smart client developers."

—*Vishwas Lele, principal architect, Applied Information Sciences, Microsoft Regional Director*

Smart Client Deployment with ClickOnce

Microsoft .NET Development Series

John Montgomery, *Series Advisor*
Don Box, *Series Advisor*
Martin Heller, *Series Editor*

The Microsoft .NET Development Series is supported and developed by the leaders and experts of Microsoft development technologies including Microsoft architects. The books in this series provide a core resource of information and understanding every developer needs in order to write effective applications and managed code. Learn from the leaders how to maximize your use of the .NET Framework and its programming languages.

Titles in the Series

For more information go to www.awprofessional.com/msdotnetseries/

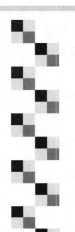

Smart Client Deployment with ClickOnce

Deploying Windows Forms Applications with ClickOnce

■ Brian Noyes

✦✦ Addison-Wesley

Upper Saddle River, NJ • Boston • Indianapolis • San Francisco
New York • Toronto • Montreal • London • Munich • Paris • Madrid
Capetown • Sydney • Tokyo • Singapore • Mexico City

Many of the designations used by manufacturers and sellers to distinguish their products are claimed as trademarks. Where those designations appear in this book, and the publisher was aware of a trademark claim, the designations have been printed with initial capital letters or in all capitals.

The .NET logo is either a registered trademark or trademark of Microsoft Corporation in the United States and/or other countries and is used under license from Microsoft.

The author and publisher have taken care in the preparation of this book, but make no expressed or implied warranty of any kind and assume no responsibility for errors or omissions. No liability is assumed for incidental or consequential damages in connection with or arising out of the use of the information or programs contained herein.

The publisher offers excellent discounts on this book when ordered in quantity for bulk purchases or special sales, which may include electronic versions and/or custom covers and content particular to your business, training goals, marketing focus, and branding interests. For more information, please contact:

U.S. Corporate and Government Sales
(800) 382-3419
corpsales@pearsontechgroup.com

For sales outside the United States please contact:

International Sales
international@pearsoned.com

This Book Is Safari Enabled

The Safari® Enabled icon on the cover of your favorite technology book means the book is available through Safari Bookshelf. When you buy this book, you get free access to the online edition for 45 days.

Safari Bookshelf is an electronic reference library that lets you easily search thousands of technical books, find code samples, download chapters, and access technical information whenever and wherever you need it.

To gain 45-day Safari Enabled access to this book:

- Go to http://www.awprofessional.com/safarienabled
- Complete the brief registration form
- Enter the coupon code ZPDA-TLPC-LCGM-SUCT-T4ZK

If you have difficulty registering on Safari Bookshelf or accessing the online edition, please e-mail customer-service@safaribooksonline.com.

Visit us on the Web: www.awprofessional.com

Library of Congress Cataloging-in-Publication Data

Noyes, Brian.

 Smart client deployment with ClickOnce : deploying Windows Forms applications with ClickOnce / Brian Noyes.
    p. cm.
 Includes index.
 ISBN 0-321-19769-0 (pbk. : alk. paper) 1. ClickOnce (Electronic resource) 2. Computer software—Development. 3. Microsoft Windows (Computer file) 4. Microsoft .NET. I. Title.

 QA76.76.D47N693 2007
 005.3—dc22

                                          2006035484

ISBN 0-321-19769-0
Text printed in the United States on recycled paper at Courier in Stoughton, Massachusetts.
First printing, December 2006

To Robin, printed words can never convey how much I love you and treasure sharing every day with you. Thank you for your support and patience with my exceptional ability to over-commit myself to work.

To Nathan, it is a joy to watch you grow and learn, and my heart swells just thinking about all the experiences we will share together over the coming years.

Contents

Figures

Foreword

IN MAY OF 2003 I embarked on a smart client journey that is even more relevant and interesting today. I mean, think about it. There is a reason we switched to building Web applications in the late 90s/early 00s—and that reason was the pain of COM-based Windows application deployments and the ease of Web-based deployments. Deployment is also the single most important ingredient to the success of the smart client revolution. Because of .NET's ClickOnce, the smart client revolution is in full swing.

The most misunderstood thing about ClickOnce (and possibly the most misunderstood concept in all of .NET) is the result of the simple five-minute demo that most .NET developers have seen or done. Because of this powerful yet simple demo, most assume that ClickOnce is a simple implementation in the Visual Studio tool, when ClickOnce is actually part of the .NET Framework itself. It is true that ClickOnce is mainly driven through Visual Studio project configuration, tools, and processes—not through code. But ClickOnce is so much more than that simple demo. This is very important and is the reason that this book is so important. This also means that ClickOnce is "industrial strength" enough to allow developers to build deployment tools based on ClickOnce so that network and infrastructure folks can deploy the applications. And there is a .NET ecosystem forming that consists of third-party tools based on ClickOnce technologies.

In addition, the reason this book is so important is also the most intriguing to me. Experts are predicting another paradigm shift in how software applications are delivered and I agree with them. This paradigm shift is the elimination of company-hosted, server-based applications and the elimination of extranet infrastructure in favor of allowing these applications to live on servers for which these companies purchase a share or processing time. It's a similar model to the one we used when I started in technology twenty-five years ago. I have some gray hair. I have been doing this a long time, which means back in my day I wrote some pretty mean JCL to allocate resources to my colleagues' COBOL applications. In those days, every compile cost money, and all application time was rented on the mainframe. Although clearly not the same, this paradigm shift is interesting because of the similarities.

Microsoft calls this software a service, and we have recently seen the popularity and success of this in a number of software vendors in addition to Microsoft with its Office-Live service. (SalesForce.com is one of them.) ClickOnce is the key technology that will facilitate this paradigm shift, and it will become popular because it is cost effective. Of course, many large companies will likely still carry the expense associated with hosting their own applications, but this type of expense will just not make sense for many small and mid-sized companies who will move to this hosted model for shrink-wrapped and custom applications. ClickOnce will pave the way for this model.

I have had the pleasure to know Brian Noyes for many years. He is a friend and a colleague. We have hiked the Malaysian rain forest together, we have ridden elephants together, and many times we have imbibed a number of malted beverages together—discussing the issues of the day, whether they be in technology or in life. I have also had the pleasure to meet his lovely wife, Robin, and his pride and joy—his son, Nathan. Brian is a fellow Microsoft Regional Director and Microsoft MVP. Brian is a fantastic author and speaker and one heck of a great software architect. There are only a few people in this world who know ClickOnce in any significant depth, and even fewer who could explain it well in a book like this. Brian is one of them. His talent and dedication to this book is a testament to his talent and character.

—*Tim Huckaby*
CEO, InterKnowlogy

Preface

DEPLOYMENT HAS BEEN a thorn in most developers' sides for a long time. Developing complex distributed applications is challenging enough just from a design and implementation perspective. Failing to plan for deployment or having the deployed environment change on you can kill an application quickly, no matter how well you plan for it. ClickOnce does not solve this problem, but it definitely takes a big step in the right direction for streamlining deployment of smart client applications.

I was first exposed to ClickOnce more than three years ago at an early adopter lab on the Microsoft campus in Redmond. At the time, I was just starting to get immersed in smart client technology and beginning to think about how to address all aspects of the application lifecycle as an architect. Having experienced a fair amount of deployment pain myself in the past, I instantly fell in love with ClickOnce as a technology. I quickly saw the potential for ClickOnce to be a key enabler for the broad adoption of smart client architectures because without a way to get those smart client applications in your users' hands, you might as well not build them.

The most common question that I got as I was working on this book was, "How can you write a whole book on ClickOnce?" This usually came from someone who had seen demos of ClickOnce but had not yet tried to use it for something real. ClickOnce is incredibly powerful, yet it seems simple on the surface. It takes only five to ten minutes to run an end-to-end demo of what ClickOnce can do for you. When people have seen this kind of presentation of ClickOnce, they do not realize that ClickOnce addresses a lot more than a single common deployment scenario. However, whenever you try to provide flexibility and power, a fair amount of complexity also comes along with it.

I think the ClickOnce team did a really good job of making the simple, straightforward use of ClickOnce as easy as possible. If you are building a new smart client application from scratch with ClickOnce in mind, using ClickOnce to deploy it requires minimal effort for both your administrators and your users. However, real applications are rarely simple and straightforward (even though, because of poor architecture, the complexity is often unnecessary or disproportionate to what the applications are designed to do). ClickOnce has many variations and options that let you address a broad range of scenarios to deal with those complexities. And once you start getting into those capabilities, you dive into the deep end of the ClickOnce pool and really need to understand a lot more about what is going on under the covers; what the effects are of setting publishing, update, and security options different from the defaults; how your application is going to behave in the ClickOnce runtime environment; and so on.

Who Should Read This Book?

This book is written for those developers and architects who need to understand the full range of capabilities of ClickOnce so that they can make educated decisions early in the development lifecycle and put those decisions into practice when the product is getting close to complete. You will need this understanding to make sure you can get your smart client applications deployed through ClickOnce and to address the complexities of real-world applications in that environment. It is primarily written for intermediate to advanced developers or architects, but IT professionals who are responsible for deploying and maintaining ClickOnce applications can also get a lot out of most of the chapters as well.

This is not a book about programming, although there are aspects of ClickOnce covered in several of the chapters that require coding to use. ClickOnce is mainly driven through Visual Studio project configuration, tools, and processes, not through code. So a fair percentage of the book will describe these aspects, and only a small portion will discuss code directly.

There is a programmatic API that is discussed in several chapters, and there are other coding practices that are important from within your application that can affect the deployment and execution of a ClickOnce application. For the sections that cover coding, I expect that readers already know how to code .NET applications. I will point out appropriate references when necessary for complex topics, but to understand the code samples, you need to have some experience developing Windows Forms applications in .NET.[1]

Conventions

Deploying ClickOnce applications is mostly about tools and less about code. However, there are a number of code samples in this book, and to help make things easier, I have adopted some common conventions.

First, any time I refer to classes, variables, namespaces, and other artifacts that manifest themselves in code, I will use a monospace font to make it clear if I am talking about an instance of the `ApplicationDeployment` class as opposed to talking about a coding construct in a conceptual way. Short code listings will be presented inline within the text using a monospaced font as well:

```
private void Form1_Load(object sender, EventArgs e)
{
    if (ApplicationDeployment.IsNetworkDeployed) { ... }
}
```

Longer listings will use a similar font, but will be broken out into labeled listings that can be referred to throughout the text (based on listing numbers). Within code listings, I will sometimes set in **bold** particularly relevant portions of the code, especially to highlight "evolving code." I may remove details that are not relevant to a discussion, and if so will

---

1. *Windows Forms 2.0 Programming* by Chris Sells and Michael Weinhardt (Addison-Wesley, 2006) is the best overall reference and tutorial for learning all aspects of Windows Forms programming. My other book in this series, *Data Binding with Windows Forms 2.0* (Addison-Wesley, 2006), will give you a deep dive on how to present data in your applications. *Programming .NET Components, Second Edition*, by Juval Löwy (O'Reilly & Associates, 2005) is an excellent deep dive on overall .NET programming, and many of the topics covered in that book are prerequisites for the more advanced code samples in this book.

insert a comment that indicates that there are more details, identifiable by a comment with an ellipses (//...). What this means is that more code is needed to complete the example or that there exists more code generated by the designer, but you don't need it to understand the concept. On occasion, I will add explanatory comments to code in order to show context:

```
private void OnCheckForUpdates(object sender, EventArgs e)
{
    // Always confirm you are running through ClickOnce
    if (ApplicationDeployment.IsNetworkDeployed)
    {
        // Hold a reference to the current deployment
        ApplicationDeployment current =
            ApplicationDeployment.CurrentDeployment;
        // Check to see if an update is available on the server
        if (current.CheckForUpdate())
        {
            //...
        }
    }
}
```

System Requirements

This book was written using the released version of Visual Studio 2005 and the .NET Framework 2.0. ClickOnce capabilities are available in all versions of Visual Studio, including Visual C# 2005 Express and Visual Basic 2005 Express. You do not need Visual Studio to use ClickOnce because it is a core capability of the .NET Framework, but to use ClickOnce for any serious project, you will need Visual Studio to do the initial publishing. Throughout the book, I will refer to Visual Studio instead of Visual Studio 2005 for brevity, but you can always infer that I mean Visual Studio 2005 or one of the Express versions (even though they do not have "Studio" in their official names).

If you plan to run the samples available from the download site or the walkthroughs and code listings in this book, you will need a version of Visual Studio 2005, Visual C# 2005 Express, or Visual Basic 2005 Express installed on your machine. One of the samples uses a SQL Server 2005 Compact Edition database to provide sample data to the application, but it includes the libraries needed to run that. One sample uses the Northwind database to provide sample data. Because the particular functionality of the application is not important to the topic being covered (how to deploy and update these applications with ClickOnce), don't get wrapped up in trying to get these samples running if you don't already have the databases available; just create an empty Windows Forms application and use it.

Choice of Language

I chose to present the code samples in this book in C#. The downloadable code is available in both C# and Visual Basic. It is a fact of life that there will continue to be a mix of C# and Visual Basic available in articles, books, and code samples for a long time to come. Even though I prefer C# myself, that is just a preference, and I feel that Visual Basic is a solid choice for developers who have a strong background in earlier versions of Visual Basic.

I firmly believe that to be an effective .NET developer, you need to be able to read code from either language, even if you spend most of your time with one. If you are not already comfortable reading C# code, I encourage you to use this opportunity to get comfortable with reading C#. It will expand your horizons in terms of the amount of reference material that is available to you, it may help you in your job, and it will give you bragging rights over the many silly and close-minded C# developers who can't or won't read Visual Basic.

Chapter Overview

This book steps you progressively through all of the concepts you will need to master to use ClickOnce to deploy real-world smart client applications. It starts with the basics in the first chapter, giving you a high-level view of ClickOnce and the surrounding context of smart client applications. Then it steps through deploying and updating applications, with all the associated options. It then focuses on more of the infrastructure for ClickOnce deployment, including how to manage application files, security, prerequisites, and advanced capabilities. It ends with an appendix that tells you what is different with respect to Windows Presentation Foundation application deployment (not much).

Here is a quick breakdown of the contents of each chapter.

Chapter 1: Introduction to ClickOnce. This chapter sets the context for the rest of the book. It starts by describing what a smart client application is and what deployment challenges ClickOnce was designed to address. It describes the high-level features of ClickOnce, and then walks you through a sample deployment and update of a client application using ClickOnce. This chapter wraps up describing the system requirements for ClickOnce, how it relates to other deployment technologies, when to use it and when not to, and a quick discussion of smart client architecture.

Chapter 2: Initial Deployment with ClickOnce. This chapter covers the process of publishing an initial version of an application and deploying it to clients. It discusses all of the publishing options that you have available for getting your applications placed on the deployment server and what that process involves using Visual Studio. It describes what happens when the user deploys the application to the client machine using Click-Once from an end user's perspective, and what is going on under the covers. It finishes by describing the process of manually publishing your application using the SDK Mage tools for an environment where Visual Studio cannot access the production servers.

Chapter 3: Automatic Application Updates. This chapter covers the capabilities of ClickOnce for automatically deploying application updates to users. The publishing for updates is discussed briefly because it is effectively the same as for initial deployment. Then the deployment process is detailed, showing what the experience is for users and what the options are. The chapter describes all of the options you have for configuring when and how updates occur. It discusses what happens behind the scenes on the deployment server as well as on the client machine when an update is detected and deployed. It also covers how to manage rolling back an update either from the client or the server side.

Chapter 4: On-Demand Updates. This chapter builds on Chapter 3, showing how to use the programmatic API for ClickOnce to trigger updates from your application code. It discusses performing synchronous and asynchronous updates, detecting updates, and pulling them down when desired using the API. It covers several strategies for doing the updates asynchronously to avoid blocking the client application. It also describes other functionality exposed through the API, including the ability to check detailed update information and find out about the version of the application that is currently deployed on the client machine.

Chapter 5: Application and Data File Management. This chapter discusses in detail managing the files that your application is composed of. It describes how ClickOnce treats those files, how to select and control what files get deployed with your application, and where they will end up on the client machine. It discusses download groups, which provide a way to download portions of your application files on demand. It discusses managing application data files, and how those files are migrated by ClickOnce when an application update occurs. It covers using plug-in DLLs in a ClickOnce application to enhance your application's functionality with individual optional modules. The chapter closes by covering how to manage the application files that get published using the SDK Mage tools.

Chapter 6: ClickOnce Security. This chapter discusses the security features and protections of ClickOnce in detail. It covers the deployment time and runtime protections for the client machine, and discusses the tamper protections for the application files both on the server and client sides. The chapter describes how to configure and control what permissions the application requires, and how those permissions are evaluated and granted on the client machine. It discusses how user prompting can be used for permission elevation, and how to use the Trusted Publisher mechanism to automatically elevate permissions based on an administrator's predeployed publisher certificate. It covers managing the ClickOnce manifest digital signature with publisher certificates. Finally, the chapter covers how to protect sections of your application from malicious code and includes a quick introduction to using role-based security in .NET to restrict permissions in the client application based on user roles.

Chapter 7: Prerequisite Deployment with the Bootstrapper. This chapter covers how to get things preinstalled on the client machine that cannot be deployed through ClickOnce. It discusses the Bootstrapper's features for wrapping multiple installer packages and running them through a single launch experience on the client machine. It describes creating and configuring Bootstrapper manifest files, and what the runtime experience is when deploying prerequisites. The chapter steps through several scenarios of types of files you might want to deploy with the Bootstrapper.

Chapter 8: Advanced ClickOnce Topics. This chapter covers a variety of additional questions that often come up for ClickOnce applications to address specialized scenarios. The chapter discusses using command line parameters, debugging ClickOnce applications, deploying non-.NET applications with ClickOnce, working with the Firefox Web browser, and deploying COM components with your application, to name a few.

Appendix A: ClickOnce Deployment of WPF Applications. The appendix covers the differences in using ClickOnce with Windows Presentation Foundation (WPF) applications. For the most part ClickOnce works the same with WPF, but there are some subtle differences. The appendix covers the Web Browser Application model, what you need to do differently when creating and publishing the project, and how the application deploys and runs on the client machine.

Book's Web Site and Sample Download Code

The Web site for this book is at www.softinsight.com/clickoncebook. All of the sample code in this book is available for download on that site. Links are available on the site to other ClickOnce-related resources, including the author's blog (www.softinsight.com/bnoyes/).

Acknowledgments

WITH EACH BOOK that I complete, I grow to appreciate even more how much of a collaborative effort a book is. Despite the single author name on the cover, there are many people who have contributed to this book to make it what it is. For all that you find good in the book, thank them. If you find fault with anything, blame me—it was my responsibility to transcribe the knowledge and insights that they shared into a readable and understandable form.

My wife, Robin, was—as always—very supportive and understanding of all the long hours, missed opportunities for spending time with her, my son, Nathan, friends, and family. I am truly blessed to have found a beautiful, intelligent, loving, and caring person like her and lucky to have held onto her for more than fifteen years now.

On the technical side, I am not overstating things in any way, shape, or form by saying that this book would not have been possible without the constant and unflagging support of Jamie Cool, Saurabh Pant, Patrick Darragh, and Sameer Bhangar from the ClickOnce product team at Microsoft. There are a lot of hidden nooks and crannies in ClickOnce, and they helped me find and shed light on all of them. Adding to their inside knowledge of the product was the outstanding review support from my technical review team: Bill Woodruff, Sameer Bhangar, Vishwas Lele, and Cristof Falk.

Everyone I work with from Addison-Wesley continues to reinforce my conviction that they are the best technical book publishers in the world to work with as an author. In particular, Joan Murray's constant attention, guidance, and understanding throughout the writing and publishing process was essential. Joan, you are a treat to work with! Sheri Cain did a wonderful job managing the technical editing process for me, Rebecca Greenberg once again did a great job turning my geek-speak into English, and Curt Johnson and Eric Garulay are always there to answer my questions on the marketing and promotion of my books.

I also want to thank my friend and mentor, Tim Huckaby, for writing the foreword for this book. I was lucky enough to meet and become friends with Tim a few years back. Besides being a really smart guy and running a very successful company (InterKnowlogy), Tim has been very influential in evangelizing smart client technology. I couldn't think of a more perfect person to introduce the topic of the book for me.

Last, but not least, thanks to my colleagues Juval Löwy, Michele Leroux Bustamante, and Mark Michaelis from IDesign. I am privileged to work with the smartest people in the industry, and my knowledge and abilities continue to grow as a direct result of my association with them.

About the Author

Brian Noyes is a software architect, trainer, writer, and speaker with IDesign, Inc. (www.idesign.net), a premier .NET architecture and design consulting and training company. He is a Microsoft Regional Director and Microsoft Most Valuable Professional (MVP), and has been developing software systems for more than sixteen years. He speaks at many major software conferences around the world, and writes for a variety of software journals and magazines. He lives in Alexandria, Virginia, but is a Southern California surf bum at heart, having grown up there. Prior to becoming a full-time software developer, Brian flew F-14 Tomcats (yep, that's them on the cover!) in the U.S. Navy and graduated from the Navy Fighter Weapons School (TopGun) and the U.S. Naval Test Pilot School. Brian has a master's degree in computer science from the University of Colorado, Boulder, a master's degree in aerospace engineering from the Naval Postgraduate School, and a bachelor's degree in aerospace engineering from the U.S. Naval Academy.

■ 1 ■
Introduction to ClickOnce

I T HAS NEVER been easier to build rich, interactive, stateful applications than it is today with Windows Forms and the .NET Framework 2.0. With the combination of the Windows Forms features and controls and the Visual Studio 2005 design and coding capabilities, you can build rich client applications quicker and better than ever before. However, it doesn't matter how easy it is to build an application if you fail to get it into your users' hands. Ask almost any software architect or software project manager what phase of the development lifecycle causes them the most headaches, and you are likely to get "deployment" as the answer from a large percentage of them. The cost and effort involved in successfully deploying an application is often far greater than development organizations plan for. Deploying applications incorrectly can easily corrupt other applications or data on a machine, and wasting resources on complicated deployments keeps you from delivering functionality that users really care about.

ClickOnce is a new deployment technology that is part of the .NET Framework 2.0, and it addresses this challenge directly. ClickOnce can make it dramatically easier to deploy client applications and to support them with updates than any preceding technology that I have experienced. It is easy to employ, has many options that give you a lot of flexibility in the way you deploy your applications, and yet provides a lot of protection to prevent your deployment from harming other applications or data on the client machine in any way. The fact that it comes for free as part of the .NET Framework makes it that much more compelling.

ClickOnce targets client applications only, but it can be used for almost any .NET Windows Forms client application, regardless of size. It was specifically designed to reduce the pain of deployment for the Intranet environment enterprise client applications that need to be deployed to large numbers of desktops in corporate environments. But it also works well for broad-reaching consumer applications over the Internet, and for smaller utilities and internal applications as well.

This chapter will give you a high-level pass over ClickOnce and the surrounding smart client context. You will learn what smart clients are, why ClickOnce is important for smart clients, what deployment challenges exist, and how ClickOnce addresses them. You will see a quick example of using ClickOnce for the deployment and update of a simple sample application, which will be followed in subsequent chapters by much more detailed coverage of how the different aspects of ClickOnce work.

On the surface ClickOnce seems very simple, and if you deploy with the default settings, it is. But there are many options that you need to understand to take full advantage of the technology. There are also a number of subtle nuances to these ClickOnce options that you need to understand to employ ClickOnce in complex, real-world scenarios. This book will give you a deep understanding of those aspects that will let you fully exploit ClickOnce and have successful client application deployments, which will save you significant time and effort in getting your application into users' hands and keeping it updated and running throughout its lifecycle.

What Is a Smart Client Application?

Client applications can be created with a number of different technologies. You can create a client application that runs in a Web browser with any number of Web technologies that render HTML over a network. You can create a client application with dumb terminals attached to a mainframe. You can create a client application that runs from a command line in Windows or other operating systems. However, the best kind of client application for most users is an application with a graphical user interface.

Smart clients are a subset of all the Windows applications running out there, and they are distinguished by a number of common attributes. Smart clients

- Are rich client applications
- Are typically distributed applications
- Run securely on the client machine
- Support offline operations
- Are automatically network deployed and updated

An application does not have to support all of these attributes to qualify as a smart client. The only required attribute is that the application must have a rich client user interface to be considered a smart client, but many smart client applications share one or more of the other attributes as well. Let's step through each one to clarify what they mean.

Smart Clients Are Rich Client Applications

The term **rich client** is commonly used to describe a client application that runs as a Windows desktop application. This means it is a graphical user interface application running on the users' local machine desktops. It is an application whose windows are presented directly on the screen by the OS, taking advantage of the full range of presentation capabilities of the OS. These kinds of applications are also sometimes referred to as a *thick client* or a *fat client* to distinguish them from a **thin client,** which typically means an application that runs in a Web browser or as a special-purpose terminal that does not have a full end-user OS available.

Smart clients are first and foremost rich clients. They are designed to take advantage of the client OS and give users the richest, most interactive and stateful experience possible to make them more productive. This usually means a Windows Forms or Windows Presentation Foundation application in the .NET technology domain. It could also mean a Visual Studio Tools for Office application through one of the Microsoft Office client applications, or it could be a forms application on a smart device such as a PDA or mobile phone.

Smart Clients Are Typically Distributed Applications

The term *smart client* is typically used in the context of business applications. Business applications often need to have access to resources on other machines to satisfy the requirements they were designed to address. They are generally not stand-alone, monolithic applications that run completely on users' desktops only accessing local machine resources; they are applications that remotely communicate with code executing on another machine. That could be as simple as executing procedures or queries against a database on another machine on the local network, or it could involve invoking services on multiple machines distributed over the Internet, with those machines talking to other machines to get their work done. This is not a hard-and-fast rule, but the majority of applications that architects would classify as a smart client application are distributed across at least two tiers (machines).

Smart Clients Run Securely on the Client Machine

In order for smart client technology to be as successful as Web applications, they have to provide some of the same benefits as well. One of the advantages of Web browser-based applications is that they are well isolated inside the browser and cannot easily cause any harm to the local machine, including other applications installed on the machine and user data stored on the machine. There are certainly ways that those protections can be violated, but short of security bugs that usually get fixed very quickly, it usually involves a conscious decision by users to allow something to run in the browser that the browser would have blocked by default.

Smart client applications need a similar degree of protection that ensures that just because the application makes it onto their machine and is running, by default it should not be able to do any harm to the applications or data on the machine. In a .NET world, these protections are normally provided by .NET Code Access Security (CAS). ClickOnce adds its own configuration and enforcement mechanisms on top of CAS that help provide similar protections to browser-based applications. Chapter 6 will investigate the security mechanisms of ClickOnce in detail.

Smart Clients Support Offline Operations

Another common attribute of smart clients, although definitely not required to be considered a smart client, is that the application is designed to support offline or occasionally connected operations. This means that the application can be run on the client machine even if it is not currently connected to a network or able to communicate with the back-end services of the distributed application it is a part of.

This includes applications designed for mobile workers to go out into the field with some preloaded or cached data on their machine, interact with that data, and possibly create more. At some point the mobile worker reconnects the machine to a network, such as through a wireless connection in an airport or hotel, or by returning to the home office, and the data gets synchronized back with the rest of the system. It also addresses applications that are designed to work in low- or intermittent-bandwidth scenarios, such as a wireless-connected application in a factory or warehouse, or a medical services application that can roam in a hospital.

This requirement for offline capability immediately forces you to choose smart clients over browser-based applications. There is no sensible or practical way to design a browser-based application that can run when the browser cannot connect to the Web server that hosts the application. It is possible but overly complex and still does not satisfy the first goal of a rich user experience, so it is strongly discouraged. Usually offline functionality is a subset of the full capabilities of the client application. Some functionality may not make sense to allow users to perform if it requires live back-end data to function properly. For those functions, you will typically want to disable the functionality based on network connectivity and give users an indication of why some things are not available.

As far as ClickOnce is concerned, it supports offline operations by letting you launch a ClickOnce installed application even if you are disconnected from the network. ClickOnce is only about deployment and update of application files, so its only concern with respect to connectivity is whether it can connect to the deployment server or not. ClickOnce does not address or care whether you can access back-end services or data when you run. However, because most smart client applications are also distributed applications, you will need to decide whether offline operations even make sense for your application and what functions you will support when you are offline. All of those considerations go beyond the scope of ClickOnce and this book.

Smart Clients Are Automatically Network Deployed and Updated

Ah, finally we get to the meat of it! This attribute is what ClickOnce is all about. As will be discussed soon in the section Smart Client Deployment Challenges, there are lots of things that can go wrong when using traditional means of installing applications on a client machine. It also takes an immense amount of effort to perform client application deployments for large networked environments like the enterprise landscape of many companies today. Using an automated, distributed, network-based deployment and update mechanism can solve most of those problems. ClickOnce is specifically designed to provide that mechanism. ClickOnce also supports initial deployment via CD or DVD, but allows updates via the network for that mode of deployment as well.

Why Choose Smart Clients?

From the previous section's descriptions of the attributes of a smart client, the reasons should be fairly apparent. You should choose a smart client when you want

- To provide the richest user experience possible
- To take full advantage of the local hardware and software resources of the local client machine
- To support offline operations
- To have the fastest possible development timeline

The first three reasons were already explained in the previous section. The last one may not be apparent, but given a common baseline of developer knowledge, it is far quicker to develop rich, interactive, and stateful applications with Windows Forms or Windows Presentation Foundation than it is with Web browser application technologies. The complexities of the stateless nature of HTTP, combined with managing shared resources on the server, dealing with the fact that your code runs on a server in a multithreaded environment, and a number of other factors make Web server development much more complex than smart client development. As a result, you can usually provide equivalent or better capabilities in a smart client application than in a Web browser-based application and in a lot less time (assuming equal training in either technology).

Smart Client Deployment Challenges

The barrier to using rich clients in the past has always been the deployment problems associated with a rich client. To get a rich client running on a user's desktop, you have to get all of the files placed on the local machine's drive. With past development technologies such as COM, you also had to do different kinds of registration of the files or modules once they were on the machine. It was far too easy and common to have one application's installation cause problems for another installed application.

Specifically, the most common challenges that IT organizations faced when trying to put their client applications into production included

- DLLs deployed to system directories overwriting other versions of the same DLL, which corrupted other applications on the machine (otherwise known as "DLL Hell")
- COM registration of components replacing the registration of another version of the component on the same machine, also corrupting other applications (another form of DLL Hell)
- Poorly designed installer packages corrupting other data or files on the machine
- File permissions or access controls preventing remote installation of applications
- Users currently using an application or leaving an application running, preventing the administrators from being able to install an update to that application
- Installing the application on every user machine is costly, time consuming, and error prone
- Ensuring that the directory an application's files are placed in will be accessible to users and that it will not overwrite other application files

Using .NET as a development platform solves some of these problems. There is no longer any registration that is necessary to use a component on the machine. .NET applications can be deployed by simply copying them into a folder—they are then ready to be run. There is a deployment model of registering .NET assemblies in the Global Assembly Cache (GAC) that may make sense for some scenarios, but that is more designed for server-based applications and for components that are not installed directly as part of a single application. And for most assemblies, you could choose to run them locally with the deployed application to avoid the need for a system-shared registration. Even if you deploy to the GAC, the GAC supports side-by-side installation of multiple versions of the same assembly.

Deploying .NET applications through normal file copying mechanisms or Windows Installer technology still has its risks. Windows Installer packages have to be developed individually for each application you want to deploy. This involves choosing where to place files, registration steps, executing custom install scripts, and other things that present many opportunities to introduce errors that can cause damage to other applications and data on the machine. ClickOnce addresses those challenges directly.

Design Goals of ClickOnce

ClickOnce is designed to provide a trustworthy, flexible, and easy-to-use deployment and update mechanism for smart client applications. It lets you get rich client applications up and running on the client machine with minimal effort on the part of both the administrators and the users, while still presenting you with a lot of flexibility through the many update and deploy options that are exposed. Despite the number of options, the design of ClickOnce still makes it difficult to inadvertently cause errors on install.

The following are some of the key design goals of ClickOnce.

- Deployment of smart client applications should be as easy as deploying Web applications. The administrators should only have to place the application files on a single machine, and the deployment mechanism can take over from there to get those files out to all user's machines.

- Allowing users with low-privilege accounts (nonadministrative) to launch and install the application on their machines with minimal effort.

- The deployment process should be transparent and easy from a user's perspective. Running a ClickOnce-deployed application should be as easy to a user as going to a Web site, and should also be as easy as launching an application that is already installed on his or her local machine.
- Different applications have different requirements for when updates occur. ClickOnce lets the application developers determine what the update policy is, including when the application checks for updates and how the updated files get downloaded.
- The application being deployed in a distributed manner needs to be protected against compromise and needs to protect the client machine from installation-caused problems. ClickOnce provides install-time and runtime protections along these lines.

The goal of this book is to help you understand and master the features of ClickOnce in a step-by-step and systematic way, exploring its various options and capabilities, so that your applications can benefit from Click-Once deployment.

ClickOnce Features

I think it is useful to have an idea up front of all these features and options I keep mentioning before you dive into the details of each in the subsequent chapters in this book. At a high level, ClickOnce includes the following features.

- **Initial deployment:**
  - Automated initial deployment of applications to end users through the simple act of clicking on a link.
  - Ability to deploy applications via an HTTP or Universal Naming Convention (UNC) file path from the client machine.
  - Ability to do an initial deployment of an application via a CD or DVD, yet still allow automatic updates over HTTP or UNC from an online update server.

- **Updating applications:**
  - Automatic update of an installed application when updates become available on the deployment server.
  - Numerous update options specifying when updates occur.
  - Efficient downloads for updates that only download the files that have changed.
  - Isolation of individual versions on the client that allow users to restore the previous version.
  - Support for user- or application-invoked on-demand updates using a programmatic API.
- **Security:**
  - Security mechanisms that protect the files on the deployment server.
  - Security mechanisms that protect the client machine from harm at installation and runtime.
  - Authenticode certificate-based security infrastructure for identifying trusted publishers to avoid user prompting for permission elevation.
- **Application and data file management:**
  - Ability to explicitly manage which files are deployed when, along with separate handling of data files and application files.
  - Ability to predeploy components that require special permissions or access privileges to the client machine through the Visual Studio 2005 Bootstrapper.

In addition, there are a number of other advanced options and features to address complex scenarios with ClickOnce. All of these features will be explored in more detail in the remaining chapters of this book.

Terminology

There is a bit of terminology you should get comfortable with as early as possible when you are learning ClickOnce, so you can understand these terms in this book and can communicate effectively with other developers about ClickOnce.

No Touch/Href-exe/Zero deployment—These were competing names for a capability in previous versions of .NET that was an early attempt to achieve automatic deployment and update of smart client applications. It let you point users to a .NET .exe file at a URL, and that .exe file and all of its dependent DLLs would be downloaded and run on the client. The basic capabilities were similar, but there were a number of problems and challenges that made it difficult to employ for real applications. ClickOnce replaces this technology.[1]

One-click deployment—The most common misnomer for ClickOnce, and an easy inversion of the name to make.

xcopy deployment—Deploying an application by simply copying the files to a folder and running the application. Named after the xcopy command, the term is used more broadly to describe any form of file copying mechanism: DOS copy, xcopy, Windows Explorer drag and drop, FTP, and so on.

Deployment manifest—A file used by the ClickOnce engine to figure out what application to deploy, when to deploy it, and where to find the application files.

Application manifest—A file used by the ClickOnce engine to determine what files an application is composed of and what permissions the application requires to run. This is different from the application configuration file, which is sometimes referred to as a *manifest for the application*.

Deployment server—The server on which you place your manifests and application files, which lets end users perform a ClickOnce deployment.

Deployment provider—The URL or address that gets embedded in the deployment manifest. It is used by ClickOnce to determine the address used to launch the application.

Publisher—The organization or company that produces an application that is deployed through ClickOnce or that is responsible for exposing the application through ClickOnce to users.

Publish—The term used to describe the act of getting all the right files placed on a deployment server so that end users can install the application from their machines.

---

1. The first edition of *Windows Forms Programming* by Chris Sells (Addison-Wesley, 2003) has a chapter on No Touch Deployment if you need more information for .NET 1.1 applications.

Deploy—When used in the context of ClickOnce, this describes the user-initiated process of downloading and caching the application files on the client machine and running the application, all initiated through a single click on a link to the deployment manifest on the deployment server.

Update—Replacing the version of an application on the client with a newer version that has been published by the application publisher.

Mage—A set of tools (mage.exe and mageui.exe) included in the .NET Framework 2.0 SDK that let you create and edit manifest files for manually publishing or updating published ClickOnce applications without Visual Studio.

Manual publishing—Many of the examples in this book use Visual Studio to publish the application for ClickOnce deployment. When I talk about manually publishing the application, I mean using some other means, including either the Mage tools or a custom tool, to get the application files placed on the deployment server and the manifests generated and ready to go.

ClickOnce Deployment Modes

ClickOnce supports three distinct deployment modes or models. The first and most common mode you will use for ClickOnce deployment is the **Install Mode,** which I call a *ClickOnce installed application* throughout this book. This is also sometimes referred to as an *offline application* or an *offline/online application*. After the initial installation from the deployment server, an installed application is available whether or not the client machine can connect to the deployment server to check for updates. Installed applications get a shortcut added to the users' Start menu, which enables them to launch the application like any other installed application on the machine, whether or not the machine can connect to the deployment server. An Add or Remove Programs item is also added at install time, so users can remove the application from their machines if desired. The Add or Remove Programs item also supports allowing users to rollback, or restore, the previous version of the application after an update has been applied, as long as that update is not a mandatory update (discussed in Chapter 3).

Most ClickOnce deployments will likely be done using the installed mode. This will feel more natural to users, and even if your application is only designed to work on user workstations that are always connected to the network, the ability to launch the application from the Start menu gives a more natural experience to users. There are also a lot more options on configuring other ClickOnce options, such as update policies, when you deploy the application as a ClickOnce installed application.

The second mode of installation is the **online-only Install Mode.** With this mode, users must always launch the application with a full URL to the deployment manifest on the server, and therefore must be connected to the network whenever the application is run. No Start menu or Add or Remove Programs items are added, so this mode of installation feels a little more like a Web application to users. The application will always check the server to see if a new version has been published to the server, and will download any files that have changed if there is a new version there. I'll cover more on the update process in Chapter 3.

In fact, the most common scenario to use the online-only deployment mode is when you will be linking to a ClickOnce deployed application from an existing Web application, such as a company portal. For example, if you wanted to give users a smart client application to let them fill out their time card information or submit travel claims, you could do that through a Web application. However, a better user experience could be provided through a smart client. You could simply put a link in the company portal Web site where they are supposed to go to perform these tasks and have that link point to a ClickOnce deployment manifest. When they click on the link, the ClickOnce application deploys or updates on their machines, and then they will always be running the latest version of the application.

The last model is a **CD deployment**, which lets you deploy your application initially via a CD or DVD. ClickOnce lets you publish your application and burn the ClickOnce application files onto a CD. When your users pop in the CD, it will automatically run the ClickOnce install (through an auto-run.inf file) using a similar process to how it deploys from a server. You can configure separately an update URL that can be used to check for updates over the network after the application has been installed from the CD. You can use this option if the initial installation of your application is expected to be very large or if your users have limited connectivity options.

When you deploy via CD, you actually have the option to configure the application's Install Mode to be an installed application or online-only application. However, you will typically only use installed mode with CD deployments because online-only mode would require users to always have the CD in their CD drives to launch the application, even though the application will actually run from a cached version on their machines. You could possibly use this as a form of license enforcement, the way many consumer games do (requiring the game disk to be in the drive).

These modes are discussed in more detail in Chapters 2 and 3 and are referred to as the *Install Mode* in those chapters.

ClickOnce Deployment Architecture

At this point, it may not be entirely clear to you what software runs and goes where when working with ClickOnce. The section Software Requirements for ClickOnce later in this chapter discusses the specific requirements on the client and server sides of things, but first let's cover a high-level view.

Before any ClickOnce deployments occur, the client machine is devoid of ClickOnce software. It needs to have the .NET Framework 2.0 installed as discussed in more detail later. On the server side of things, you need to publish the application to the server. So the first step in a ClickOnce deployment architecture looks like Figure 1.1.

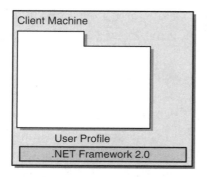
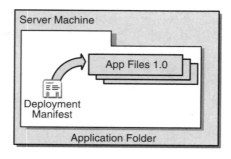

FIGURE 1.1: After Publishing, Before Deployment

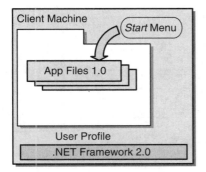 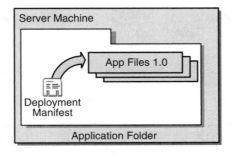

FIGURE 1.2: After Initial Deployment

After the user clicks on a link to the deployment manifest on the server, the application will be downloaded and cached under the user's profile on the client machine. If it is configured for the installed deployment mode, a Start menu shortcut and Add or Remove Programs item will be added, and then the application will be launched on the client machine. The user can continue to relaunch the application from the Start menu, and the application will continue to run from the locally cached version (see Figure 1.2).

At some point in the future, the application publisher may publish an update to the deployment server. This can be done through Visual Studio or manually by placing the files on the server and updating the deployment and application manifests. At this point, the architecture looks like Figure 1.3.

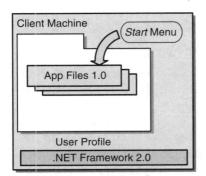 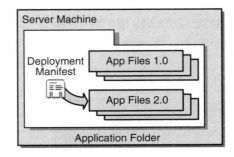

FIGURE 1.3: After Publishing Update

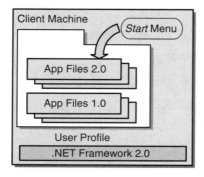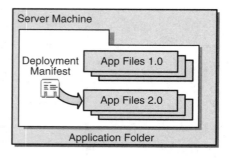

FIGURE 1.4: After Update Accepted on Client

The next time the user launches the application (with the default Click-Once settings), the new version of the application will be detected on the server, the files that have changed will be downloaded, the ones that have not will be copied over from the old version folder to the new version on the client side, and the new version of the application will be deployed and launched on the client machine. Note that with an installed application, the previous version is not discarded yet. One previous version will be retained by ClickOnce, allowing the user to restore the previous version. The publisher can prevent the user from restoring the previous version by marking the new version as the minimum required version. Now the configuration is as shown in Figure 1.4.

This process will continue for each subsequent version of the application that is published to the deployment server.

ClickOnce Deployment Process Overview

In order to use ClickOnce, you will need the following.

- A Windows Forms application that is built, tested, and ready to deploy.
- A deployment server that can serve up files via HTTP or UNC paths to client machines. For development purposes, this can be your local machine (localhost). To do HTTP publishing and deployments, you will need Internet Information Services (IIS) installed.

- Visual Studio 2005 and the .NET Framework 2.0 installed. Although you can publish applications manually using the tools in the .NET Framework SDK and even build applications using the command line tools in the SDK, for productivity reasons you will want to have Visual Studio. ClickOnce can be used from the Express versions of Visual Studio as well.

The following are the high-level steps required to accomplish a Click-Once deployment.

1. Design, build, and test your application. This is obviously no trivial task and will consume the bulk of your project timeline, but it is the subject of many other books on .NET development.
2. Publish the application to the deployment server.
3. Provide a link (HTTP URL or UNC path) to your end users. This can be done through a variety of means including a link in an e-mail, a link on a portal Web site, or a shortcut placed on a user's desktop by an administrator.
4. The user clicks on the link, responds to any install prompts, and the application is downloaded and launched on the user's machine. The application is "installed" in a sense after the first launch has occurred and will run from the locally cached version on each subsequent launch. Updates will be automatically detected and applied by default whenever the user launches the application. The user can launch the application from the Start menu after the initial installation if the offline mode is selected.

First ClickOnce Deployment: ClickOnce Hello World

Enough with the lofty goals and concepts; it's time to do your first ClickOnce deployment and update if you have never played with this technology before. The default settings of ClickOnce make it easy and straightforward to use for simple scenarios. For more complex scenarios, things get a little more complicated, but you will learn how to address those scenarios in the other chapters in this book.

Creating an Application to Deploy

To make this more concrete, let's step through a sample deployment and update with an extremely simple application: a Windows Forms Hello World example. To create the application that you will deploy with Click-Once, perform the following steps.

1. Open Visual Studio 2005.

2. Create a new Windows Application project. Select File > New > Project from the main menu.

3. Select the Windows Application project template from the New Project dialog (see Figure 1.5), give the project a name of **HelloWorld**, set the Location to a desired folder, and click OK.

4. Change the Text property for the form to Hello World (just for something trivially more interesting to see run than Form1).

5. Build and run the application to make sure all is well.

Publishing the Application

At this point you have a Windows Forms application that is ready to run and deploy. To prepare the application for deployment to end users, you

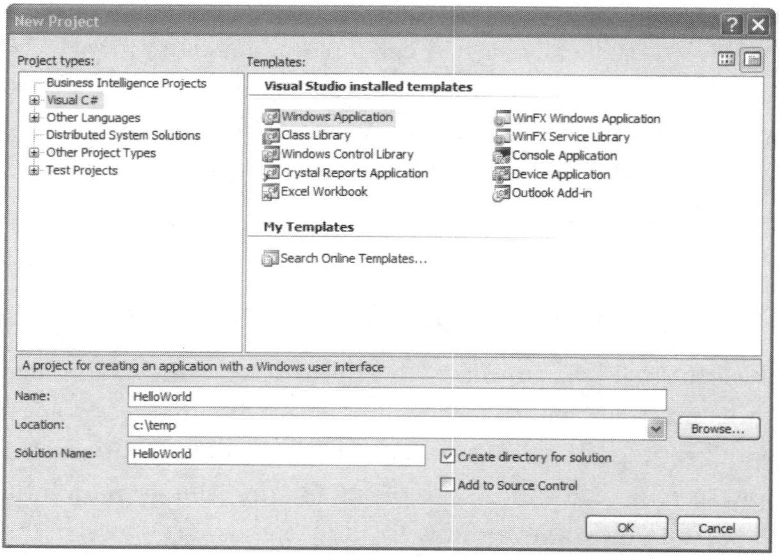

FIGURE 1.5: New Project Dialog

need to publish the application. For this exercise, and for most first testing of a ClickOnce application, you will simulate publishing to the deployment server by publishing to your local machine, so that you can test the ClickOnce publishing and deployment in a simple environment. To publish the HelloWorld application, perform the following steps.

1. Select Build > Publish HelloWorld from the main menu in Visual Studio. This will bring up the Publish wizard shown in Figure 1.6. This step lets you specify the path to the deployment server folder where you want Visual Studio 2005 to publish the files. As you can see from the dialog, the default will publish to your local machine Web server (IIS) installation, and will create a virtual directory under the Web server root directory to contain the files for this application. You can also deploy with FTP, a network file path, or to a local directory, which will be covered in Chapter 2. Accept the default and click the Next button.

2. The next step of the Publish wizard lets you select the installation mode (see Figure 1.7). The default mode is what I will call a *ClickOnce installed application* and lets your application be used online or offline by users after the first time they have launched it. The initial deployment, of course, requires them to be online to get the files from the

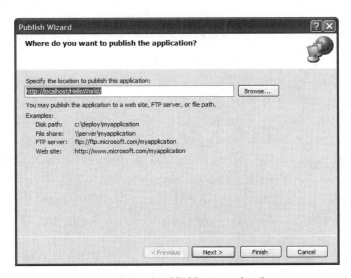

FIGURE 1.6: Publish Wizard Publishing Location Step

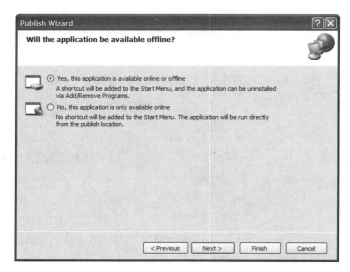

FIGURE 1.7: Publish Wizard Install Mode Step

deployment server, but subsequent launches will not require a network connection. The other mode (online only) does require users to
be online any time they launch the application. These options will be
discussed in more detail in Chapter 2. For now, just accept the default
and click the Next button.

3. The final step just summarizes what the publishing process will do
(see Figure 1.8). Click Finish to initiate the publishing process.

After you click Finish in the Publish wizard, Visual Studio will rebuild
your project to make sure it is up to date. It will then create the target publishing directory if it does not exist. Visual Studio will then copy all of the
application files into the publish directory along with two manifest files—the
deployment and application manifests—which Visual Studio will generate
from the project settings for ClickOnce. These settings will be discussed in
detail in Chapters 2 and 3. The last thing Visual Studio does is to pop up a
browser window with a publish.htm test deployment page that is generated as part of the publishing process (see Figure 1.9).

Deploying the Application with ClickOnce

At this point, you need to pretend that you are now on the client machine and
have been provided a URL to this test page. Your development machine is

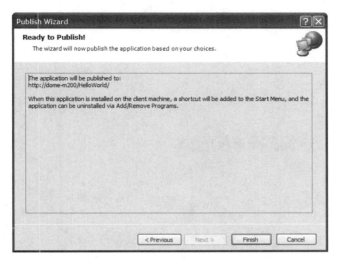

FIGURE 1.8: Publish Wizard Summary Step

FIGURE 1.9: Publish.htm Test Deployment Page

now the client machine from a ClickOnce deployment perspective. To deploy the application, click on the Install button in the browser. This will initiate the ClickOnce deployment from the client machine. You will briefly see a Launching Application dialog like the one shown in Figure 1.10. You will see

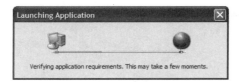

FIGURE 1.10: Launching Application Dialog

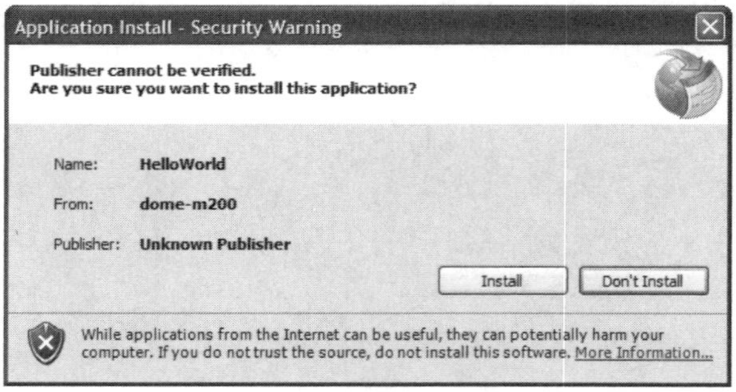

FIGURE 1.11: Application Install - Security Warning Dialog

this dialog briefly every time a ClickOnce application launches. You will then be prompted with the Application Install - Security Warning dialog shown in Figure 1.11.

The dialog shown in Figure 1.11 is the reason that people like to joke that the name of this deployment technology should have been *ClickTwice.* When using the default settings for a ClickOnce deployment, users will almost always have to click twice—once to initiate the installation process, and another time to acknowledge and accept the security warning. The reasons for getting this dialog will be discussed in more detail in Chapter 2, and options for avoiding this user prompting are covered in Chapter 6.

Click the Install button in the Application Install - Security Warning dialog and you will see (very briefly for this sample) a progress dialog like the one shown in Figure 1.12. Figure 1.12 was captured by adding a bunch of image files to the application so that it would take long enough to capture the dialog. That is why you see a download size of approximately 40MB in the figure. In your example, the application size will be a few tens of kilobytes and will happen before you can blink since you are just copying the files to a different location on your local machine. This dialog provides important feed-

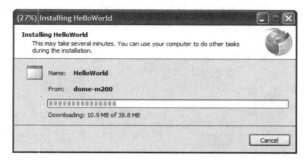

FIGURE 1.12: Install Progress Dialog

back to users when they are launching a ClickOnce application of any significant size over the Web so that they won't wonder what is going on.

After the download is complete (again, a blink of the eye if you are following along), the application will be up and running on your desktop. You can shut down the application and run it again from the Start menu. The shortcut will be placed under a programs grouping matching the name of the publisher, with a shortcut under that matching the name of the application. For this example, the name of the application is *Hello-World*. The publisher will be set to whatever company your machine has set for your operating system installation or Visual Studio installation. This is the company name that shows up under your user name in the upper left of the Visual Studio 2005 splash screen when you run Visual Studio.

Creating an Updated Application Version

To see how updates happen, you need to make a modification to the application that you can publish as an update, so you need to switch roles again and pretend you are back on the development machine. To create a simple change that will be instantly visible when it runs on the client side, perform the following steps.

1. Open the HelloWorld project if it is not already open in Visual Studio.
2. Open the Form1.cs in the designer (double-click on Form1.cs in Solution Explorer if it is not already open in the designer).
3. Select the form by single-clicking on the form's title bar in the designer.

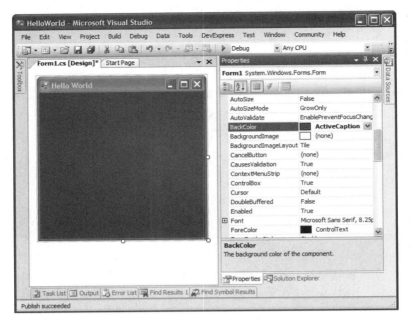

FIGURE 1.13: Setting the Form BackColor Property

4. Go to the Properties window (or press F4) and find the BackColor property.

5. Set the BackColor property to a different, easily identifiable color such as *ActiveCaption* (see Figure 1.13).

Publishing the Update

Publish the new version of the application by selecting Build > Publish HelloWorld from the main menu of Visual Studio. This will again trigger the publish process.

- You will be presented with the Publish wizard. Just click the Finish button to accept the defaults.
- The application's Publish Version revision number will automatically be incremented.
- The project will be rebuilt.

- The application files will be copied to a new subdirectory for this version on the deployment server (which is just your local machine in this example).
- The manifests will be regenerated for this version.
- The publish.htm page will be regenerated and presented in the browser.

This time, do *not* click the Install button on the publish.htm page—just close the browser.

Applying the Update from the Client

Now you need to switch roles to the user again.

1. Go to the Start menu and select Start > All Programs > [Your Company Name] > HelloWorld (see Figure 1.14). The application will begin to launch with the Launching Application dialog shown in Figure 1.10, and the new version on the deployment server will be detected by ClickOnce. You will then be presented with the Update Available dialog shown in Figure 1.15.

FIGURE 1.14: Start Menu Shortcut

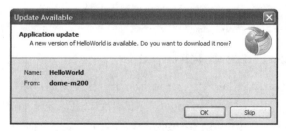

FIGURE 1.15: Update Available Dialog

2. You can see from Figure 1.15 that, by default, updates are optional in ClickOnce. Users can choose to accept the update, or to skip it and continue using the version that is already installed on their machine. Chapter 3 covers ways to override this behavior and make updates mandatory. Click on the OK button to accept the update. You will again briefly see the installation progress dialog, and then the new (colored) version of your HelloWorld application will be up and running on the desktop.

HelloWorld Wrap Up

In this little sample, you have seen the basic capabilities of ClickOnce. You were able to easily publish your application to the Web server on your local machine, and with a single selection in Visual Studio to make it available to users. With a single click on a link, you were able to initiate the install and launch process from the client. You had to click a second time to accept the installation because of the security warning, but after that the application was automatically downloaded, cached, and launched on the client machine. When a new version became available on the server (because you published an update), the client automatically detected the new version and lets users choose whether to accept the update. When you accepted, the updated version was installed and run.

As you will see in the rest of this book, there is a lot of stuff going on under the covers that you need to understand to employ ClickOnce in the real world that goes beyond this simple example. There are also a lot of variations on what you can do in terms of update behaviors, security settings, how ClickOnce prompts occur, and so on. That is what the rest of this book will teach you.

Software Requirements for ClickOnce

One important and commonly asked question about ClickOnce is, "What software requirements are there for using ClickOnce?" To answer that question, you have to discuss things in terms of the client-side and server-side requirements.

Client Requirements

ClickOnce is a client-side-initiated deployment mechanism. Through a user action on the client (clicking on a link or shortcut), the ClickOnce runtime makes file requests for the manifests and application files on the deployment server. Once the runtime gets all the files it needs, it launches the application. As a result, the minimum bar for launching a ClickOnce application on a client machine is that the machine be a Microsoft Windows machine with the .NET Framework 2.0 installed.

You will also need Internet Explorer 5.5 or later installed for things to work right. ClickOnce can be made to work with other browsers, but using another browser usually requires some manual configuration of the browser to let it know about ClickOnce and what action it should take when it is pointed to a ClickOnce deployment. See Chapter 8 for a discussion of how to get ClickOnce working with Mozilla Firefox.

If the requirement for the .NET Framework 2.0 sounds like a major impediment, read Chapter 7 to see how you can use the Visual Studio 2005 Bootstrapper to get the Framework installed easily from the client machine. You can also use something like Microsoft Systems Management Server (SMS) for administrators to push a Framework installation out to all user machines in an enterprise environment and to avoid needing to run an install on every user's machine manually.

Depending on what your application is designed to do, you may have other prerequisites including things like Microsoft Data Access Components (MDAC), DirectX, language packs, and other things. These prerequisites can also be addressed using the Bootstrapper or by using push technologies such as SMS or group policy to get them installed on the client machine before attempting the ClickOnce installation of your application.

Server Requirements

Perhaps surprisingly, there are very few software requirements on the server side. In fact, the server does not even have to be a Windows operating system. The following are the only requirements on the server side.

- The server must be able to return file requests for the deployment manifest, application manifest, and individual application files via HTTP or a UNC file path.

- The server must return appropriate MIME file types in the HTTP headers so that they are handled correctly on the client side. See Chapter 8 for information on how to configure an IIS server to meet this requirement.

One important fact to be aware of is that when you install the .NET Framework 2.0 on Windows XP, IIS gets configured correctly to serve up ClickOnce deployments. However, on Windows Server 2003, IIS is not configured correctly after a .NET 2.0 install, and you will have to perform the steps described in Chapter 8.

What to Deploy (and What Not to Deploy) with ClickOnce

One key question to consider is, "What kinds of applications are appropriate for ClickOnce deployment?" If you followed the description of a smart client application's attributes at the beginning of this chapter, you might already be forming a good picture of what kinds of applications fit that description and thus would make good candidates for a ClickOnce deployment.

ClickOnce is a client application technology driven by end users. That means you cannot use it to deploy server applications such as Web applications or services to a machine. You also cannot use it to deploy an application that must be deployed using Windows Installer (MSI) packages.

The following are some examples of application types that are perfect candidates for ClickOnce deployment, including both line-of-business applications and consumer applications.

- Business intelligence/decision support applications
- Customer resource/relationship management applications
- Financial management applications
- Administrative applications and utilities
- Enterprise resource planning applications
- Games
- Media applications

In reality, suitability for ClickOnce deployment is not determined by what specifically an application is designed to do, but is more driven by how it goes about doing it, and what it requires from the client machine to get it done.

For example, if a client application requires a number of other applications to be deployed on the client machine and communicates with those applications using specific local file/folder paths, it may not be a good candidate for ClickOnce because ClickOnce applications are explicitly isolated from other applications on the machine and their location is dynamically determined by the runtime. If your application has heavy requirements for customizing aspects of the client machine that could affect other applications or users on the machine, such as customizing the desktop, requirements for locating your application files in a specific directory, or dependencies on numerous custom install steps, then you may not be able to satisfy your application requirements using ClickOnce.

When designing a client application with the goal of using ClickOnce to deploy it, you should always try to minimize the coupling of the client application to other things on the client machine. You should specifically avoid the use of custom application registry keys, installation of assemblies in the GAC, and placing custom application files in specific shared system directories. If you cannot avoid these things, then ClickOnce may not be for you because of the following limitations that are part of the ClickOnce design.

- You cannot control your application's location on the client machine when it is deployed through ClickOnce.
- Other applications cannot determine the location of your application through any supported means because it will move locations as each update is applied.
- You cannot perform any custom install steps as an inherent part of the ClickOnce deployment. See Chapters 7 and 8 for techniques and capabilities to address custom install steps for prerequisites and initialization steps.
- ClickOnce security mechanisms may prevent you from performing certain actions (for example, accessing your runtime application directory when running as a partial-trust application).

You can use the Bootstrapper or custom startup behaviors to support these requirements even with a ClickOnce application, so it doesn't mean that you are out of luck with ClickOnce if you need to do these things. But they are definitely things to avoid if at all possible. The easiest way to think about succeeding in ClickOnce deployment is that if you can get your application up and running on another machine just by copying the files to a folder on that machine (known as **xcopy deployment**), then you should have no problem deploying your application with ClickOnce.

ClickOnce provides certain security guarantees at install and runtime. To provide these guarantees, it means that the ClickOnce runtime has to have complete control of the process of installing and running the application. This means that you do not have control over where the application files go on the machine, and you do not have explicit control over the application startup process.

If it is an absolute requirement that you place your application files in a particular location, such as under the Program Files folder, then you cannot use ClickOnce. This is done because you might choose a folder path that is already being used by another application and overwrite its files. For most other things, there is a way to get it done with either a custom Bootstrapper installer or through post-startup application code, but you cannot control the location of your application files on the client machine, and you won't have anywhere to execute code until your application is already up and running other than Bootstrapper installer modules.

ClickOnce Versus Other Deployment Technologies

ClickOnce is not intended to be a single deployment solution for every application in the future. As mentioned before, ClickOnce is only for client applications; server applications will continue to need their own means of deployment. Additionally, some client applications have heavy configuration requirements for the client machine, such as needing to explicitly place the application files in a specific location, adding registry entries before startup, multiple Start menu shortcuts or groups, desktop icons, QuickLaunch bar shortcuts, creating databases, and so on. For these kinds of applications, Windows Installer technology may still be the best option.

Windows Installer is a core operating system component designed to provide centralized management of application installations. It provides maximum control and flexibility in doing whatever you need to do when you put an application on a machine. It can be controlled remotely by administrators through products like SMS. You can create custom installer packages with Visual Studio Setup and Deployment projects, or you can use a third-party tool like InstallShield or Wise Installer. There are a couple of downsides of using Windows Installer compared to ClickOnce.

- The complexity of creating an installer package is fairly high, even for simple installation needs.
- The potential to accidentally corrupt other applications on the target machine is high if artifacts are added or placed incorrectly when the installer package is run.

Despite the downsides, Windows Installer remains a key deployment technology, even in combination with ClickOnce. Chapter 7 discusses the Bootstrapper in more detail, but one of the capabilities of the Bootstrapper is to run Windows Installer packages as prerequisite steps to get things ready on the client machine for you to do your ClickOnce deployment of your client application. This includes doing things like making sure the .NET Framework 2.0 is installed, getting third-party components installed in the GAC, and running custom installers to create databases, registry keys, or whatever else you need to support your ClickOnce deployed application.

There are other alternatives out there to ClickOnce as well. SMS provides a mechanism for pushing applications out to client machines in an enterprise environment. Third-party companies provide more robust and centrally managed solutions for client application deployment that go well beyond what ClickOnce provides out of the box. Solutions like these include features for pushing applications to client machines as well as a pull model similar to ClickOnce. They include monitoring and tracking features for knowing what version is on what client at any given time. However, they also include a fairly hefty price tag and learning curve to figure out how to use them. ClickOnce is intended as an easy and flexible deployment mechanism for the masses. It may not be as feature-rich as some of the other options, but it doesn't come with their baggage either.

As mentioned earlier in the chapter, there was a precursor technology available in .NET 1.0 and 1.1 known by a variety of names including No Touch deployment, Href-exe deployment, and Zero deployment. All of these were meant to describe a capability that was included in the Framework that let you enter the address of a .NET executable (.exe file) into Internet Explorer. Instead of the normal prompting behavior to save or run the executable, the file would instead just be downloaded and cached in the Internet Temporary Files cache of Internet Explorer, and then the application would be launched in a restricted security sandbox provided by the .NET runtime. The permissions of that sandbox are determined by the launch URL used to get to the executable.

No Touch deployment had a number of limitations that deterred most people from using it. There was no direct way to control the security context—you had to install a custom security policy on each client machine ahead of time to let users do anything meaningful from a No Touch deployed application. You also had no control over the download and update process—DLLs were downloaded automatically when they were first called, which could result in significant freezing of the UI. There was also no support for offline use of the application. ClickOnce was specifically designed to address all of these shortcomings.

Smart Client Architecture Overview

Smart client applications come in many shapes and sizes. They may support any combination of the attributes of a smart client described earlier in this chapter as long as they are a rich client application at a minimum. Figure 1.16 depicts a typical smart client architecture.

The client itself is, of course, a rich Windows application running on the user desktop machine. If the application supports offline operations, it will usually need to have a local data cache on the client machine to store data used by the application while in a disconnected state. If it is a distributed application, as most smart clients are, it will need to communicate with back-end systems via some communications mechanism. This could be a direct database connection for small scale applications, or it could be a remote connection to a middle-tier application server running business logic and data access services as shown in Figure 1.16.

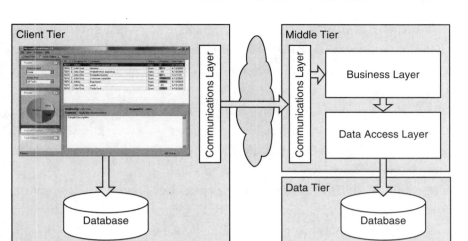

FIGURE 1.16: Smart Client Architecture

The key thing to be aware of with respect to ClickOnce is that you should try to minimize the complexity of the client application's involvement with the client machine. The local data cache for offline operations should be as lightweight as possible. SQL Server Compact Edition is a perfect data store for many scenarios—it provides a lightweight relational data engine for storing tabular data using common ADO.NET coding patterns, but only requires you to deploy a few extra DLLs as local files along with your application at a minimum. It also supports a model for deployment as a prerequisite through the Bootstrapper that will allow it to be part of Microsoft Updates if there is a need to roll out a patch to the SQL Compact Edition engine.

If you are working with custom objects and need to cache them, you can use serialization to the ClickOnce data directory as a way to keep you compatible with ClickOnce. However, if you are doing local file storage on the client machine, you should favor the ClickOnce data directory (covered in Chapter 5) or isolated storage to avoid coupling yourself to local file and folder structure and permissions.

For your communications with the middle tier, you can use .NET Remoting, Web services, or Windows Communication Foundation (WCF), but you should avoid certain features of those technologies that would tie you to a particular machine configuration on the client. Web services and WCF provide the loosest coupling, so they should be your first consideration if their performance and security are sufficient for your needs. WCF should always be sufficient, because it combines the best features and capabilities of all of the current remoting technologies in the .NET world. You would probably want to stay away from Enterprise Services because it requires the installation of a COM+ proxy on the client using an installer, and you cannot run custom installers as part of a ClickOnce deployment. You could deploy the proxy installers using the Bootstrapper, but then you would have to do this each time your interfaces to the server changed.

Many of these kinds of considerations come into play in your architecture and design, which requires you to have a firm understanding of the features, capabilities, and limitations of ClickOnce to properly design your client application so that it can be deployed using ClickOnce. Keeping the client application decoupled from the client machine as much as possible will let you do this.

Where Are We?

In this chapter you learned about the high-level context of ClickOnce. You learned what a smart client is and why you would want to choose the smart client model. You learned what ClickOnce was designed to achieve, what the challenges are that it addresses, what features it has to address those challenges, and a little about how it works. You learned what the platform requirements are on the client and on the server, what kinds of applications are good candidates for ClickOnce deployment, how ClickOnce relates to other deployment technologies, and have a taste of the kinds of smart client architecture decisions you will need to make to keep your application suitable for ClickOnce deployment. Along the way, you got a chance to try out ClickOnce to deploy a simple sample application and saw what its default behavior was for doing the initial deployment and update of an application.

The following are some of the key takeaways from this chapter.

- Smart clients are always rich client applications, not browser-based applications, and they are often distributed applications, have security features to protect the client machine, support offline operations, and have automatic network deployment and update features.

- ClickOnce combines the best aspects of both rich clients and Web applications—they provide a rich, stateful, interactive experience for the user, but they are as easy to maintain and update as Web applications because the administrator only has to publish the application files to a single machine.

- ClickOnce is a feature of the .NET Framework 2.0 and runs on the client machine to pull down and execute application files over the network using HTTP or UNC file paths.

- ClickOnce gives users the experience of an installed application through a Start menu shortcut, execution from locally cached application files, and an Add or Remove Programs item, but it avoids the risks of corrupting other applications or data due to the installation.

- ClickOnce supports initial installation on the client, as well as many options for how and when updates occur, what security the application requires, what files the application is composed of, and what the prerequisites for the application are.

- ClickOnce deployment needs to be considered early in the design process to ensure that the client application architecture is compatible with the low-impact deployment model of ClickOnce.

In the next chapter, we will dive deeper into the initial deployment of applications with ClickOnce. You will learn what all your options are for controlling that process, what happens when you publish, and when the application gets deployed.

■ 2 ■
Initial Deployment with ClickOnce

A S DISCUSSED IN CHAPTER 1, ClickOnce makes it easy to get your smart client application into your users' hands. From their perspective, all they have to do is click a link that you provide. From your perspective, all you have to do is drop some files on a deployment server and your application is accessible to end users. As developers, you are probably used to hearing statements like this only to discover that when you sit down and try to actually employ a technology that claims to be this easy, it never is. However, as developers, you will discover that if you use the built-in capabilities of ClickOnce, it really is this easy. And your users will find that it really is that easy to get their application up and running. This chapter will explore what the process is to get the application deployed, what all your options are, and what is going on under the covers to take away the magic.

After the initial deployment of an application, updates work a little differently for ClickOnce, so Chapter 3 will cover the updating process in detail. This chapter will just focus on the first deployment of an application using ClickOnce. For aspects covered by other chapters, such as updates in Chapter 3 and security in Chapter 6, I will stick to the defaults in this chapter and will explore the options and variations of those aspects in their respective chapters.

Publishing an Application with Visual Studio 2005

The first step in deploying an application with ClickOnce is to publish the application to a deployment server. Publishing an application requires you to place all of the application files in a directory on the deployment server along with two manifests: the deployment manifest and the application manifest. These manifests are used by the .NET Framework 2.0 on the client to manage the deployment of the application to users' machines. You can publish a ClickOnce application from Visual Studio 2005 if you have network access to the deployment server and permissions to place files in the target directory. You can also do it manually by creating the manifests on another machine with the appropriate entries and then simply copying all the files to the deployment server. This chapter covers both approaches, starting with publishing from Visual Studio.

Before you publish the application, you have to decide on some deployment options that you will set up before publishing. When you publish from Visual Studio, you configure these settings through the Publish tab of the project properties editor (see Figure 2.1). You bring up the project properties editor in one of three ways.

- From the Project > Properties menu
- Right-click on the project in Solution Explorer and select Properties from the context menu
- Double-click on the Properties node in the project tree in Solution Explorer in a C# project (My Project node in a Visual Basic project)

Through the Publish tab settings, you can configure most of the deployment options relevant to ClickOnce publishing. You use the Security tab to configure ClickOnce security settings (discussed in more detail in Chapter 6), and the Signing tab to configure the publisher certificates used to sign the deployment and application manifests.

ClickOnce Publishing Options

Before you jump in and publish your application with Visual Studio 2005, you first need to consider some of the options you have in terms of how users will access your application and where you are going to publish it to.

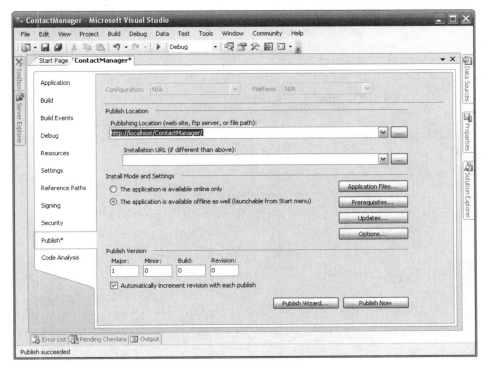

FIGURE 2.1: Publish Properties

Deployment Protocols or Media

Before you do anything, you should decide how end users are going to access your application. Your choices with ClickOnce are to distribute your application via HTTP, a UNC network file share path, or a CD-ROM or DVD-ROM disc (I'll just say *CD* from now on, but you can extrapolate this to mean CD-ROM, DVD-ROM, or one of the many other variants of writable discs). Distributing your application via HTTP will probably be the most commonly used option, as it offers the most flexibility in terms of network configuration and gives the greatest reach for your application. Using HTTP, you can still benefit from Windows integrated security to restrict access to your application (see Chapter 6), but you can also let anyone who can get to your Web server launch and use your application if desired. With UNC, you need to configure a network file share to the deployment server folder where users will launch the application from, you will be tied more directly to your network topology, and only users on your network will be able to access the application.

If you want to roll out a large application (in terms of file size) and get it into the hands of users for the first time, you may want to package that application on a CD. ClickOnce supports using this for an initial deployment, and lets you configure a separate URL that the application can check in a distributed environment for updates if you want online updates.

Publishing Location

Testing is an important part of any development process, including the deployment phase. Before you put your application into production, you should first test it locally on your development machine. Depending on your development organization, you might then publish it to an integration or QA server on your network, where you and others can test the ClickOnce deployment and execution of your application in a more distributed environment. If you have network access to the production server, you might then publish the application directly from Visual Studio to put it into production.

For any of these options, you need a deployment server address to which you are publishing the application. Visual Studio 2005 can publish your application using a number of different path types. The path you type into the Publishing Location field on the Publish tab (see Figure 2.1) is somewhat coupled to your planned deployment protocol. The default path that shows up in this setting uses HTTP to publish to the local machine, and uses the project name as the virtual directory to which it will publish (e.g., http://localhost/MyApplication/).

HTTP Publishing

If you deploy the application from a Web server, you will probably want to use the default option of using an HTTP URL to the deployment server virtual directory, such as http://mydeploymentserver/MyClickOnceApplication/. Doing so will use FrontPage Server Extensions to create the specified virtual directory if it does not already exist, and will copy the application files into a standard file and subfolder structure discussed later in this chapter. Using this approach assumes that the address you specify is a valid URL to a server that you have sufficient permissions on to create files and folders through FrontPage Server Extensions; otherwise, you will get errors in the publishing process from Visual Studio reflected in the Output window and Task pane. If your server does not support FrontPage Server Extensions, then you will need to use FTP, a UNC path, or manual publishing means to get the application published to the server.

UNC Publishing

Regardless of the protocol that end users will use to deploy the application, if you have network file access to the folder on the deployment server where you will be publishing the application, you can use a Universal Naming Convention (UNC) file path to a network file-share folder on the deployment server (e.g., \\mydeploymentserver\ClickOnceDeployments\MyClickOnceApplication\). You will need to have write access through Windows networking and Access Control Lists (ACLs) to copy the files to that directory.

FTP Publishing

Even though end users cannot deploy ClickOnce applications via FTP, you can use FTP to copy the application files to the deployment server from Visual Studio 2005. The deployment server needs to have an FTP server running with a virtual directory set up to the folder where the ClickOnce application files need to go. You would just use normal FTP addressing to this folder location (e.g., ftp://someftpserver/SomeFolder/). When you use FTP, you will be forced to specify the Installation URL, since the application will have to be launched by end users with either an HTTP URL or a UNC path to the deployment manifest. You will also be prompted when you publish the application with a log-in dialog (see Figure 2.2), which lets you specify the credentials to use to log on to the FTP server.

In the dialog in Figure 2.2, you can specify whether to use passive mode, whether to log on anonymously, and if not, what username and password to use. Passive mode changes the way the client (your Visual Studio machine) and the server communicate, and may be required to get through some firewalls.

Drive Letter Publishing

You can choose to use a drive letter path to publish your application as well (e.g., C:\SomeFolder\MyClickOnceApp\). The drive letter can map to either a local disk or to a network file share. You will typically use this

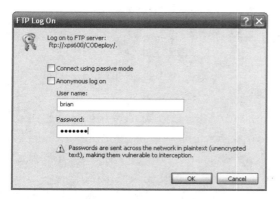

FIGURE 2.2: FTP Log On Dialog

option to stage the files for CD deployment before burning them to a writable disk drive. When you choose this option, you will have to either provide an HTTP or UNC Installation URL that you will use to launch or test the deployment, or you will have to step through the Publish wizard when you publish so that you can specify that the application will be launched from a CD. The Publish wizard can be launched in Visual Studio 2005 from either the Publish tab in the project properties editor (see Figure 2.1) or from the Build > Publish menu.

Installation URL

The **Installation URL** is specified through the Publish properties as well. This should be the full HTTP or UNC path to the folder that will contain the deployment manifest generated by Visual Studio. The deployment manifest filename is implicitly set by Visual Studio based on the project name. For example, if your project name is MyApplication, then the deployment manifest generated will be MyApplication.application, and it will be placed in the root folder specified for the Publishing Location (e.g., http://mydeploymentserver/MyApplication). The URL you provide to your users to launch the application will typically be whatever you set as the Installation URL with the deployment manifest name appended to it (e.g., http://mydeploymentserver/MyApplication/MyApplication.application or \\myfileserver \MyApplication\MyApplication.application).

An important concept to understand is that the Installation URL is also embedded in the deployment manifest as a setting named the deployment provider (the deploymentProvider element in the XML of the manifest). This is done as a security measure so that the application cannot be moved to another deployment server without re-signing the manifest with a new publisher certificate. This ensures that it is the publisher's intent for users to launch the application from a given URL.

By default, the Installation URL setting is blank and will use the same URL that is specified in the Publishing Location setting. If you specify an FTP or drive letter path for the Publishing Location, you will be forced to specify an installation location in order to publish the application from Visual Studio. You can get away with not specifying an Installation URL or deployment provider if you disable updates (uncheck the option to check for updates in the update options discussed in Chapter 3).

■ NOTE   Deployment Provider Naming

The Visual Studio setting named Installation URL gets written to the deployment manifest in the deploymentProvider element. However, if a different Update Location has been specified through the update options (discussed in Chapter 3), then the Update Location will be written to the deploymentProvider element instead. The deployment provider can also be set through the .NET Framework SDK Mage tools (mageui.exe and mage.exe). When you use the Mage UI tool (mageui.exe), this setting is labeled Start Location. When you use the command line Mage tool (mage.exe), the command line parameter that sets the deployment provider value is named providerURL. I will refer to this setting as *deployment provider* since it is the entry in the manifest that really drives the application launch behavior.

Install Mode

One of the key features of ClickOnce is the ability to execute a deployed ClickOnce application on the client machine even if the client machine cannot communicate with the deployment server. This lets ClickOnce applications be used like any other installed application on the client machine, even if the client machine is disconnected from the network or if the deployment server is unavailable due to maintenance or network connectivity problems. This facilitates using ClickOnce to deploy mobile applications to users on laptops or Tablet PCs.

If you choose to make your application available online only, it means that the client machine will need to be able to communicate with the deployment server every time users launch the application. Additionally, if you choose this launch mode, the application will always check the server to see if the application is up to date, and it will download any changes if a new version has been published. This may sound overly restrictive for many applications, and it is. But it has the advantage that you can guarantee that there is connectivity with the deployment server and that the client will never run an old version of any application file as long as you have published the application correctly to the deployment server. The connectivity guarantee may be useful if your application also uses back-end services exposed from the same server or from one within the same subnet, because it can be used as an indication that you should be able to talk to the application's back-end services at runtime. You can achieve the same update policy even with ClickOnce applications that are available offline through appropriate management of the update policy, but online-only mode ensures that the application is always up to date.

Most application developers will likely choose to use the Install Mode, which lets your ClickOnce application be available offline as well as online. I will call this an **installed application** throughout the book for brevity. This Install Mode has a number of advantages.

- It supports occasionally connected client applications. This means that users who run applications on devices such as laptops or Tablet PCs can disconnect from the network but still get work done while disconnected.
- It also supports desktop PCs that may be connected to a network or stand alone in an office or home environment, where the network connectivity to the deployment server is intermittent or unreliable.
- It gives users a Start menu item and an Add or Remove Programs item in the Control Panel, giving the application a similar presence on the local machine as other applications installed through Windows Installer technology.
- Installed applications give you a lot more flexibility in when and how updates occur.

Chapter 3 covers these options in detail.

Selecting an Install Mode in Visual Studio is as simple as selecting the appropriate radio button in the Publish settings in Figure 2.1. The default will make your application an installed application (available offline as well as online). To select the online-only mode, just check that option.

Update Policy

Chapter 3 details the various update options, but you do actually need to decide what your update policy will be before you publish your first version. The reason is that the update policy gets embedded in the deployment manifest that is placed on the server. The deployment manifest also gets cached on the client machine after the application has been deployed. If the application is an installed application, the deployment manifest is checked on the client side each time users launch the application through the Start menu shortcut to figure out whether the check for updates should occur before or after launch. As a result, the update policy you set when you first deploy the application through ClickOnce will affect how update checks occur until the next version of the application is downloaded and executed on the client machine.

For the purposes of this chapter, I am going to stick to the default policy for updates. The default ClickOnce update policy is that the check for updates will occur before the application launches every time it is launched. Additionally, any updates that are published are optional and can be skipped by users if desired. Chapter 3 discusses configuring the other combinations of update settings and the impacts that those settings have. But the default model gives you a good starting point—applications will be kept up to date automatically every time they run unless users choose to skip an update or the deployment server is unavailable. In the latter cases, users will still be able to run the version that is current on their machines. This update mode was chosen as the default mode because it is the most convenient for development.

To optimize startup performance in production applications, you will give users a better experience by checking for updates after launch on a scheduled basis. However, that option also gives you the most latency when updates are published. If updating users as soon as possible after an update has been published is your biggest concern, then using the Click-Once API to perform on-demand updates will be your best option. The default setting of checking before startup provides a decent middle ground between these two extremes.

Publish Version

When you publish a ClickOnce application, one of the pieces of information that goes into the deployment manifest is the **Publish Version.** This represents a version number for the application as a single logical unit that is accessible through ClickOnce. When you need to deploy updates, you will update the version in the deployment manifest and point to a different set of files on the deployment server; ClickOnce will take care of updating the application on the client machine based on that version number. Chapter 3 goes into more detail on this update behavior.

You set the Publish Version on the project properties editor's Publish tab (see Figure 2.1). Like other version numbers in .NET, the version number is composed of four parts: major, minor, build, and revision numbers. By default, Visual Studio will auto-increment the revision number portion of the Publish Version each time you publish the application. However, you can and should explicitly set the version number when you publish new versions from Visual Studio for the purposes of integration or QA testing, or when putting the application into production. In large enterprise applications, you probably won't even do your production or QA builds from Visual Studio. You will more likely use MSBuild or another automated build tool. If that is the case, the version will be set by that process.

Publish Options

There are a number of additional options that you can set through Visual Studio that affect the way the application is published. To set these, you select the Options button on the project properties editor's Publish tab. This brings up the Publish Options dialog, which is shown in Figure 2.3.

The following are the options in the Publish Options dialog.

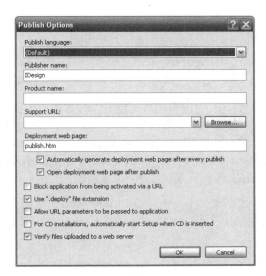

FIGURE 2.3: Publish Options Dialog

- The *Publish Language* setting specifies the locale for the application, which lets your application adapt to different locales in globalization scenarios.

- The *Publisher name* and *Product name* settings let you further identify your application with descriptive information. If you do not specify a Publisher name, Visual Studio will use the registered organization for your Windows installation (set through the \HKEY_LOCAL_ MACHINE\Software\Microsoft\WindowsNT\CurrentVersion registry key RegisteredOrganization string value). If you do not specify a Product name, the Visual Studio project name will be used. These settings also determine the Start menu programs group (set to *Publisher name*) and shortcut label (set to *Product name*).

- The *Support URL* setting lets you provide a place where users can go for product support. This URL will be available to users through the Add or Remove Programs item that is added to the Control Panel for an installed application. If you set a support URL, a shortcut will also be placed in the Start menu under the programs group (*Publisher name*).

- The *Deployment web page* setting lets you specify the name of the HTML file that will be used to test the deployment. You can choose whether this file should be generated automatically, and whether to launch it in the browser when the application is published.

- The *Block application from being activated via a URL* setting can be used to prevent the launching of the application via a URL. When this is selected, an initial install can be done via the URL, but the application will have to be launched via the Start menu shortcut. This is designed to protect against advanced security-attack scenarios; for example, where a malicious site could post a URL to an internal application with URL parameters designed to exploit the application. Since URL parameters can only be used through a URL-launched application, this blocks that attack approach.

- The *Use ".deploy" file extension* setting determines whether a .deploy file extension will be appended to all of the application files when they are placed in their folder on the Publishing Location. This helps with the administration of a Web site that will host the application, because it limits the number of file extensions that have to be mapped to MIME types and served up by the Web server.

- Enabling the *Allow URL parameters to be passed to application* setting lets users include query string parameters in the launch URL for HTTP-launched applications. This lets your application adapt its behavior or initialize properties based on information passed in from individual users. URL parameters can only be used from URL-launched applications (see Chapter 8).

- Enabling the *For CD installations, automatically start Setup when CD is inserted* setting creates an autorun.inf file in the Publishing Location folder that points to the setup.exe file. Thus, if you burn that folder to a CD's root, when a user pops in the CD, the ClickOnce deployment and launch of the application happens automatically.

- Enabling the *Verify files uploaded to a web server* setting tells Visual Studio to download each file after uploading it via HTTP to confirm a successful upload.

Figure 2.3 shows the default settings for these options.

Security Settings

Chapter 6 is dedicated to the security features and options in ClickOnce. You will want to read and understand that chapter and select the best security configuration for your ClickOnce application before you put it into production. For getting to know ClickOnce in this chapter, though, I will just stick with the default options for ClickOnce security, similar to what was discussed for the update policy.

The default setting for ClickOnce security is that the application will request full trust on the client machine. The user will be prompted, as discussed in the Launching the Application section later in this chapter, and if she installs the application, the permissions for that application will be elevated to full trust on the client machine for that user only. I will explore other security options in Chapter 6, but for the samples and discussion in this chapter, I will just stick to this default.

Publisher Certificate

To publish an application with ClickOnce, you need to sign your deployment and application manifests with an Authenticode Class 3 Code Signing publisher certificate. You can obtain a publisher certificate to use for signing in a number of ways.

- You can purchase a third-party verifiable Authenticode certificate from a certificate authority such as VeriSign or thawte. This is a recommended path if you will be publishing applications publicly to consumers or to third-party organizations.
- You can obtain a publisher certificate from your domain administrators in an enterprise environment. They can generate certificates from a Windows Server 2003 certificate server for the domain. This is the best approach for Intranet applications that will only be distributed throughout your enterprise.
- You can generate a certificate with Visual Studio 2005, either manually through the project properties editor's Signing tab or automatically the first time you publish your application. This can be used for development purposes or any other scenario. The downside of this is that the application will show up as being published by your login

account on your development machine, and it will be listed as an unknown publisher instead of coming from a known publisher name.

- You can generate a certificate with the makecert.exe Windows utility. This is really all Visual Studio is doing for you under the covers. It has the same usage and downsides as mentioned in the previous bullet.

If you create a Windows Application project in Visual Studio 2005 and publish it without configuring a certificate, a publisher certificate will be automatically created for you. It will be named <project-name>_TemporaryKey.pfx and will be added to your project files. This will be a password-protected publisher certificate with a blank password.

You can also create your own certificate ahead of time. To do so, do the following.

1. Go to the Signing tab in the project properties editor (choose Project > Properties).
2. Click the Create Test Certificate button (see Figure 2.4).
3. Enter a password in the dialog that appears (see Figure 2.5).

Doing so will add a .pfx file to your project with the same naming convention (<projectname>_TemporaryKey.pfx). You can change the name of the file after it has been created automatically, or manually simply by renaming it in Solution Explorer (right-click on the file and select Rename from the context menu).

When the certificate file is added to your project and configured as the certificate being used for signing ClickOnce manifests, it is also added to the Personal certificate store under the current user's account in Windows.

Chapter 6 discusses the use of publisher certificates for security purposes, and what happens when the manifests are signed later in this chapter in the Manifest Generation and Signing section.

Visual Studio Publishing Step by Step

To help you understand everything that is going on when you publish an application, this section steps you through the process for a sample

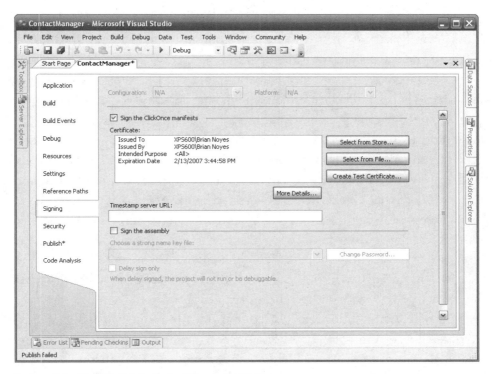

FIGURE 2.4: Signing Tab in Project Properties Editor

FIGURE 2.5: Password Dialog for Certificate Creation

application and discusses each step in more detail. It highlights the things you need to do, where the options exist, and what is happening automatically behind the scenes. The step-by-step procedures for applying an update in Chapter 3 use the results of this procedure, so if you plan to follow the update procedures in that chapter, you will want to follow them here as well.

Designing the Application

Obviously for any real-world application, designing the application is not a trivial step. And for most applications, you do not have to do anything specific in your application code to let you deploy it via ClickOnce. You will certainly have to factor in the environment where the application is going to run (i.e., client machine operating system and configuration, network connectivity, user sophistication, etc.). If it requires back-end resources such as middle-tier components, a database, or a Web service, you will need to design those capabilities to call into those resources. If you are going to support offline operation of the application, you will need data caching and synchronization capabilities for when users connect back to the network. However, these aspects of the application are all outside the scope of what ClickOnce is concerned with. At its core, ClickOnce is just a fancy wrapper around copying some files to the user's machine and launching the application. Everything the application does after it launches is beyond the scope of what ClickOnce is concerned with, other than the fact that it will be limited by the runtime security context that ClickOnce provides for the executing application.

You will want to build and test your application first *without* ClickOnce involved to get the basic functionality of your application working correctly. It is a good idea to include deployment testing throughout the design process to ensure you are not designing capabilities that have unanticipated side effects as a result of running through ClickOnce deployment. But you will need to get your application fully implemented and tested before you go through a full deployment to production.

The walkthrough in this section uses the EmployeeManager sample application that is available from the book's Web site sample code downloads. This is a simple data application that presents employee data from the Northwind database in a form for viewing or editing (see Figure 2.6). This application is composed of just a single form that uses data binding to a typed data set definition that is part of the project. The typed data set includes a table adapter class that executes SQL queries against the Northwind database to get and update the customer data.[1] You could also just use a blank form application like the example in Chapter 1 since there is nothing specific to ClickOnce about this sample application.

---

1. For more details on Windows Forms data binding, see my other book in this series, *Data Binding with Windows Forms 2.0* (Addison-Wesley, 2006).

FIGURE 2.6: EmployeeManager Application

Publishing the Application via HTTP from Visual Studio

Once you are ready to perform a ClickOnce deployment, you will need to publish the application. Publishing can be initiated from several places in the Visual Studio 2005 IDE.

- Select Build > Publish <projectname>.
- Right click on the project in Solution Explorer, and select Publish... from the context menu.
- Click the Publish Wizard button in the Publish tab of the project properties editor (see Figure 2.1).
- Click the Publish Now button in the Publish tab of the project properties editor (see Figure 2.1).

When you initiate publishing in one of these ways, a sequence of events occurs to complete the publishing process. Visual Studio does the following as part of publishing the application.

- When the Build menu, the Solution Explorer context menu, or the Publish Wizard button is used, the user is prompted with the Publish Wizard. This wizard steps through confirming the Publishing Location and Install Mode.
- The application is rebuilt to make sure all the build outputs are up to date.

- The Publishing Location address is checked to ensure it is accessible and ready to accept files. If publishing to an HTTP URL, the virtual directory specified as part of the URL will be created on the Web server if it does not already exist.
- The application files are copied to the Publishing Location in the folder structure discussed in the next section.
- Two manifest files are generated, signed, and placed in the folder structure as discussed in the following sections.
- A publish.htm test page is generated (depending on Publish tab project settings) and is loaded into the browser to let you test the deployment.

Let's step through this with the EmployeeManager application to make this all more concrete. Perform the following steps.

1. In Visual Studio 2005, open the EmployeeManager.sln solution file from the download samples.
2. Choose Build > Publish EmployeeManager.
3. The first step of the Publish Wizard is displayed, as shown in Figure 2.7. This step lets you customize the Publishing Location if you forgot to do so through the project properties editor before attempting to publish. For this first example, accept the default of http://localhost/ EmployeeManager.
4. Click Next to display the second step of the wizard. In this step you confirm what Install Mode you want for the application (see Figure 2.8). This again corresponds to the selection in the project properties editor's Publish tab, and lets you specify whether you want the application to be available online only or both online and offline. Accept the default of *Yes, this application is available online or offline.*
5. Click Next, and you see a summary step telling you what the publishing process is going to do (see Figure 2.9). Just click the Finish button to initiate the publishing process.

When you complete the wizard, the steps discussed at the beginning of this section will be done by Visual Studio—building the project, copying the

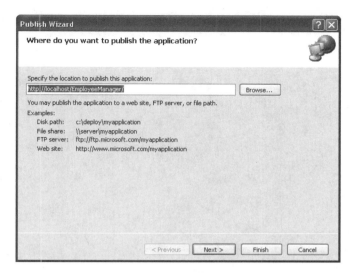

FIGURE 2.7: Publish Wizard Publishing Location

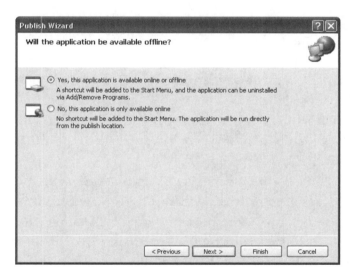

FIGURE 2.8: Publish Wizard Install Mode

files to the Publishing Location, generating the manifests, and presenting the test publish page in the browser.

Publishing the Application to CD

The Publish wizard experience is a little different when you publish to a drive letter. When you do this, Visual Studio assumes you are doing so to

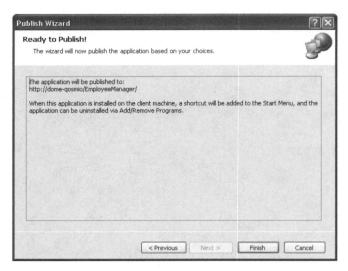

FIGURE 2.9: Publish Wizard Summary Step

stage the application files prior to burning them to a CD. In this case, Visual Studio does not use the Publishing Location as the Installation URL, because you can only deploy a ClickOnce application via an HTTP or UNC path. The ClickOnce launch mechanisms are capable of using the local path as the Update Location, but it does not really make sense for real-world scenarios, so Visual Studio does not expose it this way. As a result, for CD deployments the wizard will prompt you to confirm a couple other deployment settings as well.

If you enter a Publishing Location such as C:\temp\testdeploy, you will get two additional steps in the Publish wizard. After the wizard confirms the Publishing Location, it will then prompt for the Installation URL as shown in Figure 2.10. If you will deploy the application via CD, then you should select the last option (as shown). But if there is a valid HTTP URL or UNC Path to the same folder that you specified with a drive letter path as the Publishing Location, you can specify that here instead. But in those cases, you should just specify that path as the Publishing Location to make things simpler.

When publishing to a CD, the next step in the Publish wizard is to confirm where updates will come from (see Figure 2.11). This corresponds to the *Update Location* setting that is available through the Updates button in

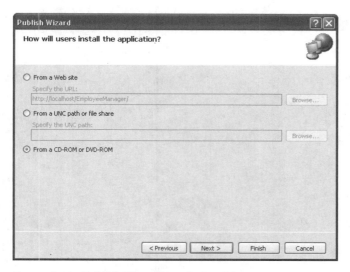

FIGURE 2.10: Publish Wizard Installation URL

the project properties editor's Publish tab. This setting gets written to the deployment provider value in the deployment manifest. After the application has been launched on the client machine via the CD that you distribute, it will use this URL on subsequent launches to check and see if updates are available, and it will download the updates from there to keep the application up to date. If the application is an online-only application, it always checks for updates at the launch URL; therefore, updates will never occur for an online-only application unless a deployment provider URL is included in the deployment manifest and the on-demand API is used to check for updates. In the case of a CD-distributed application, the Install Mode affects whether the CD has to be used to launch the application, or whether a Start menu item will be used to launch from the locally cached files after the initial deployment from the CD.

Publishing Location Folder Structure

When Visual Studio copies the application files to the Publishing Location, it creates a particular folder structure within the specified directory for each version of the application that is published. The deployment manifests (.application files), publish.htm, and setup.exe files are all placed in the root Publishing Location folder. A separate subfolder is created for

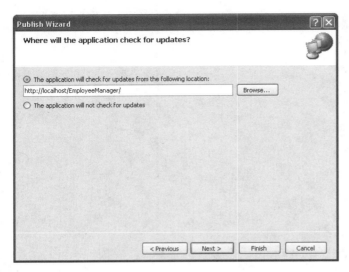

FIGURE 2.11: Publish Wizard Update Location

each version that you publish, and all of its application files are placed there along with that version's application manifest (.exe.manifest file). Figure 2.12 shows this folder structure for the EmployeeManager application.

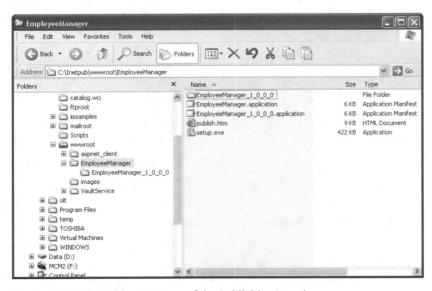

FIGURE 2.12: The Folder Structure of the Publishing Location

Manifest Generation and Signing

As mentioned earlier, two manifests are generated as part of the publishing process. The deployment manifest contains settings that affect how the application is launched and updated, and the application manifest contains settings that describe the composition of the application—specifically what files it contains and what permissions the application needs to run. In the case of the EmployeeManager sample application, the deployment manifest is named EmployeeManager.application and the application manifest is named EmployeeManager.exe.manifest.

> ### ■ NOTE   Manifest File Naming
>
> Unfortunately, the file extensions selected for these manifest files and the way they show up in Windows Explorer can make it confusing as to which is which. The *deployment* manifest has an .application file extension and is identified as an Application Manifest file type in Windows Explorer. The *application* manifest has an .exe.manifest file extension and shows a MANIFEST (all caps) file type in Windows Explorer. However, the ClickOnce documentation refers to these files as the deployment manifest and application manifest, respectively, so you will just have to get used to the fact that the .application file is the deployment manifest and the .exe.manifest file is the application manifest.

The manifest files are just XML files that comply with a particular schema. However, as a part of generating these files, Visual Studio also digitally signs these manifest files. That digital signature guarantees two things.

- The ClickOnce deployment of this application has not been tampered with since it was published. Any direct modifications of the manifest file's contents will invalidate the digital signature, and ClickOnce will refuse to launch the application unless the manifest has been re-signed after the modifications are made. Because the deployment and launching of a ClickOnce application is all done by the runtime based on the manifest files, this ensures that the application cannot be launched through ClickOnce if the manifests have been tampered with.

• The ClickOnce application was signed by whoever the publisher is that holds the certificate containing the private key used for signing. Especially with third-party-verifiable publisher certificates, this provides an authentication identity of the publisher that can be used for trust decisions (discussed in more detail in Chapter 6).

Because manifests are signed, you cannot edit them directly even though they are just XML text files. You will need to either generate the manifests by publishing through Visual Studio, or you can edit or create manifests from scratch using the Mage tools available in the .NET Framework 2.0 SDK (mage.exe and mageui.exe). Mage.exe is a command line tool that lets you automate the process of generating and signing manifests. Mageui.exe is a Windows application that provides a property-sheet-style editor for setting the various settings contained in deployment and application manifests, and for signing them as part of the process of saving the file after editing. You could also write a custom tool to edit and/or sign the manifests, because both Visual Studio and these SDK tools are just using APIs defined in the `Microsoft.Build.Tasks.Deployment` namespaces of the .NET Framework.

I'll cover using mageui.exe and mage.exe in the Moving an Application into Production with Mage section in this chapter, and will cover more details of the signing process and how it works in Chapter 6.

Deployment Manifest

The deployment manifest (the .application file) is the launch target for a ClickOnce application. When you provide a URL to your users to launch the application through ClickOnce, you should give them a URL or link to the appropriate deployment manifest file for your application. When you publish your application with Visual Studio, a default manifest is created for the application with the file name <projectname>.application. This should be the deployment manifest you point your users to. In addition, for each version of the application that you publish, a second, version-specific deployment manifest is created with a file name of <projectname>_<major>_<minor>_<build>_<revision>.application, as you can see in Figure 2.12. This file lets administrators easily perform a server-side rollback to a previous version by just overwriting the default deployment manifest with the version-specific one for the version that they want to activate. Each time you publish a new version, the default deployment manifest is updated to point to the new version of the application.

The deployment manifest contains the settings that tell ClickOnce how to go about launching the application. It contains the identity information for the application (name, version, public key token, locale, and processor architecture). It contains descriptive information about the application including the publisher, product name, and an optional support location. It contains deployment options including the Install Mode and the deployment provider, and the update settings for the application to drive how the application performs updates from the client side. Finally, it contains the application reference information to point to the application's appropriate application manifest.

The deployment provider that is placed in the deployment manifest is used to initially launch the application, and it checks for updates for installed applications. The deployment provider URL is set from one of the following three values in Visual Studio.

- The Publishing Location if no Installation URL or Update Location is specified.
- The Installation URL if no Update Location is specified.
- The Update Location if one is specified.

The deployment provider URL must be a valid address to the deployment manifest that is used by the ClickOnce runtime to launch the application. Typically, the deployment manifest, application manifest, and application files are all placed on the same machine. In that case, the URL used to launch the application from the client machine must match the deployment provider URL in the addressed deployment manifest. The URL in this context could be either an HTTP URL or a UNC file path.

The reference to the application manifest in the deployment manifest is used to determine which version of the application to launch. The ClickOnce launch mechanism will use that reference to download the application manifest, and it will continue the launch or update process based on what it finds in that manifest.

> **▪ NOTE**   Deployment Provider Indirection
>
> ClickOnce actually supports placing the deployment manifest on a different machine than the application manifest and files. Additionally, the deployment provider URL in the deployment manifest addressed by the user can point to a different deployment manifest on a different machine. This helps support forwarding calls from a client to a different deployment server. As a result, the address to the deployment manifest used by the user to launch the application may be different than the one contained in the addressed deployment manifest. The deployment provider URL in the addressed deployment manifest can point to a different deployment manifest on another server (in the same code access security zone). That deployment manifest can reference an application manifest on either the same server or yet another server in the same security zone. So a single ClickOnce launch request could result in downloads of files from up to three different servers: the one the user first addresses, the one the first deployment manifest lists as the deployment provider, and the one that the second deployment manifest refers to for the application manifest.

As you saw in the Publishing Location Folder Structure section, Visual Studio creates a separate folder for each version of the application that is published, and the application files and application manifest are placed in that folder. This folder structure is arbitrary; the deployment manifest, application manifest, and application files can be placed in any folder structure if you are manually publishing the application. The only restriction is that the application files have to be on the same server as the application manifest, specified with a relative path that is in the same folder as the application manifest or in a child (or descendant) folder.

Application Manifest

The application manifest contains all the information about what the application is composed of and what it needs to run. This includes identity information (name, version, public key token, locale, and processor architecture), what files the application is composed of (along with their file types and file groups), and the permissions required for the application to run. The relative path (from the application manifest's location on the same server) to each application file is included so that ClickOnce knows where to download the files from. The application manifest also includes a hash value for each application file; this value is used when a new version is detected on the deployment server to figure out which files have changed. Additionally, this hash value helps ensure that the application files themselves have not been tampered with. The digital signature of the manifest ensures that the manifest can't be tampered with. And since the application manifest includes the hash values for the application files, it ensures that the individual files have not been modified since the manifest was signed. This protects the integrity of the application as a single logical unit.

Setup.exe File

In addition to the manifests, Visual Studio generates a setup.exe Bootstrapper file when it publishes your application. This file, which is not part of the ClickOnce deployment, lets you install any necessary prerequisites (discussed in more detail in Chapter 7). By default, the setup.exe file will also launch the application through a reference to the deployment manifest after it has completed prerequisite checks and installs the prerequisites.

A common misconception about ClickOnce is that you need to point end users of your application to the setup.exe file to launch the application. As mentioned before, this is not really correct. You should be pointing end users to your deployment manifest for launching your application. Pointing them to setup.exe will work fine in most cases, because if the Bootstrapper does not see any prerequisites that need installation, it will just launch the application through a reference to the deployment manifest. However, the setup.exe might try to run prerequisite installers that might require administrative privilege. Also, the setup.exe file can be configured not to launch the application after installing prerequisites, so pointing users to setup.exe is not guaranteed to work in all cases.

Publish.htm Test Page

The last thing that Visual Studio does as part of publishing the application is to generate a test HTML page named publish.htm by default. The page that is generated includes some script code to check the user agent string to help detect whether certain prerequisites are installed, such as whether .NET 2.0 is already installed on the client machine. If the script code does

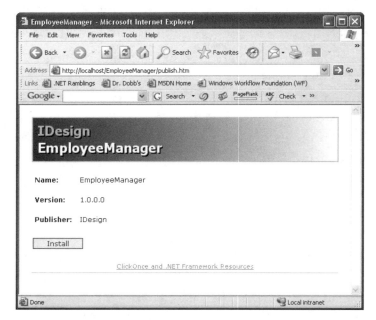

FIGURE 2.13: Publish.htm Page

not see the right information in the request's headers, it will alter the presentation on the page to state what prerequisites are missing and will provide a link button to the setup.exe file instead of the deployment manifest. If the .NET Framework prerequisites are met, then the page will simply present a link button that refers to the deployment manifest. Clicking on the button lets you test the deployment on the local machine. The link button will alter its text based on whether the application is configured for online-only or online/offline Install Mode. If online only, the button will have its text set to *Run*; otherwise, it will be set to *Install* (see Figure 2.13).

ClickOnce Application Initial Deployment Step by Step

The point of ClickOnce deployment is to easily put your application at your users' fingertips so that they can enjoy the rich functionality you have built into your smart client application. This section covers how things work for an initial deployment from the user's perspective: what the user needs to do, what they see, and also what happens behind the scenes when launch a ClickOnce application is launched the first time on a given machine.

From 40,000 feet, the ClickOnce deployment process consists of some fairly straightforward high-level steps.

1. The user clicks on a link to the deployment manifest provided to her.
2. The application files are downloaded and cached under the user's profile on the client machine.
3. The application is launched in a security execution context determined by the runtime (see Chapter 6).
4. If the application is an installed application (that is, available offline), a Start menu item is added as well as an Add or Remove Programs item.

> **■ TIP   ClickOnce and Roaming Profiles**
>
> ClickOnce applications are isolated per user, per application, and per version. The application is cached under the user's Windows profile after deployment. In a domain network environment, the users profile can be configured to "roam." That means that whatever machine the user logs on to, their profile is downloaded and cached on that machine while they are logged on, but it is then saved back to a central server when they log off. When they log on to some other machine, their profile on that machine looks just as it did on the last machine they logged on from. However, not every aspect of a user's profile roams. The cached ClickOnce application files do not roam. As a result, when a user with a roaming profile launches a ClickOnce application from a different machine, they will get a fresh install on that machine.

Installation Prerequisites

The first thing to keep straight is that ClickOnce is not meant to be a replacement for all other deployment technologies. ClickOnce is intended to be a lightweight, trustworthy deployment mechanism that can be accomplished safely by end users (nonadministrators). In order to live up to that goal, the ClickOnce deployment mechanism needs to have some severe limitations in terms of what kinds of modifications it is allowed to make to the user's machine. Thus, when a user clicks on a link to a deployment manifest and the application is downloaded and cached on the user's machine, ClickOnce cannot allow anything to happen as part of the deployment process that could harm other applications or data on the client machine.

However, sometimes your ClickOnce deployed application needs resources to be available on the client machine that cannot themselves be deployed through this lightweight mechanism. This includes things like optional operating system components (e.g., the .NET Framework 2.0 itself, Microsoft Data Access Components, DirectX, etc.), third-party products, or custom installers you create for your application's other infrastructure prerequisites.

The Bootstrapper is a mechanism that is part of the .NET Framework 2.0 and is covered in more detail in Chapter 7. At a high level, the Bootstrapper lets you wrap multiple installer packages (MSI files, executables, and scripts) into a single setup.exe launch point that you can let users run to install all of the heavyweight prerequisites that your application needs. You can configure the Bootstrapper through the Prerequisites button on the project properties editor's Publish tab. This button displays the dialog shown in Figure 2.14, where you can configure the items that you need to ensure are installed on the client machine before your application attempts to launch through ClickOnce.

Some prerequisites may not be suitable for deployment through the Bootstrapper. For example, if you only support certain versions of the operating

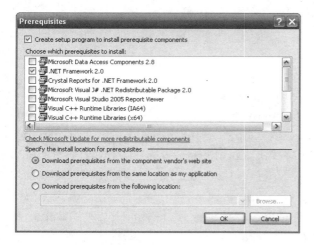

FIGURE 2.14: Prerequisites Configuration Dialog

system, you are not going to be able to deploy a new OS through the Boot-strapper. Some products may not be suitable for inclusion in the Bootstrapper due to their packaging or license model (e.g., they need to be installed from CD). In these cases you will just have to document the logical prerequisites for your application and enforce getting them in place through organiza-tional policy or other configuration management mechanisms (e.g., Active Directory or Systems Management Server) before users try to use an applica-tion through ClickOnce.

> **TIP Prerequisites and Administrative Rights**
>
> Most of the examples in this book assume that your prerequisites are already in place. Chapter 7 will cover configuring the Bootstrapper in more detail with examples. Many prerequisites will require the user to be an administrator to run them, which is why those are treated as a separate mechanism than ClickOnce. ClickOnce is designed to let end users install, execute, and update their applications even with limited user privileges.

Launching the Application

All that an end user needs to run your ClickOnce application is for the pre-requisites to be installed and to have a link to the deployment manifest. That link can come in the form of a URL in an e-mail, a link on a portal Web site, a Windows desktop shortcut, or just a URL written on a sticky note that they have to type into their browser's address bar. All it takes is for them to "click" on that link to initiate the ClickOnce installation and launch process. The process proceeds from that point as follows.

1. If the link is an HTTP address, the browser on the user's machine will attempt to access the deployment manifest file that the URL points to and download it. If the link is a UNC path, the same thing happens, but it is done through Windows Explorer and networking instead of through the browser. The first thing the user will see is a launch dia-log (see Figure 2.15), which shows the user that launching is in progress.

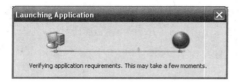

FIGURE 2.15: Launching Application Dialog

2. Once the deployment manifest is downloaded, the runtime first checks the deployment manifest digital signature to make sure the file has not been tampered with. If it has, or if the file appears corrupted in some other way, the user will see an error dialog like the one in Figure 2.16. See the section Manifest Validation for more details on this process.

3. The runtime then looks inside the manifest to determine the Installation URL (the deployment provider). For a typical ClickOnce deployment, this URL will need to match the URL being used by the client to launch the application. There is an extra level of indirection supported by the ClickOnce runtime that lets the deployment provider point to a deployment manifest on another machine, and ClickOnce will follow that URL and try to install from that location. If the deployment provider does not contain a valid path to the deployment manifest, the user will get a launch failure at that point with the dialog shown in Figure 2.17.

FIGURE 2.16: Formatting Error Dialog

FIGURE 2.17: Application Start Error Dialog

4. Next, the location of the application manifest will be determined from the deployment manifest reference, and the application manifest will be downloaded.

5. The runtime will determine from the application manifest's contents what code access security permissions are required by the application. The permissions requested by the application are compared to what permissions the application would be given by the current security policy based on the launch URL.

6. What happens next depends on the client machine's configuration. By default, what happens next is that if the application requires more permissions than it would be granted based on the security policy and its launch URL, the user will be prompted to elevate permissions (see Figure 2.18). Even if the application does not require elevated permissions, the user will be prompted at this point if the application is an installed application because visible modifications will be made to the user's environment. Specifically, a Start menu item and Add or Remove Programs item will be added as mentioned earlier. So before making these modifications, the user needs to be notified so he can prevent the change if desired.

7. If the user accepts the installation, or if the user does not need to be prompted (online-only applications that do not need any elevated permissions), a custom user-code access-security policy is created for the application to grant the required permissions.

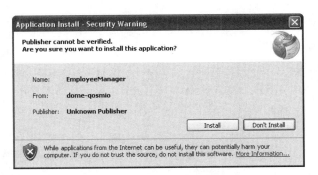

FIGURE 2.18: Security Installation Prompt

FIGURE 2.19: Download Progress Dialog

8. ClickOnce does a prerequisite check at this point to verify that certain prerequisites are met before proceeding to download the application files. These prerequisites include the proper version of the operating system, .NET Common Language Runtime, and GAC-referenced assemblies. This information is all included in the application manifest.

9. After the prerequisite check is complete, the rest of the application files are downloaded. Each file download is a separate request from the client machine to the deployment server. While the downloads are in progress, users see a progress dialog so that they can tell what is going on (see Figure 2.19).

10. Once the download is complete, the application will launch from the local file cache. It will execute in a secure execution context, only allowing those permissions granted to the application based on the security policy and the permissions requested in the application manifest.

Manifest Validation

Deployment and application manifests are validated as part of the install process. This includes schema validation, digital signature validation, and semantic validation. **Schema validation** involves comparing the XML schema of the received file and ensuring it complies with the schema defined for manifests.

Digital signature validation checks to ensure the digital signature embedded in the manifest is valid based on the file's current contents. It is able to do this because an encrypted hash is embedded in the manifest, along with the publisher certificate's public key, and the encrypted hash is generated using the publisher certificate's private key. As a result, Click-Once can recompute the hash after downloading the manifest, decrypt the embedded encrypted hash using the public key, and compare the two. As long as the two hash values match, ClickOnce can be sure that the manifest was not altered since it was signed.

In the context of application updates, ClickOnce can also determine whether this application in fact came from the same publisher as the previous version that is installed based on the publisher's public key in the signature. ClickOnce can also check to ensure that the new version of an application is signed by the same publisher as the previous version. Click-Once does not let you publish updates to an application using a different publisher certificate than was used for previous versions. If you need to switch publisher certificates, you will need to deploy the application as a whole new application.

For elevating trust for the application, the publisher's identity is validated through signature validation. This can be used to prompt users with the publisher name to let them decide whether to install the application. It can also be used to elevate permissions automatically with the trusted publisher concept (discussed in Chapter 6).

Semantic validation checks for constraints defined by ClickOnce for the allowable values for settings contained in the manifest files; for example, whether an update schedule falls within the allowable range of values for time spans of different types. Also, semantic validation compares the digital signature to the one for the previous manifest. If the signatures do not match, the update is terminated. You cannot deploy updates signed with a different publisher certificate than the one used for previous versions of the application. Semantic validation also checks to see whether a specified update interval is within the allowable values for that setting.

Install and Runtime Security

At install time, ClickOnce provides a trustworthy deployment mechanism; a ClickOnce application deployment cannot corrupt or interfere with any other application or user data on the machine. It achieves this by having the runtime control the download process and place the downloaded files in an obfuscated folder structure under the user's profile that is isolated per user, per application, and per version.

At runtime, the executing ClickOnce application is only granted the permissions it received when it was installed on the machine. This again is based on the launch URL; the location-based, code-access, security-code group permissions; and the permissions that the application manifest required. If the application requests full trust (the default), and the user accepts the risk and installs the application, the application can then do whatever it wants at runtime. Windows access control list protections still apply, since the application process will run under the identity of the logged in user. If the user does not have permission to do something, such as access the registry, the application itself will not have permission to do that either.

User Cache

As previously discussed, all of the application files are placed under a set of folders dynamically created by the runtime under the user's profile when the application is deployed to the client machine. The folder names are obfuscated by design for security reasons, so that a Web application or other applications cannot guess the location of another application to try to compromise it. As a side effect, the folder naming also makes it difficult for someone to be able to "accidentally" go into those folders and launch the application from there, since a ClickOnce deployed application should always be launched by ClickOnce. If the executable is launched by navigating to the folder it is placed in and double-clicking on it or running it from a command line, then it is no longer running through ClickOnce activation. It will then run with the security policy for assemblies running from the My Computer zone—which is full trust by default. Additionally, depending on what that application does with its data files, the application may not run correctly, because you manage data files differently in code when you know they will be running under ClickOnce, as discussed in Chapter 5.

The specific location and folder structure for the client side is considered an undocumented aspect of the way that ClickOnce works, so you should not write any code that tries to work directly against the folder structure where your application resides. There are APIs in the Framework that let you dynamically determine the application's location, and you can use those as discussed in Chapter 5. However, you should not try to infer the location of your files based on any current knowledge of the pattern used to create and determine the ClickOnce client-side folders, because that is subject to change in future releases of the Framework. That being said, it is sometimes helpful for advanced troubleshooting of launch failures or runtime problems to be able to inspect the folders and see if the artifacts you are expecting are there.

The user cache folders are all stored under the user's profile in the Local Settings\Apps folder (C:\Documents and Settings\<username>\Local Settings\Apps by default on Windows XP, c:\users\<username>\App-Data\Local\Apps on Windows Vista). Under there, a bunch of obfuscated subfolders get created to isolate each application and version. Additionally, there are separate data folders created for each application to help with data migration between versions. You can see the basic folder structure in Figure 2.20 for the EmployeeManager application. This is on a machine with no other ClickOnce applications installed and only a single version of the EmployeeManager application installed. As additional applications and versions are installed, more and more of these folders are created under the Apps root.

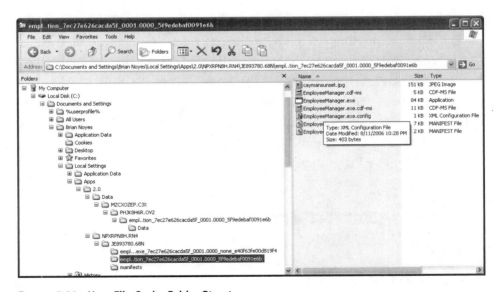

Figure 2.20: User File Cache Folder Structure

For an installed application, the cache will contain the current version of the application. Additionally, if there was a previous version of the application installed by this user and the current version is not a minimum required version, then the previous version of the application will also be maintained in the cache. Users can roll back to this previous version through the Add or Remove Programs item that is added. For online-only applications, the cache's maximum size can also be controlled by administrators by setting the HKEY_CURRENT_USER\Software\Classes\Software\Microsoft\Windows\CurrentVersion\Deployment\OnlineApp-QuotaInKB registry key, which is a DWORD value that expresses the cache size in kilobytes.

Start Menu Item

When an installed application (one that is available offline) is launched the first time, a Start menu item is added under All Programs. The group name for the item is set by the Publisher name setting, and the item name is set by the Product name setting. The icon used for the application shortcut is determined by the Resources Icon property in Visual Studio on the project properties editor's Application tab. Figure 2.21 illustrates an example for the EmployeeManager sample. If you enter a support location URL in the Publish Options dialog, you will get an additional help shortcut in the Start menu group for your publisher.

This Start menu item should be the usual way of launching the application after its initial installation through the URL to the deployment manifest on the deployment server. Any time the application is launched through the Start menu item, normal update checking will be done before launch if that is what the application was configured for. The Start menu item will be removed when the application is completely removed through its Add or Remove Programs item in the Control Panel.

FIGURE 2.21: Start Menu Item

Add or Remove Programs

When you first launch a ClickOnce installed application, it adds an item to Add or Remove Programs in the Control Panel to let you uninstall the application. Figure 2.22 shows an example for the EmployeeManager application with the Support Info dialog that displays when you click on the link to show support information.

Additionally, if the application is updated with an optional update which the user accepts, the previous version is retained on the client. When the user clicks on the Change/Remove button in Add or Remove Programs for the ClickOnce application item, the maintenance dialog shown in Figure 2.23 will display. Selecting the Remove option in this dialog will remove the files from the user profile cache for all versions of the application, will remove the Start menu items for this application, and will remove the security application trust policy for the application—everything that ClickOnce created on the client machine at the initial install and subsequent updates of that application. Selecting the Restore option will roll the application back to the previous version that is cached locally. If the user rolls the application back, the user will

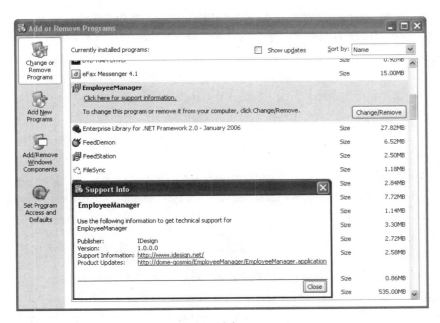

FIGURE 2.22: Add or Remove Programs Dialog

FIGURE 2.23: Application Maintenance Dialog

continue to run that version until a new update becomes available. Only one previous version is retained on the client when an update occurs.

Moving an Application to Production

So now you know how to publish an application using Visual Studio, along with all the gory details about what is going on behind the scenes. However, for large enterprise environments, you as a developer are not going to have direct access to the production servers where your Click-Once applications will really be hosted. The publishing mechanisms of Visual Studio are really just a fancy file-copy mechanism: Visual Studio just copies your application files over to the Publishing Location and generates the deployment and application manifests. You might think that you could just publish the application to a local directory using Visual Studio, and then zip up the folder and send it to your administrators for placement on the production server. Unfortunately, this will not work without a little additional effort, but luckily that additional effort is minimal. You just need to understand what is needed and how to do it, which is what you will learn in this next section.

Moving a Published Application into Production with Visual Studio

In most situations, you will at least use Visual Studio to publish your application locally to a place that you can use to test it, such as your local installation of IIS or an integration server on the development network. Once you have tested it there and it is ready to be moved to a QA or production server that you do not have direct access to from your Visual Studio development machine, you will need a way to get the files ready for placement on the target server.

If you recall, the Installation URL you specify from Visual Studio sets the deployment provider setting in the deployment manifest, and the setting will be checked at launch time on the client to ensure that the application that the user is launching is in the location intended by the publisher.

When you move the application files (including the application manifests) to a different server, the deployment provider URL in the deployment manifest will need to be updated to the desired deployment manifest's address. Typically this is the same URL that users launch the application with, but as mentioned before, ClickOnce also supports a one-hop redirect to a different deployment manifest at a different URL.

To get the deployment provider set correctly in the deployment manifest, you could approach it in one of two ways. One way is to just republish the application from Visual Studio to some local directory, but specify the appropriate Installation URL in the project properties editor before publishing, and set to the address that users will use to launch the application from the target server. You would then be able to copy all the files from the Publishing Location folder to the production target server folder and you would be good to go.

There is a slight hazard to this approach: whenever you publish from Visual Studio, your project will be rebuilt before publishing. This means that the bits that you put into production will not actually be the exact same assemblies that you tested up to that point. A safer way to do things is to use the mageui.exe GUI tool or the mage.exe command line tool to just update the deployment manifest without changing anything about the published binaries at all.

Moving an Application into Production with Mage

Mageui.exe and mage.exe let you create, modify, and sign deployment and application manifests for ClickOnce. They are part of the .NET Framework 2.0 SDK, and can be found in the \Bin folder for the SDK under your Visual Studio install (C:\Program Files\Microsoft Visual Studio 8\SDK\v2.0\Bin by default). **Mage** stands for manifest generator and editing. These are simple

.NET 2.0 applications themselves and do not depend on any other libraries other than ones that are in the Framework. So you could provide just the executables to an administrator who has a machine available with .NET 2.0 on it, and the administrator would be able to make the necessary modifications and administer the ClickOnce manifests herself.

To update the deployment provider for an application with mageui.exe, you just need to launch mageui.exe and load the deployment manifest (the .application file) for the application into the tool. If you published to a local IIS install with a URL like http://localhost/EmployeeManager, you will be able to find the deployment manifest in the root folder for the application at C:\Inetpub\wwwroot\EmployeeManager, depending on your IIS configuration. The deployment provider is called the **Start Location** in the mageui.exe editors. You can find this setting under the Deployment Options category after loading the manifest into the tool (see Figure 2.24).

After editing any aspect of the manifest, you will have to re-sign it to make sure the digital signature is valid on the file. Otherwise, no one will be able to launch the application. To re-sign it from mageui.exe, you just click the Save button in the toolbar or choose File > Save from the menu. When you do, the dialog shown in Figure 2.25 displays for you to sign the manifest. As mentioned earlier, when you add a publisher certificate to your project in Visual Studio, it is also added to the Personal certificate store in

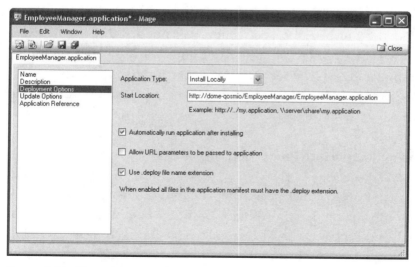

FIGURE 2.24: Mageui.exe Manifest Editor

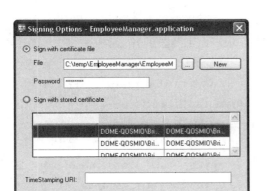

FIGURE 2.25: Manifest Signing Options Dialog

Windows under the logged in user's account. The list of certificates shown in the middle of Figure 2.25 corresponds to the publisher certificates in this store. As you can see, the problem is that every self-generated certificate looks the same in the list (every <projectname>_TemporaryKey.pfx file you have ever generated on your development machine will be in the list), so it is difficult to use that to select the certificate unless you always manually configure your ClickOnce projects to use a specially named certificate, or you are on a machine where Visual Studio has not been generating lots of certificates for you. The top of the dialog lets you browse to a particular .pfx file and use that to sign the manifest instead, which is easier to use on a development machine.

If you want to use the command line tool mage.exe instead to update the manifest, possibly as part of a script you give to your administrator to prevent her from needing to learn the tool, you just need to pass the appropriate arguments to the tool to update the deployment provider and re-sign the manifest. Just to keep things confusing, the deployment provider is called yet another thing in the command line tool—the **ProviderURL argument.** To do this, you can use a command line like the following (without the line breaks).

```
"C:\Program Files\Microsoft Visual Studio 8\SDK\v2.0\Bin\mage.exe"
-Update C:\somefolder\EmployeeManager.application
-ProviderURL http://myserver/EmployeeManager/EmployeeManager.application
-CertFile C:/SomeFolder/mypublishercert.pfx
- Password mypwd
```

Mage.exe has a ton of other parameters you can use to update other settings in either a deployment manifest or application manifest, or to generate them from scratch. But for the process of moving a tested application to a different deployment server, just updating the deployment provider is the minimum required modification. In the previous command, the `-Update` option specifies the path to the deployment manifest to be modified, the `-ProviderURL` parameter corresponds to the Installation URL setting in Visual Studio, the `-CertFile` parameter gives the path to the .pfx file you want to use to do the signing, and if that .pfx file has a password, the `-Password` parameter lets you specify that.

Where Are We?

This chapter has conducted a start-to-finish tour of all the aspects of initial publishing and deployment of an application with ClickOnce. As you can see, there is a lot more than meets the eye in a simple ClickOnce demonstration like the one you stepped through in Chapter 1. There is a lot of stuff that Visual Studio does for you when publishing that you will need to understand to handle complex deployments or troubleshoot things when they are not working as expected. There is a lot going on behind the scenes when users click on a link to a ClickOnce application to get it to run on their machines. All of this information can be very useful in understanding what occurs in a ClickOnce deployment. This is important both to educate people on what is going on when questions about security or reliability of ClickOnce applications arise, and also to diagnose and correct any problems that might arise in the publishing process. Later chapters will get into more details on some of the aspects that were introduced in this chapter, including security, managing application files, and administering Click-Once deployments.

The following are some of the key takeaways from this chapter.

- Visual Studio automates the process of publishing a ClickOnce deployed application, including copying the files to the deployment server and generating the manifests needed to launch the application from a client.

- You can launch a ClickOnce deployed application with an HTTP or UNC path to the deployment manifest (the .application file), or from a local file path with a CD deployment.

- You can publish a ClickOnce deployed application via HTTP, a UNC path to a file share, FTP, or a drive letter path.

- There are a lot of options to consider before publishing your application that all affect the installation, runtime behavior, and updating of your application.

- You deploy prerequisites through the Bootstrapper setup.exe file generated by Visual Studio.

- For a typical ClickOnce publication with all the files on a single server, the deployment provider in the deployment manifest must match the URL that users use to launch the application. If you move a published application to a different deployment server, you will have to update this property in the deployment manifest and re-sign the manifest.

- Installed applications create a Start menu item and an Add or Remove Programs item that can be used to launch or remove the application on the client machine.

- Mageui.exe and mage.exe in the SDK tools can be used on machines that do not have Visual Studio to edit or create manifest files.

The next chapter details how to automatically update applications with ClickOnce and the many variations in behavior and options that exist for performing updates. It also covers what happens under the covers during an application update in the same way that I described the step-by-step process of what is happening on the client machine during an initial install.

■ 3 ■

Automatic Application Updates

T HE LAST CHAPTER covered everything that goes on when you perform an initial deployment of an application to users through ClickOnce. It covered what you need to do in Visual Studio to publish your application with ClickOnce, what happens on the deployment server during the publishing process and how it varies depending on the publishing options you select, and the end user's experience on the client machines when they first launch the application through a deployment manifest link. This chapter focuses on updates—subsequent deployments of updated versions of the application to users.

You may need to publish updates to your application for any number of reasons. You may be putting out minor bug fixes or optional new functionality that is not essential for users to get immediately. You may be rolling out critical bug fixes or security updates that you want users to get right away. Whatever reason you have for updating your application, with ClickOnce, you have a great deal of flexibility in choosing what your update policy will be and when the updates occur. This chapter covers each of the options and what effect your selection of those options will have on the publishing process and your users. First, let's step through an update to the EmployeeManager application used in Chapter 2 to demonstrate initial deployment so that you can see the default update process in action.

Automatic Update Walkthrough

If you worked through the steps in Chapter 2, you should have a single version (1.0.0.0) of the EmployeeManager application published to your local machine, and your machine is acting as the deployment server for testing purposes. If you also launched the application from the publish.htm page generated by Visual Studio, you will have version 1.0.0.0 deployed to your local machine. You should have a Start menu shortcut under your publisher name that you can use to launch the application. If you haven't stepped through that process, you might want to do so now.

The first step in deploying an updated version of your application is to get that version built and tested in your development environment. When it is ready to be deployed to your users, you need to publish it to your deployment server.

Publishing an Update

The process of publishing your updated application from Visual Studio is no different than the process for publishing the initial version, which was described in Chapter 2. When you publish an updated version of your application to the same Publishing Location as previous versions, Visual Studio will update the default deployment manifest (<appname>.application) and will create a new subfolder and version-specific deployment manifest for the version you are publishing.

To make a visible change to the EmployeeManager application that you can see after the update is applied, you need to make a change to the EmployeeManager sample application and then publish the new version.

1. Open the EmployeeManager project in Visual Studio.
2. Open Form1.cs in the designer.
3. Click on the form's title bar to select the form.
4. Select the BackColor property in the Properties window and set it to ActiveCaption or some other color of your choice (see Figure 3.1).
5. Select Build > Publish EmployeeManager from the IDE menu.
6. Do *not* click on the Install button in the publish.htm test page that is loaded into the browser at this time—just close the browser. The reason

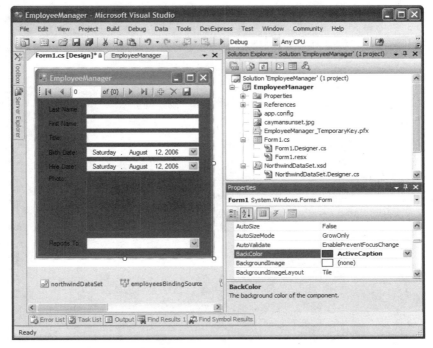

FIGURE 3.1: Setting the Form's BackColor Property

for not clicking the Install button is that if you click on the link to the deployment manifest, you would not be prompted as a client that an update is available; the update would just be immediately downloaded. Instead, you will launch the application the way users normally would, through the Start menu shortcut.

You should change the Publish Version setting in your project properties editor to the desired version before publishing to a production or QA environment. Usually you will want to have explicit control and will need to document any version that you publish for QA or production in an enterprise environment. If you don't really care and just want ClickOnce to make sure the update happens, then you don't need to worry about explicitly setting the Publish Version. Visual Studio will auto-increment the revision number portion of that version number each time you publish your application (see Figure 3.2). For this exercise, Visual Studio incremented the version to 1.0.0.1 when the first version of the EmployeeManager application was

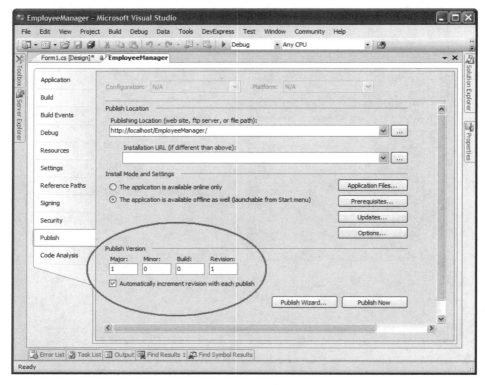

FIGURE 3.2: Publish Property Settings

published. When you published in step 5 in the preceding exercise, version 1.0.0.1 was used for the new version published to the deployment server.

Updating the Application on the Client

If you have used the default settings for updates in ClickOnce, updating the application on the client machine is automatic once the new version has been published to the deployment server. If users have connectivity to the deployment server when launching the application from the Start menu shortcut, the runtime will check for updates on the deployment server before launching. If the deployment server cannot be reached, the current version on the client machine will simply launch.

If an update is available, users will be prompted and can either accept or skip the update with the default update settings. If they accept the update, the new version will be downloaded and installed on the client machine, and the new version will be launched. Subsequent launches through the Start menu will just run the updated version from the client machine, until a newer version becomes available on the deployment server. If they choose to skip the update, they will not be prompted again to install the update for seven days. This value is hard-coded in the Click-Once runtime and is not configurable. If a new update is published, users will be prompted at that point, but they will only be prompted for the version that they skipped every seven days.

To try out updating the application, do the following.

1. Go to the Start menu and select the EmployeeManager shortcut (All Programs > IDesign > EmployeeManager).

2. The runtime will detect the updated version in the deployment manifest on the deployment server that you published in the previous section, and you will be prompted that there is a new version available (see Figure 3.3).

3. Click the OK button and the new version will download and launch.

If users choose to accept the update by clicking the OK button, and the new version requires higher privileges than were originally granted when previous versions of the application were installed, users will be warned again that the application requires elevated trust on the machine and they will have to click the Install button to install the new version (see Figure 3.4). This might occur, for example, if version 1.0 of your application just talked directly to the database and you deployed it with partial trust (as described in Chapter 6), but then later rolled out a new version that communicates with a back-end server through Windows Communication Foundation (WCF). WCF requires full trust, so the updated version would need elevated permissions to full trust in order to run.

FIGURE 3.3: Update Available Dialog

FIGURE 3.4: Application Install - Security Warning Dialog

▪ TIP   Forcing an Update

Even if users have a previous version installed on their machines, if they launch the application through a link to the Installation URL on the deployment server, the updated version will be downloaded and run without prompting the users to skip the update. This provides a way to get an update to users who mistakenly press the Don't Install button. A support person can direct them to click on a link to the Installation URL and they will get the latest version, regardless of what version was previously installed on their machines. This can also be used to get users on the current version if users have restored the application to the previous version through the Add or Remove Programs item.

Manually Publishing the Update with Mage

If you are manually publishing the new version of your application to a deployment server, you will need to update the default deployment manifest to point to the new version of the application and re-sign it with a publisher certificate. If you mimic the folder structure that Visual Studio creates, this means you need to do the following.

1. Copy your new version files into a new subfolder in the application's root deployment folder on the server.

2. Run Mage (type **mageui** and then press Enter at a Visual Studio command prompt, or execute mageui.exe in the .NET Framework SDK \bin folder).

3. Copy the application manifest (.manifest file) from the previous version's subfolder into the new version's subfolder as a starting point.

4. Choose File > Open to open the application manifest with mageui.exe.

5. Set the version number to the new version number in the first view of Mage (see Figure 3.5). This should be different than the version that was previously published so that ClickOnce can distinguish it as an update.

6. Select the Files category on the left. The list of files associated with the application will be shown, as set in the previous version (see Figure 3.6).

7. Click the Populate button to refresh the list of files. You will be prompted as shown in Figure 3.7, because the file names of any new files will be changed to include the .deploy file extension.

8. Click OK. The file list will be refreshed, and Mage will recompute the hash values for all the files. These values get embedded in the application manifest to identify which files have actually changed between versions, and to ensure that files are not tampered with on the server.

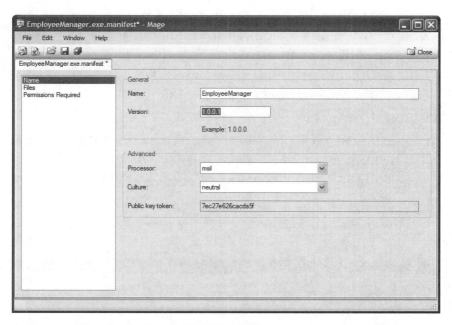

FIGURE 3.5: Mage Application Manifest Name Settings

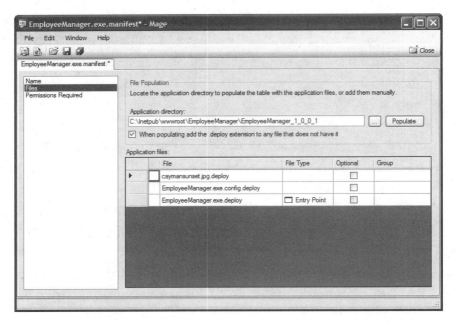

FIGURE 3.6: Mage Application Manifest Files Settings

9. Click the Save button in the toolbar. You will be presented with the Signing Options dialog shown in Figure 3.8. Either browse to the .pfx file for the publisher certificate using the button with ellipses (...) at the top of the window and enter the file password, or select an existing certificate from the list in the middle. This list shows all of the certificates installed in your Personal certificate store. Click OK.

10. Close the manifest.

11. Open the default deployment manifest in the root deployment folder using Mage (choose File > Open and navigate to the <app-name>.application file in the application root publishing folder).

12. Set the version number in the Name category to match the one you set in the application manifest.

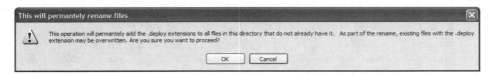

FIGURE 3.7: Mage File Renaming Warning

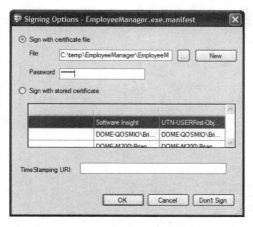

FIGURE 3.8: Mage Signing Options Dialog

13. Select the Application Reference category in the list on the left of the UI.

14. Click the Select Manifest button shown in Figure 3.9 and navigate to the application manifest (<appname>.exe.manifest) in the version subfolder that you created for the new version. This step is required any time you want to point the default deployment manifest to a new version of the application, or any time you sign the application manifest with a new publisher certificate. You can see in Figure 3.9 that the public key token for the file is part of the application reference. This is determined from the publisher certificate used to sign the file in step 9. You must use the same certificate to sign the application and deployment manifests.

15. Select File > Save from the menu bar. The Signing Options dialog will appear. Select the certificate you want to use to sign the manifest as discussed in step 9 and click OK.

ClickOnce Update Options

The default ClickOnce behavior for updates addresses the most common requirements for application update behavior—making it automatic so that users are always running the latest version, but don't tie their hands by forcing them to accept the update. The automatic aspect makes it so that users don't have to go looking for an update themselves or wait until some scheduled

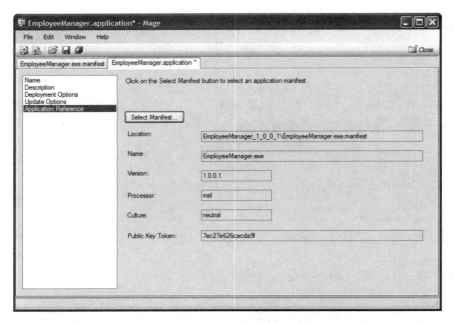

FIGURE 3.9: Mage Application Reference Settings

timer kicks in to check for them. It has the performance downside that the check will happen every time the application launches, which can be annoying and reduce user productivity. Also, users often want to have some degree of control over things that are going to change their machine.

If you, as a user, have a version of an application on your machine that is stable and that has been working fine for a while, do you really want to take an update to that application five minutes before going in to use it to present something to your CEO? You probably wouldn't want to risk that something could go wrong with the update or that the new version would change features that you need to use immediately. Of course there is also the scenario, pointed out by one of my reviewers, that if you fail to take the update, you could be presenting stale information or strategies to the CEO that were just published as the current policy for the company, and you could end up getting fired for not being up to date! In that case, hopefully the publisher of the application made it a minimum required version, forcing you to take the update.

The problem with any default behavior is that it probably won't work for everyone. ClickOnce addresses that fact by giving you a lot of flexibility as an application publisher to determine what your update policy will be. ClickOnce allows you, as the publisher, to explicitly control when users get updates. It also provides several ways that you can give users some control of the process. The next section steps you through each of the options related to automatic updates, and Chapter 4 covers how you can have even more control by using the ClickOnce on-demand API to perform updates programmatically.

Install Mode and Updates

Of all the publishing settings, the Install Mode you choose has the most significant impact on update behavior. If you choose to make the application available online only, then you have no further options with respect to update behavior. With an online-only application, no Start menu shortcut is created, so users can only launch the application through a link to the Installation URL. Every time they do launch the application, the client must connect to the deployment server to check the deployment manifest there to see if an update has been published. If there is an update, it will be downloaded immediately before the application launches, ensuring that users are always running the latest version of the application. If the client can't connect to the deployment server, the client can't run the application.

If you go with an installed application (available both offline and online), then you have a whole collection of additional options. When you select this installation mode in project properties editor's Publish tab, the Updates button gets enabled (see Figure 3.2). Pressing that button takes you to the Application Updates dialog, which is shown with the default options selected in Figure 3.10. Some of the options in this dialog are interdependent, which is why some of the options are disabled in Figure 3.10. The options available include

- Whether to check for updates
- Whether to check for updates before the application launches or after
- A schedule interval to do update checks (only available if you are checking for updates after application launch)

- Whether there is a minimum required version of the application that users must have
- An Update Location that is potentially different from the Installation URL

The following subsections discuss each of these options in more detail.

Checking for Updates

The first option you have in the Application Updates dialog (see Figure 3.10) is whether the application should automatically check for updates or not. This option is checked by default, resulting in the application automatically checking for updates when it runs. You would only uncheck this box if you did not want the application to automatically check for updates. You would typically only do this if you planned to use the programmatic API described in Chapter 4 to allow users to update the application on demand, or if you wanted to trigger updates based on some other criteria driven by your code.

If you will frequently be deploying large updates that are not essential to the operations of the applications, such as a media library update, you may want to consider using programmatic updates instead of automatic updates to do those downloads in the background while the application is

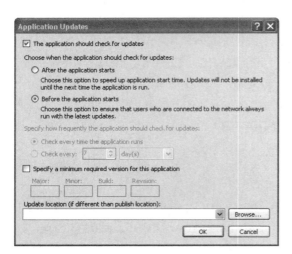

FIGURE 3.10: Application Updates Dialog

running. Doing so will prevent users from needing to wait for the entire download of an update to complete before being able to use the rest of the application. The launch of the application will always be snappy even if a large update needs to be deployed. You may also want to use programmatic updates instead of either of the automatic update options if you need users to get the update as soon as it is published, as opposed to getting it on some future execution of the application.

Checking for Updates Before the Application Launches

The default selection for when the automatic updates occur is before the application launches. This selection results in the behavior you saw in the walkthrough earlier in this chapter. Specifically, as the application is launched, it will check the deployment server for updates. If any are found, they will be downloaded and applied before the application launches, resulting in users getting the latest version of the application. If the client machine cannot connect to the deployment server, the current version of the application on the client machine will launch normally. Unless the version you are publishing is set as the minimum required version, users will be given the option to skip the update as discussed earlier.

This option is the default mainly for development convenience. If you do not need your users to get updates as soon as they are published, you should avoid checking for updates before launch because it will slow down the application's start-up time if it needs to check every time it starts up. Users will have a better experience if you select the option to check for updates after application launch, discussed next.

Checking for Updates after the Application Launches

If you select the option to check for updates after the application launches, the application will always launch immediately from the currently installed version in the user's cache on the client machine. After the application launches, the runtime will start a background thread that tries to connect to the deployment server. If successful, the background thread will check the deployment manifest on the server to see if there is an update available. If so, the runtime will set a bit that indicates that an update is available. The next time the user starts the application, he will be prompted that there is an update available (unless the update is set as the minimum required version), and the update will be downloaded and installed on that launch before the application starts. The download and install still happens in the foreground before the application launches, but it doesn't happen until the runtime already knows an update is available from the previous run of the application.

The background check only runs once when the application starts; it is not a continuous process. Depending on the application's usage pattern, this could result in a long delay between when an update is published and when the user starts using the new version. Consider an application where the user starts the application at the beginning of the day and does not shut it down until the end of the day. If an update is deployed in the middle of the day, it will not be detected until the start of the next day. Then the user will not see the update prompt and download the update until the beginning of the third day, when he launches the application.

Scheduled Update Checking

When you select the option to check for updates after the application launches, you have an additional option to perform the background checking on a scheduled basis instead of doing it every time your application launches. The default selection for this setting is to check every time the application launches. If you want to check on a scheduled basis, select the option to check after the application launches (see Figure 3.10), then select the radio button labeled *Check every*. When you do so, the two combo boxes to the right of that radio button will be enabled, allowing you to specify an interval in terms of hours, days, or weeks. The interval will be started from the point when the application is first installed, and each time users start the application, the date and time will be checked to determine whether the interval has occurred, requiring an update check. When an update check occurs, the system will record the time so that it can restart the interval.

Setting Minimum Required Version

The default settings let users skip the installation of an update, as discussed earlier in this chapter. This may not be acceptable for many applications. You may need to deploy new middle-tier application components

> ■■ **WARNING** Maximum Schedule Intervals
>
> Unfortunately, the Application Updates dialog does not do a very good job of validating your input. It will let you input interval values that are larger than what the runtime will allow. So if you put in too large of an interval value, you will be able to publish your application from Visual Studio, but ClickOnce will get a launch error when the user tries to launch it. The maximum interval is 8,760 for hours, 365 for days, and 52 for weeks. Do not enter values greater than these when you publish or your users will not be able to launch the application.

with changes to the interfaces that the client applications call through. You may also need to deploy a new version of a database with changes to its schema that would break existing clients. In these situations, the client application could fail, or worse yet, corrupt data on the back-end if you let users launch an old version of the application after the back-end deployment is performed.

You could address this situation by only deploying clients using the online-only Install Mode. With that mode you can be assured that the client that launches is always the latest version. However, that launch mode restricts users from using the application in an offline mode, which also may not make sense for many applications.

To address this situation with installed applications, you can specify a minimum required version when you publish an application. When you specify a minimum required version, this information will be published to the deployment server version of the deployment manifest when you publish the application. When the client machine detects that the new version is available and it has been set to the minimum required version, the following happens.

- The user will not be prompted that the update is available and given the option to skip the update.
- The user cannot cancel the download of the update. If she cancels and tries to launch again, the download will commence again and she won't be able to run the application successfully until the download has succeeded.

- The user cannot roll back to a version that is older than the minimum required version. If the previous version cached on the client machine has a lower version number than the minimum required version, the application's option to restore the previous application state in the Add or Remove Programs item will be grayed out.

You can use the minimum required version to ensure that a client never runs an out-of-date version of the application, particularly if that version needs to be the same version as back-end services or components that it talks to remotely. So if you deploy a new version of middle-tier components or a new database, you need to ensure that you also publish a new client with its minimum required version set equal to the new published version. By doing so, you ensure that users will not be able to run their applications in an online mode without receiving the update.

> ■ **WARNING**   No Guarantees with Minimum Required Version
>
> Using a minimum required version to ensure users get the latest version when they are online is a good way to try to keep users synchronized with the code that is running on the back-end of distributed systems. However, you need to keep in mind that this only ensures that if the client machine can connect to the deployment server, it will get the latest version of the application when it performs its updates. If the client can connect to the back-end system (middle-tier application server, Web service, or database) but cannot connect to the deployment server for some reason, you could still have a problem with the client code running out of synchronization with the server side. A defensive way of protecting against this is to include a way for your client application to check what version of a back-end system it is talking to through the API exposed to the client, and present an error to the user if the client is out of sync and unable to update. Also keep in mind that if you select the option to do updates after the application launches, the client will always get at least one more run of the old version before the new version is used for subsequent launches.

Specifying an Update Location

The Update Location option lets you specify where the application will look for updates when the application is launched on the client. This URL gets written to the deployment provider URL in the deployment manifest, which is used for launching and updating the application. You will use this setting for two situations: deploying an initial version of your application via CD, and when you disable automatic updates.

If you deploy your application via CD, you may still want to allow online updates to keep the application up to date with new features and bug fixes. When you specify that you want to initially deploy your application via CD (discussed in Chapter 2), you are prompted to provide an Update Location. The prompt in the Publish wizard is just a reflection of the settings in the project properties editor's Publish tab. The Update Location option in the Application Updates dialog lets you set the URL ahead of time so that it becomes part of your project settings for future publications of your application.

If you choose to use the on-demand API to programmatically update your application (discussed in Chapter 4) as the sole means of update, meaning that the application will never update itself automatically, then you will need to specify the Update Location to supply the URL that the on-demand programmatic API will use for update checking.

Behind the Scenes on the Deployment Server

Just like with publishing an initial version of an application, publishing an update is mostly a file-copy process. When you publish an application update from Visual Studio, the process is similar to that described in Chapter 2 for initial deployment. The following steps occur.

1. A subfolder is created in the publish location folder to contain all of the application files for this particular version.
2. The subfolder is named based on the version number with the naming convention <appname>_major_minor_build_revision.
3. The application manifest (<appname>.exe.manifest) is placed in the subfolder.
4. A version-specific deployment manifest is created with the naming convention <appname>_major_minor_build_revision .application, and it is placed in the publish location folder.

5. The application reference in the default deployment manifest (<app-name>.application) is updated to point to the application manifest for the new version.

At that point everything is in place and ready for clients to start updating their applications to the new version, either through automatic updates or through the on-demand API.

Behind the Scenes of an Update on the Client Machine

There is a lot more that goes on under the covers on the client machine to support the update process. After the user clicks on the Start menu shortcut, a large chain of steps is kicked off to check the update and get it delivered to the client machine. This all happens in a secure way that protects the user from inadvertently launching an application that has been tampered with. In the process described next, the *client manifest* means the one that was cached on the client side from the currently installed version, and the *server manifest* means the one being downloaded from the deployment server for the new version. The usual progression is as follows.

1. The user clicks on the Start menu shortcut to launch the application.
2. The client deployment manifest is checked to see what the update policy was for that version.
3. If the application is supposed to check for updates before launching, the client tries to download the default server deployment manifest.
4. If the server deployment manifest cannot be downloaded, the application is just launched from the local cached version.
5. If the server deployment manifest download is successful, the server manifest is validated. See Chapter 2 for a discussion of manifest validation.
6. If the server manifest validation succeeds, the Publish Version in the server deployment manifest is compared to the one for the client deployment manifest.

7. If the version in the server manifest is different than the one currently in use by the client, and if the current version is not less than the minimum required version specified in the update, the user will be prompted that a new version is available. It is not necessary for the new version number to be newer than the previous version. This allows the administrator to cause a server-side rollback by just republishing a previous version by updating the default deployment manifest to a previous version's deployment manifest.

8. If the user accepts the update or it is a minimum required version, the server application manifest for that version is downloaded next.

9. Once the server application manifest is downloaded, it is validated in a similar fashion to the server deployment manifest.

10. If validation succeeds, the permissions requested in the server application manifest are compared to the permissions currently granted to the application. If the new version requires more permissions than the previous version, the user is prompted to install the application (same dialog as shown in Figure 3.4). The application trust policy is updated accordingly to include the new permissions if the user chooses to install the application.

11. The application files in the server application manifest are compared to the ones listed in the client application manifest to see what has changed.

12. A progress dialog is presented to the user that shows the progress of the download process.

13. Any files that are already cached in the current version on the client that are unchanged in the new version are copied over to the new version's client cache folder to avoid redownloading those files.

14. The new or changed files in the application are downloaded into the new version's folder.

15. The previous version's data files are moved to the data folders of the new version if applicable (see Chapter 5 for more details).

16. The Start menu shortcut is updated in case the codebase, publisher, or product name changes, but the shortcut will automatically point to the new version because it is a version-independent reference to the

application. The runtime takes care of launching the current version when the shortcut is clicked.

17. The Add or Remove Programs item for the application is updated to reflect that an update has occurred.

18. The new version of the application is launched.

There are several subtle variations on this process for online-only applications or applications that do their update checking after launch instead of before. But most of the steps above apply to all updates. You don't have any direct control over the process other than to control the contents of the manifests. However, it is helpful to know what is going on under the covers both to diagnose launch errors and in case you will be responsible for educating management or IT staff of the protections that ClickOnce provides to avoid launching unauthorized applications.

File Validation

The process for comparing the files in the new version's application manifest and the currently installed version is fairly sophisticated. The application manifest contains more than just the names of the files that the application is composed of. One of the pieces of information that is included for every application file is a hash value that is computed with an algorithm also specified in the manifest. ClickOnce compares the hash values for each application file in both the client manifest and the server manifest to decide whether it needs to download the file or not. If the hash in the server manifest is different than the one in the client manifest, the new version of the file will be downloaded.

If the hashes in the client and server manifests match for a single application file, ClickOnce considers the application file unchanged on the server side compared to the currently installed version's file. ClickOnce then recomputes the hash for the current version's cached file and compares it to the client manifest hash to ensure that the application file in the cache has not been tampered with. If it has, it will download the one from the server side as if the hashes did not match to ensure that the client is running the correct version of the file.

If the hash of an individual application file in the server manifest does not match the one in the client manifest, the application file will be downloaded from the deployment server. After it has been downloaded, its hash is computed and compared to the one that was in the server manifest to ensure that the file was not tampered with on the server side.

Transactions

Obviously, with all this file comparing and copying going on as part of the update process, lots of things could go wrong. It would not be a great user experience if the update process could fail in a way that left them unable to use the application. To protect against that, the entire update process is done in a transactional way. This means that the currently installed version of the application is considered to be in a consistent state before the update process starts. All of the updating is done in a way so that the temporary, inconsistent results of the update are not accessible until a new version has been fully downloaded and cached in a similarly consistent state to the currently installed version. Once that is the case, the update transaction is completed, the Start menu item is updated to point to the new version, and the scavenging process (discussed next) then runs.

If something goes wrong during the update process, the transactional approach to updates ensures that the application's previous consistent state is never disturbed and that the temporary artifacts created during the update process are all removed.

Client Cache Scavenging

Even though disk space is cheap these days, it probably would not be a great idea to leave every version of every application ever installed by the user through ClickOnce accumulating under the user profile. As a result, ClickOnce limits what is retained in the client application cache in a couple of ways.

The first way ClickOnce controls the client cache is that at most two versions of any given installed application are retained on the client. When an update is deployed to the client for an installed application, the previous version is not removed completely. It is left in place, but the Start menu shortcut is updated to point to the new version. As long as the previous version was not a minimum required version, the Add or Remove Programs item will allow the user to roll back to the previous version. At the completion of an application update, the scavenging process takes care of removing the oldest version of the application cached on the client machine.

Additionally, if the application is an online-only application, the size of the user's application cache is limited by a quota. Each partially trusted application can only consume half of the quota, leaving room for application updates to occur. The quota size is 250MB by default, but can be set through the HKEY_CURRENT_USER\Software\Classes\Software\Microsoft\ Windows\CurrentVersion\Deployment\OnlineAppQuotaInKB registry key value (a DWORD value representing the storage size in kilobytes). Data files used by the online-only application are not subject to the cache quota limitation, and installed applications are not limited by the quota. Online application files are scavenged as needed by the ClickOnce runtime when new versions are deployed.

Removing or Restoring Applications on the Client

As discussed in Chapter 2, an item is added to the Add or Remove Programs item when a ClickOnce application is installed. If just a single version of the application is installed on the machine, the only option available from the Add or Remove Programs item is to remove the application. However, if a newer version of the same application has been deployed to the client machine through the update mechanisms discussed in this chapter, then an additional option lets the user restore the application's previous version.

This can be a handy option to have from a user's perspective. Suppose you had a stable, functioning version of an application on your machine and then accepted an update. Now things that were working fine just before you applied the update no longer work correctly, or the update is buggy and is crashing. You, as a user, are going to want to get back to that known, good version as quickly as possible.

This is precisely what the Add or Remove Programs item lets you do. If you select *Restore the application to its previous state* (see Figure 2.23), the previous version cached on the machine will be restored as if the update never happened.

Restoring an Application Version from the Deployment Server

Bugs happen. It is possible that you could publish an application and not realize until it is out in the wild that the bug exists, and you may not want your users to continue using the new buggy version. But ClickOnce is a client-pull deployment technology, so how can you push a version out to your users to get them back onto the previous stable build? Well, you can't directly, but there is an easy way to address the scenario.

Don't worry, I'm not going to say "just send an e-mail to all your users and tell them to restore the previous version through Add or Remove Programs item." That would work too, but you probably don't want to impose additional pain on your users for your mistake in publishing a buggy update. So the simple solution is to take the previous version that you want to have all users restore to, publish it to the deployment server with a new Publish Version that is newer than the Publish Version of the buggy update, and set the minimum required version setting to be that new version number. Now from a client perspective, they are forced to update to a new version, but what they will really be getting is the bits from the old version back.

Republishing a Previous Version

What if you don't want to clutter up your deployment server with another copy of an application that is already residing there with a previous version number, but you want users to get that previous version as if it were a new version? All you need to do is save the version-specific deployment manifest that is created each time you publish a version (the one with the version number as part of the name) as the default deployment manifest. You can do this by copying the file and renaming it to the default manifest name (<appname>.application).

If you no longer have the old version's deployment and application manifests available, you could just republish the old version's application files as a new Publish Version using the steps described earlier in the section Manually Publishing the Update with Mage.

Where Are We?

This chapter covered the details of what you need to do to publish an update to your application. You saw what the various options were for automatic updates and how they affected when the updates occur and how they affect what happens on the client. It discussed what happens on the server and on the client behind the scenes, as well as the actions you need to take as a publisher. The automatic update mechanisms of Click-Once are perfect for many mainstream client applications out there. If you need more explicit control over the update process, but still want to let ClickOnce do the heavy lifting, you should consider using the ClickOnce on-demand API to do your updates as described in Chapter 4.

The following are some of the key takeaways from this chapter.

- Publishing an update from Visual Studio is no different than publishing an initial version; you just have to make sure the Publish Version setting is set to a version greater than the previously published version.
- The default update model in Visual Studio is to have updates occur automatically before the application starts and be optional for the client.
- Setting the minimum required version to the current version you are publishing ensures that clients will get that new version without prompting the next time they run the application, as long as they can connect to the deployment server.
- The client only downloads the files that have changed in the new version and copies the unchanged files from the cached previous version on the client.
- The deployment process on the client is transactional and ensures that the application transitions cleanly from one consistent version to a new consistent version, with integrity checking of every file that is transferred from the server or from the previous version on the client side.

In the next chapter you will learn how to perform application updates programmatically from the client using the on-demand API exposed in the framework.

■ 4 ■
On-Demand Updates

I N THE LAST CHAPTER you learned how to use the automatic updating capability of ClickOnce to keep your applications up to date on the client machine without needing to add any code to your application. Those capabilities will probably address the deployment requirements for the majority of ClickOnce deployed applications. But when you need to do something different than the options available for automatic updates, you don't have to discard ClickOnce as an option.

The on-demand API of ClickOnce lets you programmatically check for updates and download those updates at any time when your application is running through ClickOnce. You can use this if you want to let users choose when to check for an update, or you can use it to perform background update checking while the application is executing. This chapter will explore that API, including programmatically controlling when updates occur and gathering information about the current deployment. The on-demand update code can be deployed with your initial installation or any subsequent version so that all updates are done through the API, or you can mix automatic updating and on-demand updating if it makes sense for your requirements.

When Do On-Demand Updates Make Sense?

On-demand update capability is fairly common in consumer applications these days. Most applications you buy have some kind of capability for users to tell the program to go check for updates. This is also often combined with an automatic check for updates that lets users schedule the updates, or sometimes they just occur on a scheduled basis determined by the application. As a result of the prevalence of these kinds of features, end users are coming to expect to find this ability in all consumer software that they buy. If you are offering consumer applications over the Internet, you might want to consider using ClickOnce as a deployment model for those applications.

For many applications, including on-demand updates will depend on your requirements and whether you want to let users determine what version of an application they are running. In many cases, you may want to tightly control what version of an application users are allowed to run. In those cases, automatic updates combined with minimum required version checking will work nicely, and you may not want to expose end-user-controlled on-demand updates. However, for many other kinds of applications, you may want to allow both automatic and user-controlled updating. The automatic updating could be done using the ClickOnce controlled updates as discussed in Chapter 3, or it could be done using code that you write against the on-demand API that happens in the background based on some schedule that you determine.

For example, for a consumer-oriented application, you may want to set up ClickOnce to automatically check for updates once a month in the background, but also include a menu item that lets users check for updates at any time. For an enterprise-distributed smart client, you may not want to have ClickOnce do any automatic checking, but you may want to set up a background thread that goes out every five minutes and does an update check, and then prompts users to restart the application as soon as the update has been downloaded. This helps ensure that the client application stays in sync with changes made periodically to the server components.

The ClickOnce on-demand API can be used for situations where you, as the developer, want to have more explicit control over when and how automatic updates occur, even if you don't expose an on-demand update capability to users. For example, say you have an application whose typical usage pattern is that it is started at the beginning of the workday and left running all day until users log out to go home in the evening. You may want those users to get updates that are deployed during the workday, and you may want to ensure that updates are applied within a certain period from when the update becomes available on the server. For this kind of scenario, the automatic update checking of ClickOnce will not happen until users restart the application the next day, so those updates will not be applied soon enough.

For these and other scenarios, the on-demand API gives you explicit control over when update checks occur, when the download is performed, and when the update is applied.

Introducing the ClickOnce API

The ClickOnce on-demand API is exposed through the `Application-Deployment` class in the `System.Deployment.Application` namespace in the System.Deployment.dll framework assembly. This assembly is already referenced when you create a Windows Forms project in Visual Studio. This class includes functionality for programmatically controlling the update process, gathering information about the current deployment, and managing data files.

An additional class that is not technically part of the ClickOnce APIs, but that exposes some capabilities you will use in conjunction with the ClickOnce API, is the `Application` class from the `System.Windows.Forms` namespace. The `Application` class exposes the ability to restart an application after an update has been downloaded, as well as properties that let you obtain path information for the application folders that are created by ClickOnce when an application is deployed.

One key thing you need to understand is that most of the capabilities of the `ApplicationDeployment` class do not make any sense unless the application is being launched through ClickOnce (either a URL to the deployment manifest on the server, or through the Start menu item created by ClickOnce at install time). As a result, if you do not first detect whether your application is running under ClickOnce, the `ApplicationDeployment` class will throw an exception if you try to access any of its members other than the static `IsNetworkDeployed` property. So if you just run your application in the debugger in Visual Studio and try to exercise code that tries to access properties on the instance returned by `CurrentDeployment`, you will get an exception thrown. (Chapter 8 covers debugging techniques with ClickOnce code.) But if you want to avoid having this cause you problems, you need to be prepared to catch the exception, or code defensively so that the exception is never thrown in the first place.

Avoiding these exceptions is quite easy: You just need to adopt the coding pattern so that before you access any part of the `ApplicationDeployment` class, you always first check the `IsNetworkDeployed` static property.

```
if (ApplicationDeployment.IsNetworkDeployed)
{
    // Use the ApplicationDeployment class as needed
}
```

Adding Synchronous On-Demand Updates

When you decide you want to add on-demand updating capability to your application, you need to write a little code to get it done. I know, most developers are at this point saying, "Finally! We get to write some code!!"

Performing an on-demand update consists of the following logical steps.

1. Confirm that you are running under ClickOnce.
2. Check whether an update is available on the server.
3. Download the update to the client.
4. (Optional) Restart the application to run the new version.

You can do these steps in a straightforward, synchronous manner using the `CheckForUpdate` and `Update` methods of the `ApplicationDeployment` class. To try this out, create a Windows Application project and add a button to the form. Hook up a `Click` event handler for the button and name the handler method `OnCheckForUpdates`. Add the handler code shown in Listing 4.1.

LISTING 4.1: On-Demand Update

```
private void OnCheckForUpdates(object sender, EventArgs e)
{
    // Always confirm you are running through ClickOnce
    if (ApplicationDeployment.IsNetworkDeployed)
    {
        // Hold a reference to the current deployment
        ApplicationDeployment currentDeploy =
            ApplicationDeployment.CurrentDeployment;
        // Check to see if an update is available on the server
        if (currentDeploy.CheckForUpdate())
        {
            // One is available, go get it
            currentDeploy.Update();
            // Make sure you save application state here
            DialogResult dr = MessageBox.Show(
                "Update downloaded, restart application?",
                "Application Update",MessageBoxButtons.YesNo);
            if (dr == DialogResult.Yes)
            {
                Application.Restart();
            }
        }
    }
}
```

After the code in Listing 4.1 has checked to make sure the application is running through ClickOnce using the `IsNetworkDeployed` property, the next step is to obtain a reference to the current deployment instance through the `CurrentDeployment` static property. The `Application-Deployment` class implements a singleton pattern, which means there is only ever one instance of a class. You obtain a reference to that instance through the static `CurrentDeployment` property. The constructor for the `ApplicationDeployment` class is private so that you cannot directly construct an instance yourself; it is up to the runtime to do that. This approach of exposing a static property for a singleton is common throughout the .NET Framework.

Once you have a reference to the deployment instance, you can access the rest of the on-demand API. For a synchronous update, you call `Check-ForUpdate` to see if a newer version of the application exists on the deployment server. Calling `CheckForUpdate` will use the cached client deployment manifest to obtain the deployment provider URL for the application. It will then make a request to that URL to download the server deployment manifest. The version in the server deployment manifest is then compared to the version in the client cached manifest. If the version on the server is newer, then `CheckForUpdate` will return true, indicating that an update is available.

Once you have determined that an update is available on the deployment server, then you can download it synchronously by calling the `Update` method. This method is a blocking call while the update process happens. That means that the calling thread will not progress past the call to `Update` until the entire process is complete. The following steps occur behind the scenes as part of the update process.

1. The application manifest from the server is downloaded.
2. The manifest is validated.
3. The files that have changed or that have been added to the new version are determined from the server application manifest and the cached client application manifest.
4. The downloaded files are validated.
5. The changed or added files are downloaded from the deployment server and placed in the new version's cache folder on the client.
6. The unmodified files from the current version on the client are copied to the new version's cache folder on the client.
7.   The scavenging process runs to remove the version that preceded the last version if appropriate (see the section on Client Cache Scavenging in Chapter 3 for more details).
8. The Start menu shortcut is updated so that it points at the new current version on the client.

Once the `Update` method returns, the update process is complete and you can restart the application if desired by calling `Application.Restart`. The update process has no effect on the running application. It is not until you restart the application that the downloaded changes have any effect on the application. The sample code in Listing 4.1 prompts users first to let them decide whether to restart the application. The next time the application runs, whether through a call to `Restart` or because a user shut down the application and started it again through the Start menu shortcut, the new version, which is now the current version from the client's perspective, will run. The same things happen in terms of validating the update and deciding what to download and what to copy over from the previous version as were described for an automatic update by ClickOnce in Chapter 3.

The `Update` method returns a Boolean flag indicating whether an update occurred. This is because you can call `Update` without first calling `CheckForUpdate` if you choose, in which case you should check whether an update occurred before prompting users for a restart.

After you have added the code from Listing 4.1 to your application, disable automatic update checking in the application by doing the following.

1. Open the project properties editor in Visual Studio (choose Project > Properties).
2. Select the Publish tab.
3. Copy the URL from the Publish Location field.
4. Click the Updates button.
5. Uncheck the option at the top to check for updates.
6. Enter the URL that you copied in step 3 into the Update Location field at the bottom.

You can now publish the application and install it. The first time you press the button to which you hooked up the update code in Listing 4.1, nothing should happen since you just deployed the current version and there are no newer versions on the deployment server. However, if you publish the application again (which you can do while the previous version is running) and then press the button, you should see the application prompt you for a restart after the update has been applied.

If users decide that they don't like the new version, and it was not marked as the minimum required version by the publisher, they can roll back to the previous version through the Add or Remove Programs item just like with automatic updates.

One important security requirement to be aware of is that anytime you use programmatic updates, whether synchronous or asynchronous, your application will need to have full trust permissions. This means that the

> **⬛ WARNING** Update Location Required if Update Checking Is Disabled
>
> When you publish an application with ClickOnce that performs automatic updates (either before or after the application starts), the deployment provider is set to the Installation URL if an Update Location is not specified explicitly, and the Installation URL is set to the Publishing Location if it is not set explicitly. As a result, for most ClickOnce applications published through Visual Studio, you will just specify the Publishing Location; this implicitly says that the Publishing Location URL is also the Installation URL and Update Location.
>
> If you disable the option to check for updates, you are disabling automatic update checking. Unfortunately, this causes Visual Studio to no longer write the Publishing Location to the deployment provider setting in the generated deployment manifest. As a result, if you call the update methods in the ClickOnce programmatic API, an exception will be thrown and users will see the error dialog in Figure 4.1. To avoid this error, you will need to enter the Update Location explicitly if you disable automatic checking, even if it is the same URL as the Publishing Location.

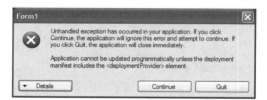

FIGURE 4.1: Launch Error Dialog with No Update Location

code in the application is unrestricted as far as .NET Code Access Security is concerned. See Chapter 6 for more details on the security features of ClickOnce and Code Access Security.

Performing Updates Asynchronously

The update process described in the previous section will block the calling thread when `CheckForUpdate` and `Update` methods are called as mentioned. This means that if you call these methods on the main user interface thread, the user interface will lock up until the update process is complete. This will not give a good user experience. To avoid that, you need to

> ## ▪ WARNING   Deployment Provider Must Be Set for Programmatic Updates
>
> In order for programmatic updates to work, the deployment manifest cached on the client has to have a deployment provider URL set. This URL is used to locate the deployment manifest on the server to see if any updates are available and to locate the application manifest for the appropriate version if so. As discussed in Chapter 2, the deployment provider is populated in one of three ways from Visual Studio.
>
> - The Update Location setting is used if you provide one.
> - The Installation URL is used if you provide one but don't specify an Update Location and you leave the updates setting to check for updates enabled.
> - The Publishing Location is used if you do not specify an Installation URL or Update Location, and you leave the updates setting to check for updates enabled.
>
> If you disable the updates setting to check for updates (automatic updating enabled), you must set the Update Location property to set a deployment provider URL in the deployment manifest. The deployment provider URL is exposed through the `ApplicationDeployment.UpdateLocation` property for programmatic access.

ensure that the update process occurs on a separate thread from the main UI thread. This means you will perform the updates asynchronously, or using another thread, from the thread that initiates the process. There are several ways to make that happen.

- Run a manual worker thread and call the update methods from there.
- Use the `BackgroundWorker` component to execute the update on a separate thread from the thread pool.
- Use the asynchronous methods in the `ApplicationDeployment` class to perform the updates.

I won't show an example of the first option because both of the other two options are easier and result in cleaner code, and the first option has no distinct advantages for this process. The `BackgroundWorker` approach is the best choice if you rarely do asynchronous operations in your client application and are using `BackgroundWorker` components for those that you do.

The asynchronous methods in the `ApplicationDeployment` class are a better option if you are comfortable with using asynchronous methods in .NET in general, and are a cleaner choice if you will be monitoring update events. The latter approach also gives you more control and flexibility over controlling the update process, such as reporting the update's progress.

Using the BackgroundWorker Component for Asynchronous Updates

The `BackgroundWorker` component lets you execute asynchronous processes without needing to worry about the intricacies of multithreading in Windows Forms. Windows Forms requires that any updates to the UI are done on the UI thread. It uses an event-driven model to let you execute a method on another thread, while providing progress and completion events that fire on the UI thread. This makes it so that you don't have to worry about marshaling calls from the background thread to the UI thread when you need to update the UI. To use it, you do the following.

- Add the component to a form.
- Hook an event handler method up to the `DoWork` event on the component.
- Place the code you want to execute asynchronously in the `DoWork` event handler.
- Call the `RunWorkerAsync` method to execute the `DoWork` event handler on a separate thread from the thread pool.
- Optionally, handle the `RunWorkerCompleted` or `ProgressChanged` events on the component.

When you use a `BackgroundWorker`, the `DoWork` event handler is executed whenever the `RunWorkerAsync` method is called against the component instance. There are two overloads of `RunWorkerAsync`: one that takes no parameters and one that takes an object parameter. At the point where `RunWorkerAsync` is called, the runtime grabs a thread off the thread pool and executes the `DoWork` event handler on that thread.

The `DoWork` event delegate is of type `DoWorkEventHandler`. The parameters to this delegate type's target methods include an object reference and a `DoWorkEventArgs` object. The latter has two properties: `Argument` and

`Result`. The `Argument` property lets you access the object parameter that was passed in to the `RunWorkerAsync` method, if any. The `Result` property lets you pass a reference to an object that is the result of the asynchronous work out to the `RunWorkerCompleted` event handler. This prevents you from needing to save the result somewhere that synchronization concerns might surface, such as a member variable. The `Result` property effectively dispatches an object reference from the worker thread that the `DoWork` event handler executes on to the UI thread that the `RunWorkerCompleted` event handler executes on.

▪️ **WARNING** **BackgroundWorker Component Does Not Remove Synchronization Requirements**

Anytime you do multithreading, you need to worry about synchronization requirements. Specifically, you should never access a memory location (member variable, local reference variables initialized to a nonlocal object, or static variable) from more than one thread concurrently. Additionally, you should never access a Windows Forms control from a thread other than the UI thread. When you use the `BackgroundWorker` component, you are still doing multithreading—the method you hook up as the `DoWork` event handler is executed on a thread from the thread pool. You need to follow the same rules about multithreaded synchronization from your `DoWork` event handler as you would from a thread method that you run in a manual worker thread. The `RunWorker-Completed` and `ProgressChanged` events fire on the UI thread, so it is safe to access controls or memory locations used elsewhere on the UI thread from those event handlers. A full discussion of multithreaded synchronization is beyond the scope of this book.[1]

Do the following to walk through an example of using the `Back-groundWorker`.

1. Create a new Windows Application project named **Background-WorkerSample**.

2. Add a button to the form.

---

1. For an excellent reference on multithreading and synchronization in .NET, see *Programming .NET Components* by Juval Löwy (O'Reilly & Associates, 2005).

3. Add a `BackgroundWorker` component to the form from the Toolbox.

4. Name the button **m_UpdateButton** and the `BackgroundWorker` **m_BGWorker**.

5. Disable automatic update checking as described for the example in the earlier section Adding Synchronous On-Demand Updates.

6. Modify the form code to look like Listing 4.2.

LISTING 4.2: Asynchronous Updates with BackgroundWorker

```
public partial class Form1 : Form
{
   public Form1()
   {
      InitializeComponent();
      // Hook up the event handlers
      // Done here instead of using the designer for
      // code listing clarity purposes
      m_UpdateButton.Click += OnUpdateCommand;
      m_BGWorker.DoWork += OnUpdateApp;
      m_BGWorker.RunWorkerCompleted += OnUpdateCompleted;
   }

   private void OnUpdateCommand(object sender, EventArgs e)
   {
      // Make the BackgroundWorker call DoWork asynchronously
      m_BGWorker.RunWorkerAsync();
   }

   private void OnUpdateApp(object sender, DoWorkEventArgs e)
   {
      // Always confirm you are running through ClickOnce
      if (ApplicationDeployment.IsNetworkDeployed)
      {
         // Hold a reference to the current deployment
         ApplicationDeployment current =
            ApplicationDeployment.CurrentDeployment;
         // Check to see if an update is available on the server
         if (current.CheckForUpdate())
         {
            // One is available; go get it
            current.Update();
            // Return true to indicate that an update did occur
            e.Result = true;
         }
      }

   }
```

```
      private void OnUpdateCompleted(object sender,
         RunWorkerCompletedEventArgs e)
   {
      // Check to see if an update did occur
      if (e.Result.Equals(true))
      {
         // Prompt for restart
         DialogResult dr = MessageBox.Show(
            "Update downloaded, restart application?",
            "Application Update", MessageBoxButtons.YesNo);
         if (dr == DialogResult.Yes)
         {
            // Has to be done on the UI thread from a ClickOnce
            // launched application
            Application.Restart();
         }
      }
   }
}
```

The code in Listing 4.2 first hooks up event handlers for the `Click` event on the button and the `DoWork` and `RunWorkerCompleted` events on the `BackgroundWorker`. You would normally hook these up in the Windows Forms designer in Visual Studio, but I chose to hook them up manually just to make it clear where the following methods were getting called from. The `Click` event on the button initiates the update process by calling `RunWorkerAsync` on the `BackgroundWorker` component. That causes the `DoWork` event handler, `OnUpdateApp`, to get executed on a worker thread. The `OnUpdateApp` method does a normal synchronous ClickOnce update process as shown earlier in Listing 4.1.

After the `ApplicationDeployment.Update` method completes, `OnUpdateApp` sets the `Result` property of the `DoWorkEventArgs` event argument to true to indicate that an update did in fact take place. When the `DoWork` event handler completes, the `RunWorkerCompleted` event will fire, calling the `OnUpdateCompleted` handler. This method checks the `Result` property on its event arguments, which contains whatever value was set as the event argument's `Result` property in the `DoWork` event handler. If this value is set to *True*, then the method prompts users to restart the application.

You might be tempted to do the user prompting and application restart from the `DoWork` event handler. However, it would not work correctly when the application is launched through ClickOnce due to a bug I discovered in writing this in the .NET 2.0 Framework. At the time of this writing, the bug has been reported through the Product Feedback Center, but it has not been resolved. This is the reason I put the restart code in the `RunWorker-Completed` event handler, which does execute on the UI thread.

You might also think about trying to hook up the `ProgressChanged` event of the `BackgroundWorker` component, which lets you report progress on your background work. However, in this case, we are doing a blocking synchronous call from the background thread (the reason we are using `BackgroundWorker` in the first place), and so there is unfortunately no opportunity to report progress by using this approach.

Asynchronous Updates Through the ApplicationDeployment API

The `ApplicationDeployment` class also exposes update methods that use a standard pattern for asynchronous method execution used in many places in the .NET 2.0 Framework. There are asynchronous counterparts for each of the update methods in the `ApplicationDeployment` class, named XXX-Async, where XXX is the name of the operation that is being performed asynchronously (e.g., `CheckForUpdateAsync` and `UpdateAsync`).

When you call the asynchronous versions of these methods, they execute their respective operations on a thread from the thread pool, similar to the `DoWork` event on the `BackgroundWorker` discussed in the previous section. As a result, if you call these from the UI thread, there will be no blocking and negative impact to the UI responsiveness that is noticeable by users. For each of the XXXAsync methods, there is a corresponding event with the naming convention XXXCompleted that gets fired when the asynchronous operation completes. If the XXXAsync method is called from the UI thread, the XXXCompleted event will fire on the UI thread as well.

To see the asynchronous methods in action, do the following.

1. Create a new Windows Application project named **AsyncUpdates**.
2. Add a button to the form.
3. Name the button **m_UpdateButton**.
4. Disable automatic update checking as described for the example in the earlier section Adding Synchronous On-Demand Updates.
5. Modify the form code to look like Listing 4.3.

LISTING 4.3: Asynchronous Updates Through the ApplicationDeployment Class

```
public partial class Form1 : Form
{
    public Form1()
    {
        InitializeComponent();
        m_UpdateButton.Click += OnUpdateCommand;
    }

    private void OnUpdateCommand(object sender, EventArgs e)
    {
        // Always confirm you are running through ClickOnce
        if (ApplicationDeployment.IsNetworkDeployed)
        {
            // Get a reference to the current deployment
            ApplicationDeployment current =
                ApplicationDeployment.CurrentDeployment;
            // Hook up async event handlers
            current.CheckForUpdateCompleted +=
OnCheckForUpdateCompleted;
            current.UpdateCompleted += OnUpdateCompleted;
            // Check for updates asynchronously
            current.CheckForUpdateAsync();
        }

    }

    void OnCheckForUpdateCompleted(object sender,
        CheckForUpdateCompletedEventArgs e)
    {
        // Check to see if an update is available on the server
        if (e.UpdateAvailable)
        {
            // Get a reference to the current deployment
            ApplicationDeployment current =
                ApplicationDeployment.CurrentDeployment;
            // One is available; go get it asynchronously
            current.UpdateAsync();
        }
    }

    void OnUpdateCompleted(object sender, AsyncCompletedEventArgs e)
    {
        DialogResult dr = MessageBox.Show(
            "Update downloaded, restart application?",
            "Application Update", MessageBoxButtons.YesNo);
        if (dr == DialogResult.Yes)
        {
            Application.Restart();
```

```
        }
      }
    }
```

In the button `Click` event handler `OnUpdateCommand`, the code checks first to make sure it is running through ClickOnce by checking the `IsNet-workDeployed` property. If so, then it subscribes event handlers for the `CheckForUpdateCompleted` and `UpdateCompleted` events. After the event handlers have been hooked up, `CheckForUpdateAsync` is called.

Just like with the `CheckForUpdate` synchronous version, this causes the download of the deployment manifest from the server and the comparison of versions between that and the client's cached manifest. When that process is complete, the `CheckForUpdateCompleted` event fires and calls the `OnCheckForUpdateCompleted` event handler on the UI thread. The `CheckForUpdateCompleted` event argument contains an `UpdateAvailable` property that can be checked to determine if an update is available. In the handler in Listing 4.3, if there is an update, `UpdateAsync` is then called to execute the update process on a separate thread. That will follow the same process as the synchronous version as well, and will then fire the `UpdateCompleted` event at the completion. The handler for that event in Listing 4.3 just prompts users at that point and lets them restart the application to the new version if desired.

Update Progress Notifications

When you do asynchronous updates, you also have the option of being notified during the download process when progress changes. To do this, you can hook the `UpdateProgressChanged` event in the `ApplicationDeployment` class and access the event argument's properties to see what the current progress is in terms of percentage, number of bytes transferred, total number of bytes, and what phase of the download process it is in.

The following code is a slight modification of the code from Listing 4.3 to hook the `UpdateProgressChanged` event and dump the information to a `ListBox` control in the application while the download process is in progress. The `DeploymentProgressChangedEventArgs` class exposes `ProgressPercent`, `BytesTotal`, and `BytesReceived` properties, whose names are self-explanatory. The State property exposes an enumerated value of type DeploymentProgressState, which has three named values: DownloadingDeploymentInformation, DownloadingApplicationIn-formation, and DownloadingApplicationFiles.

```
private void OnUpdateCommand(object sender, EventArgs e)
{
    // Always confirm you are running through ClickOnce
    if (ApplicationDeployment.IsNetworkDeployed)
    {
        // Get a reference to the current deployment
        ApplicationDeployment current =
            ApplicationDeployment.CurrentDeployment;
        // Hook up async event handlers
        current.CheckForUpdateCompleted +=
            OnCheckForUpdateCompleted;
        current.UpdateCompleted += OnUpdateCompleted;
        current.UpdateProgressChanged += OnUpdateProgressChanged;
        // Check for updates asynchronously
        current.CheckForUpdateAsync();
    }

}

void OnUpdateProgressChanged(object sender,
    DeploymentProgressChangedEventArgs e)
{
    listBox1.Items.Add("-------------");
    listBox1.Items.Add("Deployment State: " + e.State.ToString());
    listBox1.Items.Add("Deployment progress: " +
        e.ProgressPercentage.ToString() + "%");
    listBox1.Items.Add("Bytes received: " + e.BytesCompleted.ToString());
    listBox1.Items.Add("Bytes to go: " +
        (e.BytesTotal - e.BytesCompleted).ToString());
    listBox1.Items.Add("-------------");

}
```

Combining On-Demand Updates with Automatic Updates

When you do on-demand updates, you do not have to abandon automatic updates at the same time. However, if you are going to combine them, it really only makes sense to do so if you set the automatic updates to be done in the background on a scheduled basis. If you leave automatic updates on with checking before the application starts, then users will always get or deny the available update immediately on startup. Only if the application is expected to run for long periods of time (i.e., days, weeks, or months at a time) would it make sense to combine before startup checking with on-demand updates.

The most sensible way to combine automatic updates with on-demand updates is to set a policy, such as having your application automatically check for updates weekly after the application starts, but to allow users to command an update check at any time. That way, if users forget to check, they still will not get too far out of date, and if they hear that a new version was just put out by word of mouth, e-mail, or something they saw on the Web, they can go and get it immediately.

To do this, just configure your application through Visual Studio with update settings that specify update checks should happen in the background on a seven-day schedule, as shown in Figure 4.2.

Then add code such as that shown in Listing 4.2 or 4.3 to check for updates and to apply them if commanded by users. You would typically hook this up to a menu or toolbar command.

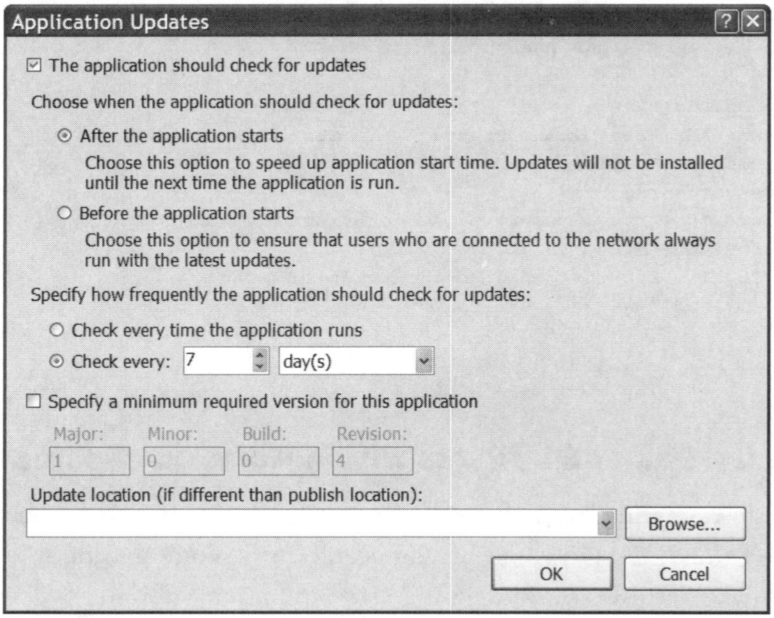

FIGURE 4.2: Automatic Update Checks Every Seven Days

Checking Detailed Update Information

If you want to gather more detailed information about an available update before deciding whether to retrieve it or not, you can use the CheckForDetailedUpdate method in the ApplicationDeployment class. This returns an instance of the UpdateCheckInfo class containing detailed information about the available update on the server. Before accessing the detailed properties on this object, you must first determine whether an update is available. To do so, you can call CheckForUpdate first, and only call CheckForDetailedUpdate if CheckForUpdate returns true. You can also call CheckForDetailedUpdate on its own, and check the resulting UpdateAvailable Boolean property on the UpdateCheckInfo instance that is returned before trying to access any of the object's other properties. If UpdateAvailable is false and you try to access the other properties, an exception will be thrown.

The code in Listing 4.4 shows an example of retrieving detailed check information. After retrieving the UpdateCheckInfo object, the code checks to see if an update is available. If so, it uses the object to data bind to a set of controls on a form for viewing through a BindingSource component. You can see the form running in Figure 4.3 after retrieving an update.

LISTING 4.4: Retrieving Detailed Update Information

```
private void OnCheckForDetailedUpdateInfo(object sender, EventArgs e)
{
    if (ApplicationDeployment.IsNetworkDeployed)
    {
        // Get a reference to the current deployment
        ApplicationDeployment current =
            ApplicationDeployment.CurrentDeployment;
        UpdateCheckInfo uci = current.CheckForDetailedUpdate();
        if (uci.UpdateAvailable)
        {
            updateCheckInfoBindingSource.DataSource = uci;
        }
        else
        {
            updateAvailableCheckBox.Checked = false;
        }
    }
}
```

FIGURE 4.3: Detailed Update Checking Application

You can see from the displayed information in Figure 4.3 that the `UpdateCheckInfo` object includes five properties. The `UpdateAvailable` property tells you whether an update is available as discussed earlier. The `IsUpdateRequired` property indicates whether this update is required, which will be the case if the `AvailableVersion` property is equal to the `MinimumRequiredVersion` property. All of these properties are of type `System.Version`, which lets you get the four parts of a .NET version number. Finally, the `UpdateSizeBytes` property tells you how many bytes total are in the collection of files that need to be downloaded to obtain this update.

Gathering Information about the Current Deployment

The `ApplicationDeployment` class includes a number of properties that let you inspect information about the current deployment. You can think of this as allowing you to read the deployment metadata out of the cached client manifests.

Table 4.1 shows the properties available in the `ApplicationDeployment` class and what they tell you.

TABLE 4.1: ApplicationDeployment Class Instance Properties

Property	Type	Description
ActivationUri	Uri	Displays the URL used to launch the application, including query string parameters if applicable. This property is only populated if the setting to allow URL parameters (trustURLParameters attribute in the deployment manifest) has been set to *True*.
CurrentVersion	Version	The full version information for the version currently running.
DataDirectory	String	The fully qualified path for the data directory created for files marked as data files for this application.
IsFirstRun	Boolean	Indicates whether the current execution of the application is the first time the current version has been run. This lets you call any custom initialization code you integrate into your application.
TimeOfLastUpdateCheck	DateTime	The date and time an update check last occurred in local time.
UpdatedApplicationFullName	String	This is a long string that contains the URL to the deployment manifest, the full identity information of the manifest, and the full assembly identity information for the application executable.

Continues

TABLE 4.1: ApplicationDeployment Class Instance Properties *(Continued)*

Property	Type	Description
UpdateLocation	Uri	The address where updates will be checked for. Corresponds to the deployment-Provider setting in the manifest.
UpdateVersion	Version	The full version information for any detected update versions.

Where Are We?

This chapter showed you how to use the `ApplicationDeployment` class to perform on-demand updates and to gather information about the current deployment and detailed update information. You saw how to perform the updates synchronously and asynchronously, and to combine programmatic updates with automatic updates.

The following are some of the key takeaways from this chapter.

- Always check the `ApplicationDeployment.IsNetworkDeployed` property and make sure the value is true before accessing any members on the `CurrentDeployment` property returned object.
- Call `CheckForUpdate` and `Update` to perform a synchronous update. Only do this if you are calling them from a background thread, such as a `BackgroundWorker` thread, so that they do not block the UI thread.
- Call `CheckForUpdateAsync` and `UpdateAsync` to perform updates asynchronously. You will need to handle the `CheckForUpdateComplete` and `UpdateComplete` events to be notified when each process completes. The runtime will take care of running the operation on a thread from the thread pool.
- The Update Location setting in Visual Studio must be set to the appropriate URL for update checking if you disable automatic

updates by unchecking the *Check for application updates* setting at the top of the Update Options dialog.

In the next chapter, we will look at configuring data files, how they are handled through automatic update API, and how you can explicitly control the download of data files through the `ApplicationDeployment` class.

▪ 5 ▪
Application and Data File Management

A S DISCUSSED IN EARLIER CHAPTERS, your ClickOnce application is
treated as a single entity from a deployment and versioning perspective. However, Windows Forms applications are usually composed of a number of individual files. At a minimum you have the application executable. You may also have a configuration file that goes with it, any number of referenced dependent assemblies, and other resource files. The referenced assemblies may be ones that you built or they may be third-party control or component libraries. These files determine the application behavior when it runs, and they are called **application files** throughout this chapter. In addition, your application may include any number of additional files that contain data used by your application at runtime, and that data may change and need to be persisted locally on the client between runs of your application. These files are called **data files** with respect to ClickOnce and have a separate deployment process from your application files.

This chapter will discuss the capabilities ClickOnce exposes for managing the individual files that your ClickOnce application is composed of, what happens with those files when ClickOnce application deployment and update occur, and how you can control the process for custom requirements. The chapter will first focus on managing application files and then will look at managing data files. This chapter delves into the deep configurability of

ClickOnce. For simple applications, you probably don't even need to read this chapter. If your application just starts up, uses the default loading behavior of .NET to use its referenced assemblies, and does not try to directly access any other files that get deployed with the application, then you can skip this chapter. But if you will be deploying complex applications that dynamically load assemblies or access local data or resource files that deploy with the application, then read on.

Application Executable Deployment

When you publish your Windows application with Visual Studio, the executable output (a Windows .exe file) will always be part of the published application, as will its configuration file (.exe.config file) if present. Any assemblies set as references in the Visual Studio project will be added to the published application by default, as long as the Copy Local project reference property is set to *True*. You can set or view this property by selecting a project reference in Solution Explorer and viewing its properties in the Properties window.

If your project reference assemblies are installed in the Global Assembly Cache (GAC) on your development machine, you will have to decide whether you want to deploy those assemblies as local assemblies (installed in the application folder through ClickOnce) on the client, or whether you want them installed in the client's GAC. Deploying referenced assemblies locally minimizes the complexity of installing prerequisites before you deploy your ClickOnce application. You may need to deploy to the GAC depending on what the assembly was designed to do. For example, if the code in a referenced assembly requires full trust to execute, but your ClickOnce application will be deployed with partial trust (see Chapter 6), then installing the referenced assembly in the GAC is a way to give that assembly full trust.

You cannot set the Copy Local property to true for .NET Framework assemblies that you have as project references. You will have to ensure that the .NET Framework 2.0 is already installed on the client machine as a prerequisite before attempting to deploy a ClickOnce application to that machine. See Chapter 7 for more information on deployment prerequisites.

Likewise, some third-party assemblies may require you to install them with a Windows Installer package on the client as a prerequisite, and their installer will deploy their assemblies to the GAC and possibly configure client license information. You will have to consult the documentation for third-party products to see which deployment models they support. Many third-party components get installed in the GAC to make them more accessible for adding them to many projects on a development machine, but they also support deployment as a local assembly. If the third-party assemblies your application depends on do support local deployment, you should set their Copy Local property to true before publishing your application so that they become part of your application for deployment to the client.

If your application project includes references to additional class library assemblies that your organization developed, then you should always try to avoid requiring GAC installation for those assemblies to make Click-Once deployment easier. The bottom line is that if you have application references that have to be deployed to the GAC, you will have to create a Bootstrapper package to get those assemblies deployed to the client as a prerequisite (see Chapter 7).

> **■ NOTE** **Strong-Named Assemblies Get a Single Copy Across Applications**
>
> One optimization the ClickOnce team made was to make sure that if multiple applications or versions of one application are using the same strong-named assembly, only one version of that assembly will be cached on the client machine. This means that if ApplicationA and ApplicationB both use strong-named assembly StrongNamedAssembly (where the name, version, locale, and public key all match up), then only one copy of StrongNamedAssembly is created in a separate cache folder on the client, and the assembly is loaded from there by the ClickOnce engine. You can think of this folder as a mini-GAC—its scope only applies to other ClickOnce deployed applications on the machine.
>
> The ClickOnce runtime also checks the hash of this file when updates occur to make sure that two different assemblies with the same strong name are not different in their contents. If the file hash is different, it is just treated as a local assembly and the strong name is ignored. But if an application is deployed with a strong-named assembly that is already present in the client cache, the one in the strong-named cache will be used instead of creating another copy of the assembly.

Adding Application Files in Visual Studio

At design time, the primary way you will manage application files (other than referenced assemblies) is by adding them to your Visual Studio project. Files must be part of your project to be included in your deployed ClickOnce application if you publish from Visual Studio. To add an existing file to a project in Visual Studio, just do the following.

1. Right-click on the project in Solution Explorer.
2. Select Add > Existing Item from the context menu.
3. Navigate to the file you want to add through the File dialog.
4. Select the file and click the Add button.

Source files and other project files are not added to your application by default. Files that are part of your project have a number of properties associated with them. One project file property that is particularly relevant with respect to ClickOnce application file management is the Build Action property.

The Build Action property indicates what will be done at build time with this file. Values for this property include *Content*, *Compile*, *Embedded Resource*, *Component*, and *None*. When you add arbitrary files to your project to have them included in your application, Visual Studio will set the appropriate Build Action based on the file extension of the file being added.

If you want to include a file in the deployed application as an individual file, you will need to set the Build Action to *Content*. For example, you might include a .gif file that is loaded dynamically by the application or an XML file that contains static settings or data used by the application. When the Build Action is set to *Compile* or *Embedded Resource*, the file will be used by the compiler to generate the application assembly. With either of these values, the file will not be included in the application files that get deployed through ClickOnce, but the resulting executable will. See the later section on Embedding Files in the Assembly for more information on embedded resources. *Component* will be set if you add a DLL to your project as a file, but it will not be included when publishing unless you change the Build Action to *Content*. See the later section Deploying Extensible Plug-In Applications with ClickOnce for an example of when you would want to do so.

Finally, if the value of the Build Action is set to *None* for a file, the file will not be included in the deployed application either.

Configuring ClickOnce Application Files

Once you have added application files to your project and set their Build Action to *Content* or *Component*, you can then configure those files with ClickOnce. ClickOnce includes two configurable properties for each application file: the Publish Status and the Download Group (see Figure 5.1). You get to these properties by opening the editor's project properties, selecting the Publish tab, and clicking the Application Files button.

The available values for the Publish Status vary depending on what kind of file the application file is. The possible values are Include, Exclude, Data File, and Prerequisite. Depending on the file type, you will see an *(Auto)* qualifier on these options for each file to indicate the default status based on the file type. You can see these values being used for a variety of file types in Figure 5.1.

Include (Auto) will be set for any project file with a Build Action of *Content*, as well as for the build output of the project (the application .exe file and application configuration .exe.config file). Include (Auto) will also be set for project references that have their Copy Local property set to *True*.

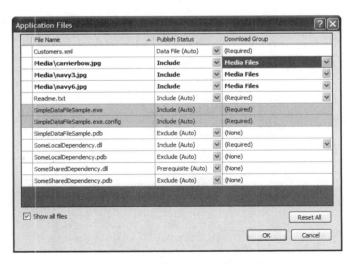

FIGURE 5.1: Application Files Publish Configuration

In fact, the application executable and configuration file settings cannot be modified; they will always be set to *Include (Auto)* for the Publish Status and *(Required)* for the Download Group. Setting a file's Publish Status to *Include* has the same effect as setting the status to *Include (Auto)*. The latter setting just indicates that the behavior is being determined by default for the file type instead of being set explicitly with the Include value. When a file's Publish Status is set to *Include* or *Include (Auto)*, the file will be copied to the application's Publishing Location (set in the project properties editor's Publish tab) when you publish the application and will be included in the application files listed in the application manifest. When the user deploys the application through ClickOnce, those files will be downloaded into the client's application cache directory.

Setting a file's Publish Status to *Exclude* or *Exclude (Auto)* will prevent that file from being copied to the Publishing Location and it will not be part of the published application in any way. Exclude (Auto) will be set by default for the .pdb debug symbols file for any application. Excluded files are not normally shown in the Application Files dialog. To show them, check the Show all files box at the bottom as shown in Figure 5.1.

Data File (Auto) is the setting that distinguishes an application file from a data file as defined at the beginning of this chapter. This setting and all of the other options and capabilities that go along with it are covered in the later sections in this chapter focused on data files.

Prerequisite (Auto) will be set for any project references whose Copy Local property is set to *False*. This applies to assemblies that are expected to be deployed to the GAC before deploying your application through ClickOnce. When this value is set, the assembly will not be copied to the Publishing Location, but it is listed in the application files in the application manifest as a prerequisite. This value serves as a reminder of which files you will need to deploy through the Bootstrapper to the client machine. The ClickOnce runtime engine also checks the GAC on the client machine at install time to ensure these prerequisite assemblies are present before installing the application. If the assembly is not installed in the GAC, ClickOnce will show an error message indicating the GAC assembly name and version.

The Download Group lets you partition sets of application files into different groups which can then be programmatically downloaded on demand. The default Download Group value for any application file with a Publish Status of *Include* is *(Required)*. Any file with a Download Group of (Required) will be downloaded with the application whenever the installation or update occurs on the client. If you add a named Download Group and set that group for an application file, that file will not be downloaded as part of a normal installation or update. It will have to be downloaded on demand using the programmatic API discussed in the later section Programmatic Download of Application Files. Download Group cannot be set for files with a Publish Status of *Data File*, only those set to *Include*.

An example where you might use a named Download Group would be to add plug-in libraries to your application based on a user selecting an add-on feature that they would like. Figure 5.1 shows three media files that are marked as being part of a Download Group named *Media Files*. You can add a new Download Group by using the field's drop-down list to change the Download Group value for any file to *(New...)*. Once you have provided a name for the new group, it will be added to the Download Group drop-down list for all the files in the application.

■. WARNING   The Application Directory Is Only Accessible from Full-Trust Applications

An important limitation to understand is that the application directory from which your ClickOnce application runs on the client is only accessible programmatically from full-trust applications. When you deploy a ClickOnce application with partial trust, the running executable is called AppLaunch.exe and the current directory is the installed .NET directory (e.g., C:\Windows\Microsoft.NET\Framework\v2.0.50727). There is no way to get to the actual installation directory of the application files. In a full-trust application, the application executable itself (e.g., MyApp.exe) is the running executable, and the current working directory is your installed application folder. If you deploy files through Download Groups that you expect to access programmatically, such as loading an image file like those listed in Figure 5.1 through a relative path, you will have to deploy your application with full trust. See Chapter 6 for more details on ClickOnce security.

Embedding Files in the Assembly

Visual Studio supports taking any file in your project and making it an embedded resource in the compiled assembly. To do so, you set the Build Action for the file to *Embedded Resource*. When you do so, the file will be turned into a byte stream and will be embedded in the application assembly at compile time.

When you embed a file, you no longer need to include that file for deployment with ClickOnce because it will be contained in the application executable assembly, which is always included. Embedding files in your application assembly has advantages and disadvantages. The biggest advantage to using embedded resources in Visual Studio 2005 is that you get a strongly typed wrapper class that makes it extremely easy to access those resources in a type-safe way. Another advantage is that because the file will be loaded into memory when the assembly loads on the client, you will have a (minor) performance improvement when accessing the file as a resource at runtime. Usually for client applications, this performance impact is insignificant. A final advantage is that if you configure your ClickOnce application to run in partial trust (see Chapter 6), you will not need to include `FileIOPermission` as a required permission for the application in order to access the embedded file. Resources also support localization better than individual files that are dynamically loaded by name.

Disadvantages to using embedded resources include that the resource is read-only and cannot be modified by the application, and that the resource will always have to be loaded into memory on the client even if the application does not use it. If you want to deploy a change to the resource, you will have to deploy an updated version of the executable or class library that contains it.

Embedded resources can be loaded into their own class library assembly that is only loaded at runtime as needed, which can address the second disadvantage just discussed. In fact, this is the best way to manage embedded resources, particularly if you will be localizing the application to multiple cultures and have the localized resources in separate assemblies for different cultures. See the next section, Localizing Your ClickOnce Deployment, for more details on this technique.

If you use embedded resources to avoid deploying additional physical files, you will want to take advantage of the enhanced features for working with resources in Visual Studio 2005. The project properties editor for all applications and class library projects has a Resources tab, where you can add embedded resources of multiple types into your application. The Resource types supported by the Resource properties page include strings, images, icons, audio files, and any other kind of file that you would like to include.

The easiest approach to adding a file as an embedded resource is to do the following.

1. Display the Resources tab in the project properties editor.
2. Select the resource type you will be adding from the drop-down list in the upper left corner of the tab.
3. Open Windows Explorer and locate the file you want to add.
4. Drag and drop the file from Windows Explorer into the content area of the Resources tab.

The result of this procedure is that the file you dragged from Windows Explorer will be added to a Resources subfolder under the project as a project file, and it will be displayed in the appropriate view of the Resources tab as shown in Figure 5.2.

Visual Studio automatically compiles embedded resources into your assembly when they are added through the Resources tab. The associated files are added to a special folder named Resources that is added under the project directory. If you select the files in the Resources folder in Solution Explorer and view their Build Action property, you will see that it is set to *None*. The associated resource will still be embedded in the compiled output because it was added through the Resources tab.

When you drag and drop a file in the Resources tab, the Visual Studio designer also generates and adds a class named `Resources` to the project in a child namespace named `Properties`. As an example, if you added an image file to the SimpleDataFileSample project as shown in Figure 5.2, the resulting fully qualified class name for the `Resources` class will be `SimpleDataFileSample.Properties.Resources`. Through this class,

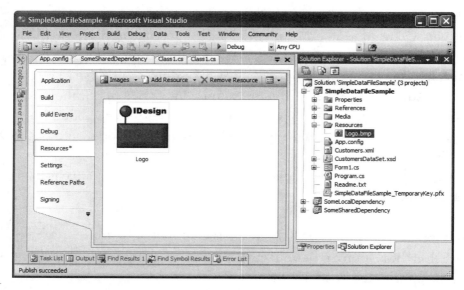

FIGURE 5.2: Adding Embedded Resource Files

you will have strongly typed access to the resources embedded in your application.

For example, for the Logo.bmp file added to the Images category of the Resources tab shown in Figure 5.2, you end up with a property named `Logo` of type `Bitmap` in the `Resources` class. You could use this to populate a `PictureBox` control as shown here.

```
using SimpleDataFileSample.Properties;

namespace SimpleDataFileSample
{
   public partial class Form1 : Form
   {
      // Rest of Form1 class ...
      private void Form1_Load(object sender, EventArgs e)
      {
         m_LogoPictureBox.Image = Resources.Logo;
      }
   }
}
```

Visual Studio will infer the appropriate Resources category based on the file extension. For example, if you drag a .bmp file onto the Resources tab, it will be added to the Images category. If you drag an XML file, it will be added to the Files category, and its strongly typed property in the `Resources` class will be of type `String`, allowing you to access the file's contents easily as a string. If the file type is unknown, it will be added to the Files category and the Resources property will be of type `byte[]`, giving you raw access to the byte contents of the file to do with what you want.

Localizing Your ClickOnce Deployment

The .NET Framework has rich built-in capabilities for globalizing and localizing your applications. Localizing an application means adapting it for a particular language and culture. Globalizing or internationalizing your application just means enabling it to be localized. This is a very big topic, and in fact there is a whole book that covers this topic comprehensively: *.NET Internationalization: The Developer's Guide to Building Global Windows and Web Applications* by Guy Smith-Ferrier, which is part of the Addison-Wesley .NET Development series. For the purposes of this book, I am just going to give you a very quick glimpse into the capabilities of ClickOnce to accommodate localization. Guy has more detailed coverage in his book that I won't attempt to duplicate here. The fact is that if you will be localizing your .NET applications, you need to dive into a lot of other aspects besides just localizing the ClickOnce deployment itself, and there are a lot of variations on localizing your ClickOnce deployment that Guy covers as well.

There are several aspects to localizing a ClickOnce deployment. There is the localization of the application itself that you are deploying, which involves changing strings, images, data formats, and so on that are presented in your application to match the language and culture of your users. There is the localization of the ClickOnce publication, which means making sure you publish the right localized resources for your application. There is also the localization of the ClickOnce prompting that is presented by the .NET Framework on the client machine to do a ClickOnce deployment. Finally, there is the prompting that is presented by the Bootstrapper (covered in Chapter 7) that needs to be localized as well. I won't go into the latter two aspects since they are fairly complicated and Guy covers them well in his book.

The language you specify in .NET is composed of two parts: the culture-neutral language (e.g., English, Spanish, Swedish, etc.) and the culture that the language is used in (e.g., British English vs. American English, Mexican Spanish vs. Spanish in Spain, etc.). These language/culture combinations are specified through culture code such as en-us, es-mx, and so on. .NET supports localizing to just the language level, called a *culture-neutral language*, or to each specific culture subdivision of the language. I'll just call this *language* for the rest of this section for simplicity where that could mean either form—culture-neutral or culture-specific language.

Usually when you set properties on Windows Forms controls in the designer, the property values are associated with your application's default language, which will match whatever your current settings are for your operating system. These settings all get compiled into your application executable by default. To localize an application, you have to first set a design property that tells the designer that you want to start localizing the application and to which language. You then set the properties to values that will be used when it is run on a machine that has that language set as the default. This results in a separate assembly that will be generated for each language that you localize property values to.

The following are the basic steps to localize a Windows Forms application.

- Set the form's `Localizable` property to true.
- Set the form's `Language` property to the language that you are localizing to.
- Modify properties on individual controls in the designer (e.g., the text on buttons and labels, images in PictureBox controls) to set them to the appropriate values for the target language/culture.

When you select a different language and start setting properties in the designer, the values for those properties are placed in a localized resource file (.resx file) that is under the form's class file in Solution Explorer. When you compile your application, this .resx file will be compiled into a separate resources assembly and placed in a subfolder under the application folder named according to the associated language/culture code (e.g., en-us for U.S. English, es-mx for Mexican Spanish, etc.). See Figure 5.3 for an

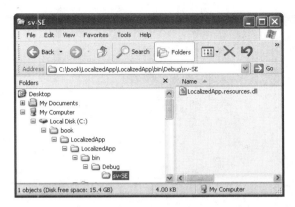

FIGURE 5.3: Localized Resource Assembly in Build Output

example of this where the language and culture are Swedish in Sweden (as opposed to Swedish in Finland). The .NET Framework will automatically load the appropriate resources assembly and use the values found in it if the application is running on a machine set to the language that you localized your application to. You will also want to make sure your clients have the appropriate language pack for the .NET Framework installed as well.

By default, ClickOnce does not include localized resource assemblies when you publish your application, even if they are present in the build output because you took the previous steps to localize your forms. It will mark those files in the Application Files dialog as *Exclude (Auto)*, as shown in Figure 5.4. The default publishing options just target your default language. If you are going to publish your application in more than one language, you have several choices for how to handle this.

- Publish a single version per target language
- Publish a single version that can be used by multiple languages
- Publish a single version that downloads multiple languages on demand

Publishing for a Single Target Language

Say that you have localized an application for at least one target language other than your default language. To publish for a single target culture,

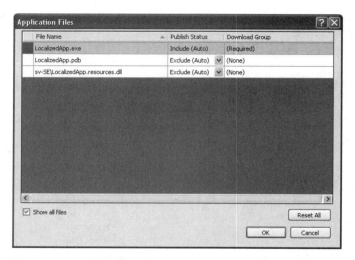

FIGURE 5.4: Excluded Language-Specific Resources

you just go into the project properties editor's Publish tab for the application and set the Publish language in the Publish Options dialog to the target language/culture (see Figure 5.5).

After setting a particular language in this dialog, the associated resource assemblies will be included in the published application files. This assumes you have localized some aspect of your application and that

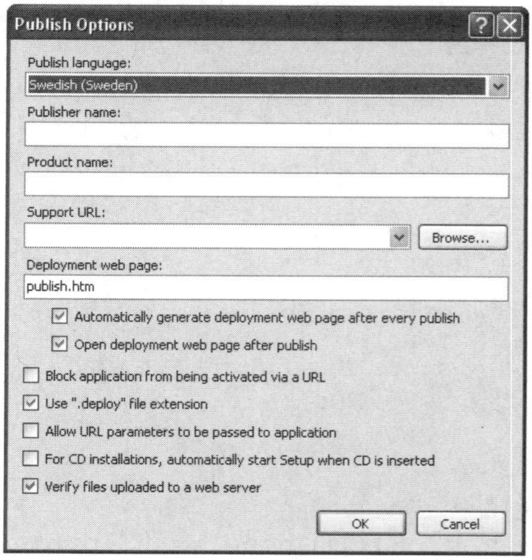

FIGURE 5.5: Setting the Publish Language

there will be localized resource assemblies for the selected language. When users deploy the application that you published to include a specific language, if their machines are configured for that language, they will get the localized version of the resources displayed by the application. If their machines are not configured for that language, they will get the default version of the application that was coded in your default language when you developed it.

Using this approach, you need to publish separate versions of your application to different URLs for each target language to which you have localized, because only one set of localized resource assemblies will be included each time you set the Publish language and publish your application. The advantage of this approach is that users will only get one set of localized resource assemblies downloaded to their machines. The disadvantage is that you will need to publish the application once for each target language and manage all of those separate publications.

Publishing for Multiple Target Cultures

If you have localized your application to support multiple languages, but you don't want to have separate publications of your application for each target language, you can publish just a single version of your application that supports multiple languages. To do so, you will need to manually configure the application files in the Publish properties to include all of the localized resources. To do so, first localize your application for each language that you want to target. This will result in a separate resource assembly in individual subfolders in the build output for each language. You will then need to open the Application Files dialog from the project properties editor's Publish tab, check the box at the bottom for *Show all files,* and then switch each of the resource assemblies to *Include* under Publish Status (see Figure 5.6).

The advantage of this approach is that you only have to publish one version of your application. Every user who launches the application will get all language resource assemblies, and thus they will get the localized version of the application based on whatever language they have set up on their machines. The big downside is that it means that a bunch of assemblies are being downloaded to every client that may never get used, because single users are likely to only ever set their system up for a single

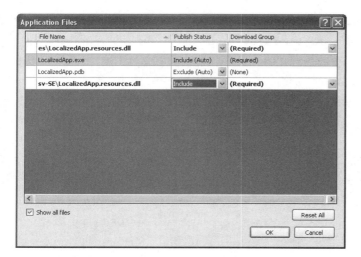

FIGURE 5.6: Including All Localized Resources

language. That means launching the application will take longer because the initial install is not complete until all of localized resource assemblies download, even though they will only be using one language at a time and will rarely switch languages. It also means more disk space consumed on the client machine once those files have been downloaded.

Publishing for On-Demand Download of Other Cultures

Another way that you could address the need to support multiple localized languages for your application with only a single publication is to use Download Groups to programmatically download the language resources after the initial application download. The process of defining and downloading groups of files is covered in the next section. This would require that you design your application to download and launch the initial files for your application, detect what the current culture is from the main application thread after it is launched, and then programmatically download the correct localized resources after the application is started. This approach is pretty complex to get right but is a possibility. You could also prompt users to select the language version that they want to use, but that would assume that they can understand the language that you use for prompting in the initially downloaded version. So in general I would stay away from this approach and choose one of the others just discussed.

Programmatic Download of Application Files

In some cases, you may not want the user to have to wait until all the application files have downloaded in order to start using your application. In that case, you can partition sets of files in your application into Download Groups. When you create a named Download Group, you can designate one or more files that are part of your application to belong to that Download Group. Once you do so, those files will no longer be downloaded as part of the normal installation and update process of ClickOnce, but can be programmatically downloaded on demand when desired.

To create a Download Group, do the following.

1. Open your application project in Visual Studio.
2. Go to the project properties editor's Publish tab.
3. Click the Application Files button to bring up the Application Files dialog.
4. For one file, from the Download Group drop-down list, select (New...), as shown in Figure 5.7.
5. Enter a name for the Download Group in the dialog shown in Figure 5.8 and click OK.
6. Select that Download Group from the drop-down list for the other files in the application that you want to be part of that group.
7. Click OK to close the Application Files dialog.

After you have done this, the files added to a Download Group will be marked as part of the application and will be published to the deployment server when you publish the application. However, when a user launches the application through ClickOnce, any files that are marked as part of a Download Group other than the (Required) group will not be downloaded and cached on the client automatically. You will need to add some code to your application to pull those files down programmatically at runtime and make them accessible to the client. You might also want to prompt users as to their availability, and let the users choose whether they want to download and use those features.

The download code for this chapter on the book's Web site includes a sample application called ProgrammaticDownloadGroups, which demonstrates

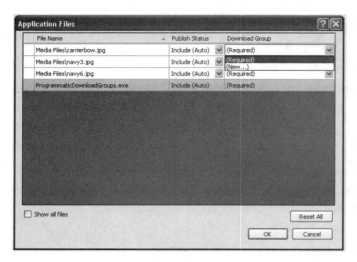

FIGURE 5.7: Adding a New Download Group

FIGURE 5.8: Naming the Download Group

this approach. The application includes three media files in a subfolder under the project, which coincidentally is named Media Files. Those three files are configured as a Download Group named Media Files using the process described in the preceding steps, and their Publish Status is set to *Include (Auto)*, meaning they will be placed in the application folder. Those three files have their Build Action property set to *Content*, and their Copy To Output Directory property set to *Copy always* in the Properties window when the file is selected in Solution Explorer. Because these files are in the \Media Files subfolder under the project root folder, they will be placed in a \Media Files subfolder both in the build output folder and in the deployed ClickOnce application folder.

When you first publish and install this sample application through ClickOnce, you can click the button labeled *Check For Images* on the main form shown in Figure 5.9 and you should get a message box indicating that no files are available yet. Clicking this button checks for the presence of the

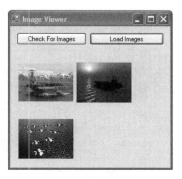

FIGURE 5.9: The ProgrammaticDownloadGroups Sample Application

image files in the \Media Files subfolder. You can then click the Load Images button and the media files will be downloaded through their Download Group and loaded into the UI as seen in Figure 5.9.

The code that performs the download is shown in Listing 5.1. The code is designed to run correctly whether you run the application in the debugger or through a ClickOnce installation. It first checks to see whether the application has been launched through ClickOnce by using the IsNetworkDeployed property as discussed in Chapter 4. If so, then it checks to see if the Download Group has already been downloaded through the IsFileGroupDownloaded method on the ApplicationDeployment instance. If not, the code hooks up an event handler for the DownloadFileGroupCompleted event and invokes an asynchronous download of the group through the DownloadFileGroupAsync method. If the application is not running under ClickOnce, or if the Download Group has already been downloaded, then the LoadImages helper method is directly invoked. The event handler for the DownloadFileGroupCompleted event calls LoadImages once the download is complete. The LoadImages helper method loads each file into a Bitmap object, creates a PictureBox control, sets the Bitmap as the image on the PictureBox, and then adds the PictureBox to the FlowLayoutPanel that arranges the images in the form.

LISTING 5.1: Downloading Files in a Download Group

```
private void OnLoadImages(object sender, EventArgs e)
{
    // If running under ClickOnce
    if (ApplicationDeployment.IsNetworkDeployed)
```

```
    {
        // Get ref to deployment
        ApplicationDeployment current =
            ApplicationDeployment.CurrentDeployment;
        // See if the group has not yet been downloaded
        if (!current.IsFileGroupDownloaded("Media Files"))
        {
            // If not, hook up event handler and download async
            current.DownloadFileGroupCompleted +=
                OnMediaDownloadComplete;
            current.DownloadFileGroupAsync("Media Files");
        }
        else
        {
            // Already downloaded
            LoadImages();
        }
    }
    else
    {
        // Not running under ClickOnce
        LoadImages();
    }
}

void OnMediaDownloadComplete(object sender,
    DownloadFileGroupCompletedEventArgs e)
{
    LoadImages();
}

private void LoadImages()
{
    string[] imageFiles =
        Directory.GetFiles(@".\Media Files","*.jpg");
    foreach (string filePath in imageFiles)
    {
        Bitmap bmp = new Bitmap(filePath);
        PictureBox pbox = new PictureBox();
        pbox.Image = bmp;
        pbox.Size = new Size(100,100);
        pbox.SizeMode = PictureBoxSizeMode.Zoom;
        m_ImagePanel.Controls.Add(pbox);
    }
}
```

Just like the CheckForUpdate and Update methods covered in Chapter 4, the ApplicationDeployment class includes both synchronous and asynchronous versions of the `DownloadFileGroup` method, along with progress and completed events and the ability to cancel a download in progress.

Deploying Extensible Plug-In Applications with ClickOnce

Many applications support the notion of extensibility and plug-ins that allow different levels of functionality to be added to an existing application based on either user desires or the license that has been purchased for an application. There are a number of ways to achieve this in a .NET application. A common way is through a combination of a factory class to dynamically instantiate the plug-in types and interface-based programming to access the components. The application has no specific type information about the plug-in components at compile time other than what interfaces they implement. Using this approach, you can decouple the application from the implementation details of the plug-ins to a great degree and add new functionality to your application after it has been deployed.

An example of a plug-in application would be an image-processing application that lets you plug in various image transformation algorithms to work against images that are loaded into the application. Those transformations do not all need to be available at the time you ship the first version of your application, can be provided by third-party vendors, and you may want to allow developers to plug in their own implementations if desired.

To support this, you have to define a contract for how the plug-in will be used by the application, since the application will not have specific type information for the plug-in type that gets added later. The best way to do this is through an interface or abstract base class definition that the plug-in type is expected to implement or derive from. You can then use the factory pattern to create an instance of the plug-in type, and cast it to the known contract type. Then the application can just program against the contract and does not have to know the specific type of the plug-in. A full exploration of this pattern and the various ways to implement it are beyond the scope of this book.[1] This approach is used in many places in .NET to add

---

1. The Plug-in Pattern is described in *Patterns of Enterprise Application Architecture* by Martin Fowler (Addison-Wesley, 2002).

extensibility to the .NET Framework. The Provider Model in ASP.NET 2.0 is based on this pattern, and the Enterprise Library from Microsoft patterns & practices also uses a plug-in architecture for extensibility.

The bottom line with plug-ins is that they are usually just class library assemblies (DLLs) that are added to an application in some known location at any point after initial deployment. In addition to providing the library in which the plug-in type is defined, you usually also specify the type information for the plug-in through an external configuration file so that the application knows what type to create after loading the plug-in assembly. Once the DLL has been placed in the appropriate location and the type information provided externally from the application through the configuration file, the application then loads those plug-ins dynamically when you call into them from the application and makes their functionality available as if it was "built-in" with the application.

Plug-ins can be added to a ClickOnce deployed application in a couple of ways. You could add new plug-ins as part of the application files in future published versions of the application. You could also let the user load a plug-in by browsing to the plug-in file.

The download code for this chapter on the book's Web site includes a sample application named ImageProcessingPlugInApp that demonstrates the deployment of plug-ins through ClickOnce updates. The sample application folder has two full versions of the application and its referenced class library projects for simplicity. The core application is composed of the following.

- The ImageProcessingPlugInApp Windows Forms application, which is the ClickOnce deployed application. It displays an image in a `Pic-tureBox` control and dynamically loads available plug-ins that perform image processing on the displayed image (see Figure 5.10).

- The DynamicFactoryLibrary class library contains a .NET generics-based `DynamicFactory` class that lets you dynamically instantiate components based on type information contained in the application configuration file. This class is extracted from a demonstration sample that I wrote and is available from the IDesign download library at www.idesign.net. A copy of the full sample is also included in the

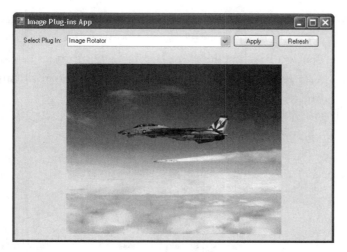

FIGURE 5.10: ImageProcessingPlugInApp Sample

download code for this chapter. See the Readme.doc file in that sample for more information on how the factory works.

- The ImageProcessingPlugInContracts class library defines the interface that plug-in components are expected to implement, `IImage-Processor`.

The glue that ties the deployed client application to the plug-ins that may be added later is the interface contract that plug-ins are expected to implement. The `IImageProcessor` interface definition is quite straightforward.

```
public interface IImageProcessor
{
    Bitmap ProcessImage(Bitmap img);
    string PlugInName { get; }
}
```

The `ProcessImage` method defines the primary behavior for a plug-in—to take in an image and to pass back a processed version of that image in the form of a `Bitmap` instance. The `PlugInName` property lets the plug-in expose a friendly name for itself that can be used for display in the consuming user interface. Any plug-in for the main application is expected to provide a component that implements this interface and that performs whatever kind of processing it is designed for on the provided image.

The plug-ins are loaded by the client application (using the `Dynamic-Factory` class) based on type information that you place in the application configuration file as shown here.

```xml
<?xml version="1.0" encoding="utf-8" ?>
<configuration>
    <!-- configuration section definitions ommitted for brevity -->
    <applicationSettings>
      <DynamicFactoryLibrary.Properties.Settings>
        <setting name="Types" serializeAs="Xml">
          <value>
            <ArrayOfString xmlns:xsi="..." xmlns:xsd="...">
              <string>ImagePlugIns1.Rotator, ImagePlugIns1</string>
            </ArrayOfString>
          </value>
        </setting>
      </DynamicFactoryLibrary.Properties.Settings>
    </applicationSettings>
</configuration>
```

The type information is specified as a string collection, where each string is in the form of:

```xml
<string>Fully.Qualified.Typename, AssemblyName</string>
```

The main application calls the `DynamicFactory` to load the plug-ins from the \Plugins subfolder when the Refresh button is pressed and adds them to a `ComboBox` for display and selection.

```csharp
private void OnRefresh(object sender, EventArgs e)
{
    IList<IImageProcessor> imageProcs =
        DynamicFactory.CreateInstances<IImageProcessor>(@".\Plugins");
    List<PlugInItem> items = new List<PlugInItem>();
    foreach (IImageProcessor imageProc in imageProcs)
    {
        PlugInItem item = new PlugInItem();
        item.Name = imageProc.PlugInName;
        item.Processor = imageProc;
        items.Add(item);
    }
    m_PlugInCombo.DataSource = items;
    m_PlugInCombo.DisplayMember = "Name";
```

```
        m_PlugInCombo.ValueMember = "Processor";
    }
```

When the Apply button is pressed, it obtains a reference to the currently selected plug-in from the selected value of the `ComboBox` and calls `ProcessImage` on it to replace the contents of the `PictureBox` control with the processed image.

```
private void OnApply(object sender, EventArgs e)
{
    // Get the selected processor from the combo box
    IImageProcessor proc = m_PlugInCombo.SelectedValue
        as IImageProcessor;
    if (proc == null)
        return;

    // Get the current image from the picture box
    Bitmap bmp = m_PictureBox.Image as Bitmap;
    if (bmp == null)
        return;

    // Call the processor to get the modified image
    // and set the result as the image on the picture box
    m_PictureBox.Image = proc.ProcessImage(bmp);
}
```

The Version 1.0.0.0 folder also includes a single plug-in library named ImagePlugIns1 that contains an image processor named `Rotator` with a simple implementation of the `IImageProcessor` interface. This project is configured to copy its build output to the main application project's \Plug-ins subfolder. The main application project has a copy of the built class library configured as a project file with a Build Action of *Content* and a Copy To Output Directory property set to *Copy always*. As a result, those files are copied into the same subfolder of the application when it is deployed to the client through ClickOnce. As long as the application configuration file has valid type information for the contained processing components, these components will be dynamically loaded at runtime by the `DynamicFactory` and will be available to the application.

The version 2.0.0.0 folder includes the whole application from version 1.0.0.0 plus an additional plug-in library named ImagePlusIns2 that is similarly configured to ImagePlugIns1 but that contains a different (simple) processing component.

To try out the initial application with a single plug-in, do the following.

1. Open the ImageProcessingPlugInApp.sln file from the version 1.0.0.0 folder.
2. Publish the application (choose Project > Publish ImageProcessing-PlugInApp).
3. Install the application from the publish.htm test page when it appears in the browser.
4. Click the Install button when prompted by the ClickOnce security warning.
5. When the application loads, click the Refresh button and you should see Image Rotator appear in the ComboBox.
6. Click the Apply button and the image should rotate 90 degrees.
7. Shut down the application.

To deploy a new version of the application with an additional plug-in, do the following.

1. Open the ImageProcessingPlugInApp.sln file from the version 2.0.0.0 folder.
2. Publish the application. This version includes the ImagePlugIns2 class library as well as the ImagePlugIns1 class library.
3. Run the client ImageProcessingPlugInApp application from the Start menu.
4. Click OK when prompted that an update is available.
5. Click the Refresh button once the application is loaded.
6. You should see both the Image Rotator and Image Flipper processing components in the drop-down list.
7. Select and apply each one to verify that the plug-ins are in fact loaded and working.

When you deploy plug-ins as updates in this manner, you can evolve the functionality of your application over time without needing to deploy new versions of the main client application. Those plug-ins could be added to Download Groups as discussed in the previous section and downloaded on demand by the user, or based on the licensed version that the user has purchased. To deploy a new plug-in with this model, you need to include the new plug-in class library in the project with its Build Action set to *Content*. You then update the application configuration file to include the type information for the new plug-in library and publish the application.

You could also employ a standard naming convention for the plug-in component types to avoid needing to specify anything in the configuration file. For example, in the ImageProcessingPlugInApp, I could have instead required that all plug-in types be named `<AssemblyName>.ImageProcessor`. I could have dynamically found all DLLs in the \Plugins folder, loaded them, and tried to create an instance of the type based on the naming convention instead of the explicit type information in the config file. There are a number of commercial applications supporting plug-ins that take this approach of putting the plug-in files in a known directory and automatically loading them from there.

Regardless of which approach you employ, the fact is that you can easily employ plug-ins in a ClickOnce application as shown here or through some other custom approach to getting the plug-ins loaded into the application directory. If you wanted to allow the user to browse and identify the plug-in files from some other folder, then you would probably want to copy the selected file to the application's DataDirectory after the user selects the source file, so that the files would be automatically copied forward to newer versions of the application after updates occur. See the section later in this chapter titled Dealing with Data Files on the Client for more information on the DataDirectory.

Managing Application Files with Mage

Once you have your application all built, tested, and published from Visual Studio for the first time, it doesn't necessarily mean you are done adding application files. Your organization may add whole new libraries of content files, media, document templates, and other such files to the application after the development team has finished the application and moved on to other things. Like with all things to do with ClickOnce, the show is driven by the manifests at deployment time, and you can change the manifests any time using the Mage tools.

Application files are all identified in the application manifest, so that is the only manifest you will be concerned with editing through Mage for this purpose. All of the settings that you can edit using Mage correlate to settings that you enter in the project properties editor in Visual Studio.

To add, remove, or replace application files, launch the Mage UI tool through mageui.exe from a Visual Studio command prompt or from the \SDK\v2.0\bin folder under your Visual Studio install. Open the application manifest (<appname>.exe.manifest file) from the folder where the version you are modifying exists. Once you have opened the file, select the Files category in the list on the left (see Figure 5.11). You will see the list of application files that are currently listed in the manifest in the grid, along with their file type, group, and whether they are optional.

The File Type selection here corresponds to the Publish Status setting in Visual Studio, and can be set to *Entry Point* for the main executable, *Data File* to be placed in the DataDirectory for the application, or *Icon* if you

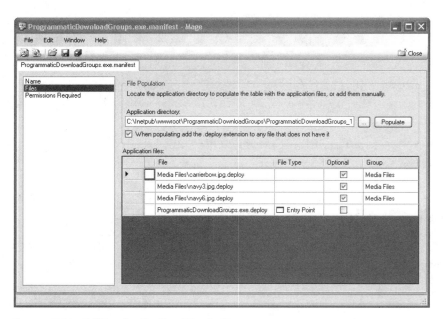

FIGURE 5.11: Editing Application Files in Mage

need to replace the application icon that is used for the Start menu item. The File Types column becomes a drop-down list when you select it. Selecting *None* from the drop-down list of File Types just blanks out the entry, making it the same as a file marked with a Publish Status of *Include* in Visual Studio.

The Optional checkbox column should be correlated with entering a Group (which is the same as Download Group in Visual Studio). You check this column if the file is expected to only be downloaded when its Download Group is programmatically downloaded.

The Group column is a simple text box entry column, in which you can type any Download Group name you want. Leaving it blank means it is not part of a named Download Group.

You cannot directly add, remove, or replace files from the Mage UI. If you want to add, remove, or replace an application file, you need to first do so by making the change to the physical files that are in the published application folder. You can simply add any new files, delete ones that you want to remove, and replace any that you want to replace through Windows Explorer or a command line tool. Once you have done that, you need to get Mage to recognize the current contents of the folder by clicking the Populate button.

You should keep the checkbox selected that adds a .deploy file extension to all application files, because it makes it easier to set up the MIME file type mappings on the deployment server to control what is exposed from the server. When you do so and then click the Populate button, a warning will pop up telling you that the file names of the application files in the folder will be changed to include this .deploy file extension. That extension is a modification to the file, and as a result it will be treated as an updated file when a client goes to update the application, even though the contents of the file may not have changed at all.

After clicking the Populate button, the list of files in Mage will reflect the current contents of the published application folder, but it unfortunately resets all the columns for those files and you will have to reenter any download file groups for individual files that you need, as well as set their File Type and Optional properties correctly.

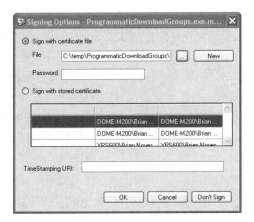

FIGURE 5.12: Signing the Manifest

Once you have made any changes to the files in the application manifest, as with any change to a manifest, you will need to re-sign the manifest with a publisher certificate. You do this by clicking the Save button. This brings up the Signing Options dialog shown in Figure 5.12, where you can select a publisher certificate from a file or from those listed in your Personal certificate store in the middle of the dialog.

If you make any change to the application manifest (such as changing the file list or signing the application manifest with a different publisher certificate than was used when the application was first published), you will also need to update the Application Reference in the deployment manifest (.application file), because it includes both a hash for the application manifest's contents and the public key token from the publisher certificate used to sign the application manifest.

Managing Data Files Through Visual Studio

Managing data files in a ClickOnce application is done through the same means as managing application files. You must first include the data file in your Visual Studio project, and you must also set the Build Action to *Content* so that the data file will be included in the Application Files listed in the project properties editor's Publish tab. Then the key discriminator between an application file and a data file is that data files must be marked with a Publish Status of *Data File* in the Application Files dialog. They will then be treated differently when the application is deployed to the client machine and when updates occur, as described in the following sections.

The Data File Publish Status value is set by default for any SQL Express .mdf and .ldf files, SQL Compact .sdf files, as well as for any .xml files in the project. Any file whose Publish Status is set to *Data File* will be copied to the Publishing Location folders along with the rest of the application files. When the application is deployed to the client machine, these files will be put in a separate folder for each application and version under a \Data root directory under the user profile. You can get the path to this folder on the client programmatically using the `Application.User-AppDataPath` property or with the `ApplicationDeployment.Data-Directory` property. I will call this folder the *DataDirectory* folder throughout this chapter for brevity.

Dealing with Data Files on the Client

If you include files in your application that you will need to load programmatically on the client, you will need to know how to obtain a path to those files so you can use them through the Framework's classes that take path arguments, such as the `FileStream` and `Bitmap` class constructors.

If a file is included with your application and its Publish Status is set to *Include*, it will be placed in the same location relative to the root folder for the application as it has relative to the project root folder in Visual Studio. For example, if you have a MyPicture.jpg file that is in a project's \Media subfolder in Visual Studio, that same file will end up in a \Media subfolder of the client's application directory. To access the files in a full-trust application, you use a relative file path (e.g., \Media\MyPicture.jpg) to access them programmatically from the client's application folder. Likewise, if that file is marked as a Data File, it will be placed in the same relative folder location from the DataDirectory that it resides in relative to the project folder.

One challenge in using data files is that the DataDirectory is only present when your application has been launched through ClickOnce on a client machine. In order for your application code to work with these files in a debug environment, you will also need to do a few things. First, set the Copy

To Output Directory property for the data files to *Copy always* or *Copy if newer*. The result of doing this is that those files will be copied to the same relative folder location under the build output folder for your project, and thus will be available during your debug session. Next, add conditional code that checks if the `ApplicationDeployment` class' `IsNetworkDeployed` property is set to *True*. If it is, you can safely get the path for the DataDirectory from the property of that name in the `ApplicationDeployment` class, and use a relative path under that (e.g., \Media\MyPicture.jpg under the DataDirectory path) to locate your data file. If the `IsNetworkDeployed` property is not true, then you should just use a local relative path to access the file under the debug folder (e.g., .\Media\MyPicture).

If you want to determine the folder for your application, regardless of whether it is running through ClickOnce or not, you can use the `Application.ExecutablePath` property in combination with the `GetDirectoryName` method in the `Path` class from the `System.IO` namespace.

```
private void DisplayAppFolder(object sender, EventArgs e)
{
    string appFolder = Path.GetDirectoryName(
        Application.ExecutablePath);
    MessageBox.Show(appFolder);
}
```

As mentioned earlier, if you are running a partial-trust ClickOnce application, the executable path will not be your application executable's installed directory on the client. If you need to programmatically access files in a partial-trust application, you should deploy those files with their Publish Status set to *Data File*. If an application file is set as a Data File, it will be placed in a separate folder on the client when it is deployed through ClickOnce, and that folder is accessible in partial trust.

To access a data file, you will need to use the `Application.UserAppDataPath` property or the `ApplicationDeployment.DataDirectory` property to obtain the path to the containing folder for the data file, then you can append the data file name. The `Application.UserAppDataPath` property will return the same result as `ApplicationDeployment.DataDirectory` if the application is running through ClickOnce, but will return a different path to a directory under the user's profile when not running through ClickOnce.

The path used by `Application.UserAppDataPath` when not running through ClickOnce is determined dynamically by the project assembly information, accessible through the Assembly Information button in the project properties editor's Application tab in Visual Studio. In the Assembly Information dialog you can set a company, product, and assembly version. The user data path for a non-ClickOnce deployed application is placed under the user's profile in the Application Data folder and partitioned using those three pieces of information. For example, for the SimpleDataFileSample application, the user data path when running in the debugger is:

C:\Documents and Settings\Brian Noyes\Application Data\IDesign Inc\SimpleDataFileSample\1.0.0.0\

where IDesign Inc is set as the company, SimpleDataFileSample is the product name, and 1.0.0.0 is the assembly version number.

If you set a file's Publish Status to *Data File*, and set its Copy To Output Directory property to *Copy if newer* or *Copy always*, then you can access the data file with code similar to the following regardless of whether you are running in the debugger as a normal application or through a ClickOnce launch.

```
private void LoadData()
{
    string dataPath;
    if (ApplicationDeployment.IsNetworkDeployed)
    {
        dataPath =
            ApplicationDeployment.CurrentDeployment.DataDirectory;
    }
    else
    {
        dataPath = ".";
    }
    dataPath += @"\Customers.xml";
    CustomersDataSet ds = new CustomersDataSet();
    ds.ReadXml(dataPath);
    customersBindingSource.DataSource = ds.Customers;
}
```

Data File Update Process

When you set a project file's Publish Status to *Data File*, the update process for that file is a little different than when a file is just an included application file. To understand what is different about data file handling during an update, let me quickly recap what happens with application files during an update first.

As discussed in Chapter 3, when an application is already installed on the client and an update is downloaded, the new version gets its own new folder on the client and the updated application files are placed in that folder. Files that are new or changed on the server in the update version are downloaded from the deployment server, and files that are unchanged between versions are copied from the previous version's client-side cache folder to the update version's folder to save on download time.

Files in the application folder for a ClickOnce application are not expected to be edited directly. As a result, as discussed in the File Validation section in Chapter 3, if an application file has been modified on the client side and is unchanged between the two versions on the server side, the application file in the update version on the server will be downloaded instead of copying the previous version's modified file across to the update version's new folder. This behavior is by design to avoid running application files that have been tampered with on the client side.

Data files are migrated differently than application files when an update is downloaded. Say you publish version 1.0.0.0 of your application with a data file Customers.xml (with its Publish Status set to *Data File*). Customers.xml gets placed in the DataDirectory on the client side after deployment. The Customers.xml file that is in version 1.0.0.0 has some default sample data in it. The application lets users interact with the data in that XML file and save changes back to the XML data file on the client side. This application gets deployed to a client, and users start using the application and editing and saving customer data over time in the application's DataDirectory folder.

Then at some point, you need to publish an update to the application to fix a logic bug. You publish version 2.0.0.0 of the application, and the Customers.xml file in that version is unchanged from version 1.0.0.0 on the deployment server. When the update happens on the client, the modified

Customers.xml file that users have been editing is copied forward to the DataDirectory folder for version 2.0.0.0, and the Customers.xml file on the server is not downloaded. When users start using version 2.0.0.0, they will see all their modified data from working with version 1.0.0.0.

This works great up to a point. As long as the server-side data file is unchanged, the users' data file will be moved forward as each update occurs, letting users continue to work with their modified data. However, what happens if the Customers.xml file is changed in the project on a subsequent version? Perhaps you decide to change the schema of the .xml file slightly or add another sample data record. Now you have a conflict. You have an intentional change to the data file by the publisher of the application, possibly one that is required for the application to work correctly with that data file. But you also have a modified version of the file on the client side that contains modified user data. Which should get copied into the data directory for the new version when an update occurs? What happens to the other file?

To understand what happens, I'll describe it in the context of a specific scenario. Say you have version 1.0.0.0 on the client with modifications in the Customers.xml file in its DataDirectory folder. Version 2.0.0.0 of the application gets published to the deployment server with a new version of Customers.xml. When a user accepts the updated version, the following happens behind the scenes.

1. The modified Customers.xml from the DataDirectory of version 1.0.0.0 is copied to a \.pre subfolder of the DataDirectory folder for version 2.0.0.0 (see Figure 5.13).
2. The new version of Customers.xml from version 2.0.0.0 is placed in the version 2.0.0.0 DataDirectory folder.

If you do nothing else, version 2.0.0.0 will run and ignore the previous version's data file and will display and use the new 2.0.0.0 default file. To deal with data file updates like this, you will need to include some data migration code that only runs if an update like this has occurred. You can access the previous data file from the \.pre folder and import that data into the new data file, or do whatever is appropriate based on the kind of change you

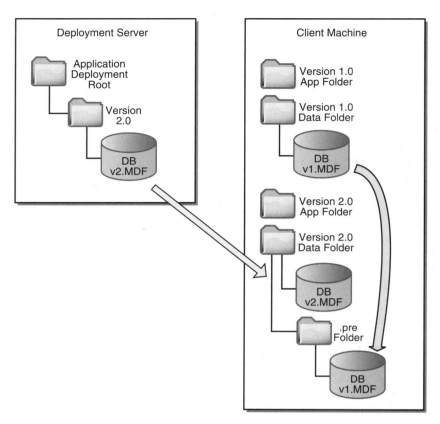

FIGURE 5.13: Data File Migration Process

made to the data file. An example of doing this will be shown in the next section for a SQL Compact database file.

If you do not do the data migration immediately on launching a new version, you risk losing the user's changes permanently. The data file from the previous version that was placed in the \.pre folder is not migrated forward to any subsequent versions. So if another update occurs before you migrate the user's changes into the new data file in the current version's root DataDirectory folder, then when the next update occurs, those user changes from the previous version will effectively be lost. Strategies for dealing with this, particularly in the context of SQL Compact data files, are discussed in the next section.

Deploying a Client Database with Your Application

One of the most common forms of data files you will need in your application is a client-side database or data cache. A great choice for these requirements is to use SQL Server 2005 Compact Edition (formerly known as SQL Server 2005 Mobile Edition). This lightweight database engine lets you create and store data on the client using standard relational data access with ADO.NET. SQL Compact does not support the full range of capabilities that SQL Server 2005 does, but its functionality is usually sufficient for single-user client applications. For example, SQL Compact supports tables, constraints, and relations between tables, but it does not support stored procedures, functions, views, or other more advanced features of the full SQL Server product, such as SQL Server Service Broker. It does support two forms of synchronization with back-end databases as well: Remote Data Access and merge replication.

SQL Compact is easy to deploy with ClickOnce applications because you can either deploy it as a prerequisite through the Bootstrapper (see Chapter 7) or by simply adding some DLL files to your project and deploying them as application files. The total size of the DLLs required is under 1.4MB, so the impact of deploying them with your application is very small, and it minimizes the complexity of deploying your application because it prevents you from needing to specify database prerequisites for your application.

To get started with SQL Compact, you will first need to download and install the SQL Compact package. As of this writing, SQL Compact is in Community Technical Preview (CTP) status. Your best bet by the time you read this is to simply search the Web for the full name (SQL Server 2005 Compact Edition) and look for the download links from Microsoft. It is a free product. Once you download and install it on your development machine, you can start developing applications using it. If you have previously used or developed applications with SQL Server 2005 Mobile Edition, SQL Compact is compatible with those applications. The release of SQL Compact is really more a rebranding and repackaging of SQL Mobile than a whole new technology.

The next section demonstrates how the database files associated with SQL Compact are migrated when an update occurs.

Migrating SQL Compact Edition Database Files

The download code for this chapter includes a sample called SQLCompactDefaultMigration that you can use to see what happens if you do not properly migrate your data when a data file update occurs. That sample includes two versions of the application: v1.0.0.0 and v2.0.0.0. They both use trimmed down versions of the Northwind.sdf file from the Mobile SDK as a client-side data store that is integrated into a data-bound form in the application.

The first version just contains the Customers table in the database and presents the Customers data in a grid, and lets you edit fields in the grid and save the changes back to the database through a `BindingNavigator` (toolbar) control at the top of the form. The second version adds the Orders table (and a couple of related tables) to the database with a foreign key relation between Customers and Orders. The second version application adds a master-details view of the data with two grids in the form (see Figure 5.14). Because the second version needs to ship a new version of the database, which is just an .sdf file being used by the application as a data file, you will run into the data file migration problems described earlier.

⬛ TIP   DataDirectory and Connection Strings

When you add a SQL Compact database (.sdf file) to your Visual Studio project, it gets placed in the project as a file with a Build Action of *Content*. As a result, it will be included in the Application Files dialog of your publish settings for ClickOnce deployment, and it will be automatically marked as a data file (Publish Status of *Data File (Auto)*). When deployed, the SQL Compact .sdf file will be placed in the Data-Directory folder for your application. You will need to make sure that you include the special |DataDirectory| placeholder in your connection string so that the path can be filled in automatically by the runtime. For example, the NorthwindConnectionString project setting for the sample application is set to:

```
Data Source ="|DataDirectory|\Northwind.sdf"
```

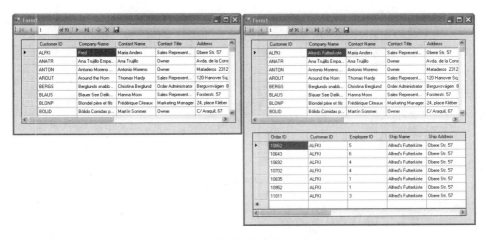

FIGURE 5.14: Two Versions of SQL Compact Edition Sample

When the first version is deployed through ClickOnce and users start making changes to the data and saving those changes, the local Northwind.sdf file in the DataDirectory is updated when the changes are saved. When the second version is subsequently deployed, the new version contains a modified version of the data file that needs to be downloaded to support the new functionality in the application (the presentation of the new Orders table as a child relation). As a result, the data migration logic of ClickOnce kicks in and downloads the new database file from version 2.0.0.0 on the server into the DataDirectory of version 2.0.0.0. The modified data file from version 1.0.0.0 is placed in a \.pre subfolder of that directory, but is not directly accessible to the application unless you write some custom code to migrate the data from the old database into the new one.

To see this in action, do the following.

1. Open the solution for v1.0.0.0. Notice that it includes the seven SQL Compact DLLs in the solution (see Figure 5.15). After adding those files from the SQL Compact installation directory, their Build Action file property is set to *Content* in the Properties window. This gets them included in the Application Files dialog of your publish settings when you deploy the application with ClickOnce, so you do not have any prerequisites for using SQL Compact in your application.

FIGURE 5.15: SQL Compact Edition DLLs in Project

2. Publish the application (Build > Publish SQLCompactDefault-Migration).

3. Install the application when the publish.htm page is presented by clicking on the Install button.

4. The application should launch and you will see customer data in the grid. Change a company name field and click the Save button in the toolbar. This will write the changed data back to the disk file (North-wind.sdf) in the DataDirectory.

5. Shut down the application.

Do the following steps to verify that the changes were persisted.

1. Run the application again from the Start menu. You should see your changed value loaded back into the grid because it was written out to the database file when you saved.

2. Close the application and the solution in Visual Studio.

3. Open the v2.0.0.0 solution in Visual Studio. This version is the same as v1.0.0.0 except that it contains extra tables in the database file and has an additional data-bound grid on the form.

4. Publish this version (Build > Publish SQLCompactDefaultMigration).

5. When the publish.htm page is presented, close the browser.

6. Go to the Start menu and launch the application.

7. You should be prompted that an update is available. Click the OK button to accept the update.

8. The application should launch and you will no longer see your changed data value in the Customers table.

The reason your changes were lost in this case is because the new version of the database file was downloaded from the server and placed in the DataDirectory in the same path for the new version that the previous database file was for the old version. The old version's database file was migrated forward to the v2.0.0.0 directory, but was placed in a \.pre subfolder of the DataDirectory. Version 2.0.0.0 did not include any code to migrate the data from the previous version forward, so it will be lost to users.

To fix this, you need to add some migration code to the application to move the data forward from the old version's database to the new version's database at the point where the new version gets deployed. It is going to be completely up to you to determine what an appropriate migration process is based on the kinds of changes that were made to the database. There is no stock, one-size-fits-all solution that you can just apply out of the box. Some changes are fairly easy to address, such as adding a column to a table or just adding new tables that didn't exist in the old version. More difficult are changes that remove information, such as dropping a table or column. In those cases you will have to decide what to do with the user data that is in the old version of the database.

The general process to migrate the data will be to run a SQL script or set of SQL queries to retrieve the data from the old database and insert the data into the appropriate tables in the new database. You might write this code as part of a separate migration utility that is invoked when the new version gets deployed.

The download code for this book shows an example of doing this in the SQLCompactScriptedMigration sample. The sample also includes a version 1.0.0.0 and 2.0.0.0 of the same application that you just saw for the default migration. Version 2.0.0.0 of this application includes a key piece of code that is called in the main form constructor.

```
public Form1()
{
    InitializeComponent();
    if (ApplicationDeployment.IsNetworkDeployed)
    {
        if (ApplicationDeployment.CurrentDeployment.IsFirstRun)
        {
            MigrateData();
        }
    }
}
```

The application checks to see if it is running through ClickOnce with the IsNetworkDeployed property, and if so, also checks to see if this is the first time this version has run. The IsFirstRun property will be set to *True* the first time any version of an application is launched through ClickOnce. You can use this to check and see if you need to do any kind of initialization steps. When you have a data migration scenario caused by a change to a data file, such as a schema change in a SQL Compact database, this flag lets you know that it is time to do your migration.

The MigrateData method is really the hard part of getting this done. This will be the place that you need to execute whatever data migration steps are appropriate for your application. For the sample application, a new table was added to the database with a foreign key relation to the old table. As a result, as long as no customers have been deleted, the code to migrate the data is fairly straightforward. If a user has deleted customers since the first version shipped, even this code will break, because the foreign keys in the Orders table will have lost their parent rows. But this will at least give you a sense of the kind of thing you will need to do to hook up to the old and new database. The code for this sample migration is shown in Listing 5.2.

LISTING 5.2: MigrateData Method Sample

```
private void MigrateData()
{
    string preFile = Path.Combine(
        ApplicationDeployment.CurrentDeployment.DataDirectory,
        @".\.pre\Northwind.sdf");
    if (!File.Exists(preFile)) // nothing to migrate
        return;
```

```
// Get a connection to the old data in the \.pre folder
string oldDataConnectionString =
    @"Data Source=|DataDirectory|\.pre\Northwind.sdf";
SqlCeConnection oldConnection =
    new SqlCeConnection(oldDataConnectionString);
// Get a connection to the new data
string newDataConnectionString =
    @"Data Source=|DataDirectory|\Northwind.sdf";
SqlCeConnection newConnection =
    new SqlCeConnection(newDataConnectionString);
// Fill a dataset with the migration data
NorthwindDataSet oldData = new NorthwindDataSet();
CustomersTableAdapter oldAdapter = new CustomersTableAdapter();
oldAdapter.Connection = oldConnection;
oldAdapter.Fill(oldData.Customers);
// Create a table adapter for the new database
// and a compatible data set
CustomersTableAdapter newAdapter = new CustomersTableAdapter();
newAdapter.Connection = newConnection;
NorthwindDataSet newData = new NorthwindDataSet();
// Fill the new data set with default data
newAdapter.Fill(newData.Customers);
// Merge the old data into the new schema
// Assumes compatible schemas--this is the hard part for
// real apps with significant schema changes
foreach (DataRow row in newData.Customers)
{
    row.Delete();
}
newData.Merge(oldData);
newAdapter.Update(newData);
}
```

The key aspect of this code to note is the way the connection string to the old database includes the \.pre directory in front of the database's file name. There is no way to avoid the complexity that is likely to ensue in your `MigrateData` method for any significant real-world schema change. There is also nothing really specific about ClickOnce with this problem other than how to address the database in the connection string. Anytime you have an existing database populated with data and you need to migrate to a new database schema while moving the old data forward, things get very complicated very quickly.

Another potential problem to be aware of with this is that the migration of a data file is triggered by *any* change to the data file in a newly published version of your application. If you connect to your SQL Compact database in Visual Studio just to check the schema or contents of the default values, you will have modified the date timestamp of the .sdf file, so the next time you publish your application it is going to be treated as a new version of the database, and the data migration process will occur even though you did not intend a real migration. *As a result, you could lose the user data from the previous version if you do not have migration scripts in place when that new version gets published.*

Where Are We?

This chapter has covered a variety of concerns that arise for specific kinds of application files when deploying applications with ClickOnce. You learned that files treated as part of the application for publishing purposes are determined by the files that are included in the Visual Studio project. Files marked with a Build Action of *Compile* for source code and *Embedded Resource* for resource files are compiled into the application executable, and the executable is always part of the published application. If you have an application configuration file, that will always be included in the published application as well. You learned how Build Action and Copy To Output Directory properties on additional files in the project influence whether they are published and whether they are available for debugging. You saw how to support data files, embedded resources, and plug-ins in ClickOnce deployed applications. You also saw how to programmatically download groups of files on demand instead of including them in the main application deployment.

The following are some of the key takeaways from this chapter.

- A Build Action of *Content* includes a file in the list of Application Files configurable through the project properties editor's Publish tab.
- A Publish Status of *Include* places files in the client's application directory after deployment, in the same relative path (subfolder) as they exist in the project folder in Visual Studio.
- A Publish Status of *Data File* places the file in the DataDirectory folder for the application on deployment.

- Data files that do not have a newer version in a published update will be copied forward into the new application version's DataDirectory folder.

- Data files that do have a newer version in a published update will be copied into the \.pre subfolder of the new version's DataDirectory, and the old data will be migrated into the new version's data file.

- The `XXXDownloadFileGroupXXX` methods and events in the `ApplicationDeployment` class expose the API for programmatically downloading groups of files on demand.

The next chapter will cover the security mechanisms in ClickOnce in more detail. It will review the default security protections that ClickOnce provides, as well as show you how to provide better protections than the defaults for enterprise environments.

6
ClickOnce Security

WHEN PLANNING FOR DEPLOYMENT, you need to consider a number of different aspects with respect to security. You need to consider

- How to protect the client machine from being compromised by your application's installation or execution
- How to protect the application files from being tampered with on the deployment server
- How to implement authentication and authorization based on the user's identity
- What you want to allow the application to do based on the identity of the application publisher

ClickOnce, the .NET Framework, and the Windows operating system provide facilities to address all of these considerations. This chapter will discuss these different aspects and give you a solid understanding of what protections ClickOnce provides, and how you can customize those protections to suit the needs of your particular application.

ClickOnce Security Overview

ClickOnce is designed to be a trustworthy deployment mechanism for smart client applications. This means that ClickOnce is designed to protect the client machine from being harmed by applications that it deploys. ClickOnce provides protection for the client machine at install time and at runtime, ensures that the client machine and users can identify who the publisher of the application is, and protects the application's files to ensure than no one can tamper with them after the publisher has published the application.

ClickOnce runtime protection is based on the application's identity, not on the user. ClickOnce is specifically designed to enable low-privilege users to deploy and launch smart client applications without adminis-trator intervention. The user identity is not used directly by ClickOnce in any way. However, that does not mean that your ClickOnce applica-tion will be unprotected with respect to user privileges either. You can take advantage of .NET role-based security to prevent users from using functionality in your application if they do not have sufficient rights. Additionally, the client machine's operating system will still enforce access controls based on the logged-in user, such as limiting access to files, folders, or the registry if the user is not part of the access control list for those resources.

ClickOnce Deployment-Time Protections

ClickOnce security protection comes into play as soon as an application or update is deployed to the client machine. When files are deployed to the client machine through ClickOnce, they are isolated per user, per application, and per version under the user's profile. The application deployment itself is nothing more than a series of files copied into an iso-lated folder under the user's profile. If you have worked with .NET iso-lated storage before, the ClickOnce cache folders are similar in concept, but located in a different place under the user's profile. You cannot exe-cute any custom installation steps that make modifications to the local machine as part of the ClickOnce deployment itself (see Chapters 7 and 8 for more information on custom installation requirements). As a result of this design, there is no way that the act of deploying an application to a client machine through ClickOnce can harm other applications or data on the machine.

ClickOnce Runtime Protections

ClickOnce and the .NET runtime provide runtime protections for the client as well. ClickOnce relies on the Code Access Security (CAS) infrastructure of the .NET Framework for enforcing those runtime protections, but ClickOnce security is configured and managed a little differently than for non-ClickOnce deployed applications. For a quick overview of CAS, see the sidebar entitled A Short Primer on Code Access Security.

A Short Primer on Code Access Security

The .NET Framework provides Code Access Security (CAS), which is a security mechanism that complements Windows access control and .NET role-based security. Both of these are based on the identity of the user who is executing the code. CAS lets you control the permissions the executing managed code has based on evidence associated with the executing code. CAS is a fairly complicated topic that many developers do not even know exists, or if they do, they do not really understand how it works.[1]

Evidence is based on either the identity of the code itself or the launch location of the code. The code's identity is determined by one of several forms of code identity that are embedded in the assembly manifest at compile time. These forms of identity include a hash of the assembly contents, an assembly strong name, or a publisher certificate. The location the code is being executed from can be determined by the .NET runtime based on the path used to load an assembly, and can be associated with a local machine directory, URL, site, or zone.

CAS is driven by security policies that can be administratively configured through the .NET Configuration tool or set programmatically. A complex schema of security objects drives the application of CAS by the runtime. Each machine has several security policies defined for it. Each *security policy* is composed of a collection of *code groups,* and each

Continues

---

1. For a deep understanding of Code Access Security, including how it works, how to configure it, and how to programmatically invoke it, I recommend *Programming .NET Components, Second Edition*, by Juval Löwy (O'Reilly & Associates, 2005).

code group is composed of a form of *evidence* (also called *membership criteria*) and an associated *permission set.* Each permission set is composed of a collection of individual *permission types,* which correspond to the discrete operations or resources that you want to protect, such as the file system, user interface, security capabilities, or the registry. For each permission type, there are fine-grained options that you can control. For example, you can control what specific set of URLs an application is allowed to access for a permission of type `WebPermission`.

For applications that are not launched through ClickOnce, CAS evaluates the evidence available for an assembly as the runtime loads it. It compares the evidence for the assembly against each code group's membership criteria (form of evidence associated with the code group). If the evidence presented by the assembly meets the code group's membership criteria, the assembly will be granted the code group's permission set. The runtime follows this process for all of the code groups in all of the policies on the system to come up with a final set of permissions that the assembly is granted for execution. As the code in the assembly is invoked, security demands can be made programmatically (typically by Framework assemblies) that ensure that the assembly and all of its callers have been granted the required permission for the operation or resource access that is being performed. If the assembly itself or any of the calling assemblies do not have the demanded permission, a security exception will be thrown.

By controlling the configuration of CAS, you can explicitly grant or deny permissions to any assembly on a machine for various operations and resources. For example, you can configure a server machine so that only .NET Framework code and code signed by your development organization's strong name are allowed to run on that machine. By doing so, you can ensure that if any other managed assemblies make it onto that server somehow, they will be unable to run unless an administrator intervenes and grants those assemblies a set of permissions.

When you install .NET, there are a predefined set of CAS policies and code groups installed on the machine. The built-in code groups are all based on the location that code is executing from. By default, any assemblies installed on the local machine have full trust (unrestricted permissions). This corresponds to the My Computer CAS zone. If assemblies are loaded from somewhere other than a local disk, the runtime can evaluate the path used to load the assembly and will compare it to the membership criteria of the other code groups. The other built-in code groups include ones for paths that evaluate to the LocalIntranet zone, Internet zone, Trusted Sites, or Restricted Sites. The LocalIntranet and Internet are the most common other security zones applied, based on the path to the assembly being loaded. The Trusted and Restricted Sites zones are based on URLs configured through Internet Explorer security settings.

ClickOnce security is applied at the application level, instead of at the individual assembly level as it is in a normal .NET application. Your entire ClickOnce application (the application executable and all assemblies that it loads) are treated as a single unit for the purposes of deployment, versioning, and security. When an application is deployed through ClickOnce, the application manifest specifies what security permissions the application needs to run. These permissions are based on CAS.

As the application is launched by ClickOnce, the runtime first evaluates what URL or UNC path was used to deploy the application to the client machine (the path to the deployment manifest on the deployment server). This path is treated as the launch path. Based on this path, the runtime associates your application with one of the built-in location-based code groups (My Computer, LocalIntranet, Internet, Trusted Sites, or Restricted Sites zones). The runtime determines what set of permissions should be granted to your application based on the zone that it was launched from and compares that to the set of permissions requested by the application.

If the requested permissions in the application manifest are less than or equal to the set that would be granted based on the launch zone, then no elevation of permissions needs to occur and the application can simply launch and run. If the application attempts to perform an operation that exceeds the granted permissions, then a `SecurityException` will be thrown.

To see this in action, do the following.

1. Create a new Windows Application project in Visual Studio, and name the project **RuntimeProtectionApp**.
2. From the toolbox, add a button to the form.
3. Double-click on the button to add a Click event handler for the button.
4. Add the following code to the event handler:

```
private void button1_Click(object sender, EventArgs e)
{
    StreamWriter writer = new StreamWriter("AttemptedHack.evil");
    writer.WriteLine("If I can do this, what else could I do??");
    writer.Close();
}
```

5. Add a using statement for the `System.IO` namespace to the top of the file:

```
using System.IO;
```

6. Open the project properties editor (choose Project > RuntimeProtectionApp Properties).
7. On the Security tab, check the checkbox labeled *Enable ClickOnce Security Settings*, and click the radio button labeled *This is a partial trust application* (see Figure 6.1).
8. Publish the application by choosing Build > Publish RuntimeProtectionApp.
9. When the Publish wizard appears, click the Next button.
10. In the second step of the Publish wizard, select the option to make the application available online only (see Figure 6.2) and then click Finish.
11. Click the Run button in the publish.htm test page when it appears in the browser. This launches the application.
12. Press the button that you added to the form in step 2, causing the application to try to write a text file to the current working directory (which in this case is the C:\Windows\Microsoft.NET\Framework\v2.0.50727 folder, since the application is marked for partial trust as discussed in Chapter 5).

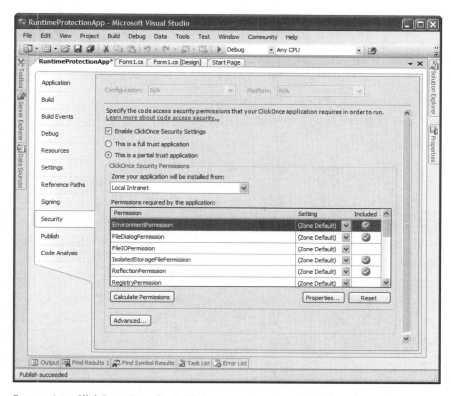

FIGURE 6.1: ClickOnce Security Settings

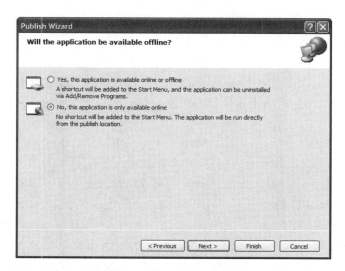

FIGURE 6.2: Selecting Install Mode in the Publish Wizard

13. A `SecurityException` will be thrown for the `FileIOPermission` type, because the default LocalIntranet zone security permissions do not include that permission. The permission is demanded by the `StreamWriter` class when you construct an instance of the `Stream-Writer`. Since the application does not catch the exception, the dialog shown in Figure 6.3 will display.

14. Click the Quit button to exit the application.

In this example, the application requested permissions that did not exceed the permissions granted by the launch zone. This is because you selected partial trust and the default zone for partial trust is the Local Intranet zone. When you installed the application by clicking on the Run button in the publish.htm test page, the address used was http://<your-machine-name>/RuntimeProtectionApp/RuntimeProtectionApp.application. The runtime evaluates this address to the Local Intranet zone (based on the server address portion of the URL: http://<your-machine-name>/) and compares the requested permissions in the application manifest to the permissions for that zone. Since they match, no additional prompting is needed based on security and the application launches.

However, just because the application only requests a certain set of permissions based on its manifest does not mean that there is not code in that application that might try to do some operation that exceeds the granted set of permissions. In this example, the application contains code that tries to perform a file write to the local directory. That operation triggers a check for `FileIOPermission` for the file that is being written. Since the Local Intranet zone does not include that permission, a `SecurityException` is thrown at that point.

These protections are designed to ensure that your application does not inadvertently do something on the user's machine that it was not designed to do. This could result from bugs in your code, debug code that was left behind unintentionally, or it could happen if your application manages to load some other assembly that does something more than you expect it to. For example, suppose you design a smart client application that acts as a data entry client for a distributed application. Based on your design, that application should only present a rich interactive user interface for the user

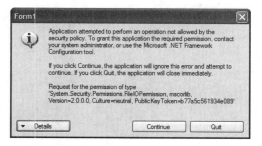

FIGURE 6.3: Unhandled Exception Dialog

to view, enter, and manipulate data that gets passed to your middle-tier application server through Web services.

Suppose you choose to use some third-party UI component to speed your development. Unknown to you, the code inside that component collects any values that are entered through its controls and transfers that data to some unknown location via a Web request for intelligence gathering. If you deployed this application with full trust, the component would be able to do just that and you may never even know it is happening behind the scenes. However, if you deployed your application with partial trust and restricted the WebPermission options to only allow calls to your middle-tier servers, then a security exception would be thrown when that nefarious component tried to do its evil deeds. By restricting the permission set, you would be protecting the user from that hidden data transfer.

Using a restricted set of permissions through partial trust is an excellent way to prevent your application from doing anything it was not designed to do. Unfortunately, for a lot of meaningful things that you might want to do in your application, such as doing on-demand updates through Click-Once or making remote calls through Windows Communication Foundation, you will be required to set your application for full trust due to the more advanced things the Framework does for you under the covers to provide those capabilities. You can still lock down permissions for specific sections of your code, however (see the section Adding Restricted Code Sections later in this chapter for an example of how to do that).

If the application manifest requests permissions that exceed the launch zone permissions, such as full trust, then those permissions need to be granted to the application somehow so it can launch. This can be done either through user prompting (the default) or automatically based on trusted publishers. Both of these approaches are covered later in this chapter.

> **■_ NOTE   ClickOnce Evaluates Permissions at the Application Level**
>
> An important distinction between the way CAS evaluates permissions and the way ClickOnce does so is where the scoping boundary is for a set of granted permissions. CAS evaluates permissions on an assembly-by-assembly basis, at the point where the assembly is loaded. ClickOnce evaluates permissions at the application boundary when the application is launched, and further checks are not done when each assembly is loaded. Additionally, ClickOnce only considers the built-in location-based code groups (My Computer, Internet, Local Intranet, Trusted Sites, and Restricted Sites zones) to determine what set of permissions the application should be given by default based on its launch URL. If you have custom code groups defined for which your assemblies would normally meet the membership criteria, those code groups will not be factored into what set of permissions the runtime will give your application by default.

ClickOnce Size Limitations for Online-Only Applications

A partial trust online-only application can run without any user prompting, depending on the permissions the application requires and the zone it is running from. To prevent such an application from filling up the hard disk by downloading many large files, ClickOnce restricts the total size of a partial-trust online-only application to be half the online cache quota on the machine. This size is checked at download time as bits are being downloaded, and the ClickOnce launch will fail once the limit is exceeded. The default cache quota is 250MB, so partial-trust applications larger than 125MB should ask for full trust.

ClickOnce Tamper Protections

ClickOnce protects the files that your application is composed of by using digital signatures. When you publish an application with ClickOnce, you have to sign the deployment and application manifest with an Authenticode Class 3 Code Signing publisher certificate. Authenticode certificates are based on public-private key cryptography. Publisher certificates contain both a public and a private key. The public and private keys have a mathematical relationship that makes it so anything you encrypt with one of the keys, you can decrypt with the other. However, the complexity of the mathematical relationship is such that it is extremely difficult to come up with one key when you just have the other. With the strength of current cryptographic keys, it would take hundreds or thousands of years of heavy-duty computing to figure out the value of one key if you just know the value of the other.

As the names imply, the intent is that you keep one key (the private key) to yourself, but you can freely hand out the public key to anyone who wants it. Once others have your public key, you can encrypt a message or file with your private key and give the message or file to them, and they can decrypt it using the public key with a strong assurance that the message or file they decrypted actually came from you (or at least someone who has access to your private key). Likewise, they can encrypt a message or file with your public key and give it to you, and they can be sure that only you can decrypt that message or file and see the contents.

When you sign a file with a certificate, the signing mechanism computes a hash of the file's contents using cryptographic methods. In computing the hash, it disregards a reserved section of the file into which it will insert the digital signature once is has been computed. Once the hash has been computed, the hash is encrypted with the private key of the publisher certificate. The encrypted version of the hash is the digital signature. This signature and the public key from the certificate used to encrypt the hash are inserted into the reserved location in the file. Now anyone who receives that file can compute the file's current hash using the same algorithm that was used to generate the original hash. They can then extract the digital signature and decrypt it using the public key embedded in the file with the signature. After they have decrypted the signature, they have the original hash that was computed by the publisher. If they compare the original hash and the hash they just computed, they can confirm that no one has tampered with the file since it was signed by the publisher, because any modifications to any part of the file will modify the computed hash and it will be different from the original hash.

This approach is used by ClickOnce to digitally sign your deployment and application manifests when you publish your application. It is also used by .NET for strong naming assemblies. Strong naming is just a similar digital signature approach. In the case of ClickOnce, the digital signature is embedded in the manifests as XML. In the case of strong naming, the digital signature is computed when an assembly is compiled, and is embedded in the assembly manifest in binary form.

In addition to digital signatures providing a guarantee that the manifests have not been tampered with since you published your application, they also provide tamper protection for all of your application files. When your application manifest is generated, a hash of each of the files in the application is put into the application manifest along with the rest of the file information. When ClickOnce deploys or updates your application, it computes the hash of each file as it is downloaded from the server and compares the hash to the one embedded in the downloaded application manifest. Since the application manifest is signed and can't be tampered with to change the hash values for application files, there is no way for someone to tamper with any of your application files, because ClickOnce will refuse to launch your application if the application file hashes don't match after they have been downloaded.

Internet Explorer Security Settings Affecting ClickOnce

Internet Explorer has several zone security settings that will impact your users' ability to launch a ClickOnce application on their machines.

- **Script Activation:** By default, script activation is disabled for ClickOnce applications coming from the Internet zone on Windows XP with Service Pack 2 and later platforms. This means that an Internet Web site cannot launch a ClickOnce .application file with a script. The setting that controls this in Internet Explorer is in the Tool > Internet Options > Security Tab > Custom Level button > Downloads > Automatic Prompting for File Downloads. If this is set to *Enable*, script activation of ClickOnce applications is allowed. If this is set to *Disable*, script activation is disallowed. The default setting is *Enable* for Intranet and *Disable* for Internet.

- **Disable ClickOnce MIME Handler:** If Downloads > File Download is set to *Disable*, launching any ClickOnce application over the Web (http or https) will result in the Security Alert message, "Your current security settings do not allow this file to be downloaded." By default this setting is enabled for all zones, so this will not usually be a problem.

- **Disable Managed Code:** If .NET Framework-Reliant Components > Run Components Not Signed with Authenticode is set to either *Disable* or *Prompt*, ClickOnce will be disabled. This setting must be set to *Enabled* for ClickOnce to work. The default value for this setting for all zones is *Enabled*.

Another Internet Explorer-related setting that you may want to be aware of is a registry key setting that determines whether users are prompted with a download dialog when they click on a link that points to a ClickOnce deployment manifest. The registry key in question is HKEY_CURRENT_USER\Software\Policies\Microsoft\Internet Explorer\Restrictions\AlwaysPromptWhenDownload. When this DWORD value is set to 1, you will always get a file download prompt before the ClickOnce launch process starts. This registry key is not set by default, which lets ClickOnce start the launch process immediately when a link is clicked on.

Configuring ClickOnce Security Permissions

The permissions a ClickOnce application requires to run are determined by its application manifest. These permissions are populated by Visual Studio when you publish your application based on the project properties. You can configure these security permissions on the project properties editor's Security tab. You can also modify them to a certain degree after you have published from Visual Studio using the Mage SDK tools. I'll cover both approaches in this section.

Regardless of which tool you use, you have two choices at the top level—you can request full trust or partial trust. Full trust means that you do not want your application constrained by CAS in any way at runtime on the client. This corresponds to the *unrestricted* permission set in CAS. When you select this setting, your application code and any code it calls will not be restricted in any way based on CAS. Keep in mind that CAS is separate and distinct from user-based security. So depending on the users' rights, they may still be prevented from doing certain things, either by role-based security code in your application or by the operating system if they try to access something on the system through your application that they do not have Windows access control privileges to use. But as far as ClickOnce and CAS are concerned, if the application has full trust, it can do whatever it likes.

When you choose partial trust, you have to specifically select a set of permissions that you want to include in the requested permissions for the application. You can base this on one of the predefined zone-based permission sets, such as Local Intranet or Internet, or you can use a custom set of permissions to request the specific permissions that correspond to the operations and resources your application uses by design. The latter is a better approach from a security vulnerability perspective.

Whether you use Visual Studio or Mage, what you end up with is a specification inside your application manifest file that says to the runtime, "My application needs these permissions to run."

Configuring ClickOnce Security Permissions with Visual Studio

Figure 6.1 showed the Security tab of the project properties editor. This is where you configure the set of permissions that are placed in your application manifest at the time that you publish your application. Checking the Enable ClickOnce Security Settings checkbox makes the rest of the options available. This box will be checked automatically the first time you publish your application from Visual Studio.

Enabling ClickOnce security settings also affects the way your application runs in the debugger. Once enabled, each time you run your application, the selected security settings will be applied to the debug executable process, so your debug runtime environment will have the same security restrictions as your target environment. For example, if you select Local Intranet as the target zone for partial trust and make no modifications to the permissions list below the partial-trust selection, and then run a debug session and your code tries to do file I/O, you will get an exception in the debugger because the process will run with only the permissions for the Local Intranet zone. This is extremely helpful in debugging and fixing problems that would otherwise only occur in the deployed environment.

If you select partial trust, you can then select the target zone as Local Intranet, Internet, or Custom. Selecting either Local Intranet or Internet selects the permissions in the ClickOnce Security Permissions table to match the target zone. Once those permissions are selected, you can then customize the settings to something different than the defaults for that zone as needed, using the zone permissions as a starting point for a custom set of permissions. Remember that ClickOnce ignores any custom security policy code groups, so setting fine custom permissions through the ClickOnce partial trust settings are the only way to explicitly grant specific permissions in a partial-trust scenario.

So, for example, if you were going to deploy an application to the local Intranet, but the application needed to call a Web service on your network other than the one where the application is being deployed from, you would do the following.

1. Check the *Enable ClickOnce Security Settings* checkbox in the project properties editor's Security tab (see Figure 6.4).
2. Select *This is a partial trust application.*
3. Select *Local Intranet* in the drop-down list labeled *Zone your application will be installed from.*
4. Scroll down in the grid of permissions required by the application to find the *WebPermission* type.
5. In the Setting column drop-down list, select *Include.*

After doing this, your application will request all of the permissions in the Local Intranet zone as well as the `WebPermission` permission with unrestricted access to the Web.

As mentioned, most permission types have a number of additional options that you can set to customize exactly what options in that permission type you need. `WebPermission` includes the ability to set a list of URLs that you will let your application either call out to or be called

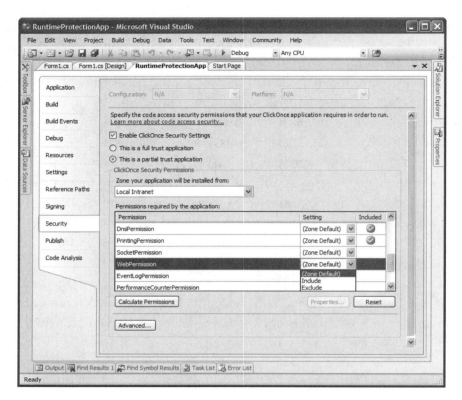

FIGURE 6.4: Adding Permissions to a Selected Zone

on. Unfortunately, the permissions editor in the Security tab for Click-
Once does not allow you to access all the options for all of the displayed
permission types. WebPermission is an example. You can see in Figure
6.4 that the Properties button below the grid is disabled. If there are configurable properties for a selected permission type, this button will be
enabled and will take you to a dialog that lets you edit the finer-grained
options for that permission type. Figure 6.5 shows an example of one of
these dialogs for the SecurityPermission type.

There are some permission types that are not shown in the grid at all.
The only way to add these permission types is to either select full trust for
the application (see Figure 6.4) or use the Mage tool to configure the permission type based on its XML declaration. See the next section for more
information on how to do that.

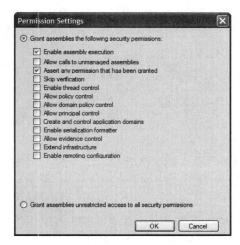

FIGURE 6.5: Options in the Permissions Settings Dialog

If you do not want to run your debug sessions in the ClickOnce security zone selected, you can disable this capability by doing the following (see Figure 6.4).

1. Open the project properties editor for your application.
2. Select the Security tab.
3. Check the *Enable ClickOnce Security Settings* checkbox if it is not already checked.
4. Select *This is a partial trust application* if it is not already selected.
5. Click on the Advanced button at the bottom of the Security tab. This brings up the Advanced Security Settings dialog shown in Figure 6.6.
6. Uncheck the box labeled *Debug this application with the selected permission set.*

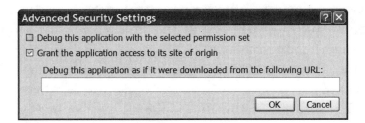

FIGURE 6.6: Advanced Security Settings Dialog

Notice that you also have the options in the Advanced Security Settings Dialog to do the following.

- Grant the application access to its site of origin (selected by default)
- Debug the application as if it were downloaded from a different URL

Granting the application access to its site of origin lets you expose a Web service from the same site that the application is launched from that the application calls for back-end services. You can also use this to download additional files on demand. By doing this, you do not need to ask for `WebPermission` specifically to make those calls. Debugging the application as if it were downloaded from a different URL lets you test and see what will happen with different security zones based on the URL—without needing to understand the exact logic that the runtime is using to evaluate the URL and match it against the location-based security zones.

The settings that you select in the Security tab are saved as part of your Visual Studio project file and will be used each time you publish your application from ClickOnce. The appropriate entries in the application manifest will be created when you publish.

Calculating Permissions with Visual Studio

At the bottom of the project properties editor's Security tab, there is a Calculate Permissions button (see Figure 6.4). If you click this button, Visual Studio will do a static analysis of your code, and every assembly that your code calls out to, in an attempt to determine what permissions your application will require to run. After you run the permissions calculator, it will configure the individual security permissions required for your application to include the permissions that it determined your application needs.

Using the permissions calculator is only appropriate if you plan to deploy your application under partial trust and are not sure what permissions your application requires based on its design. The thing to be aware of with the permissions calculator is that it makes a conservative estimate of what permissions your application will require. Based on my experience trying to use this tool, it always overestimates the permissions required by your application. In fact, it often grossly overestimates the permissions required.

As a result of this overestimation, you will be better off keeping track of what permissions your application needs based on its design and configuring only those permissions. Then test the application rigorously, running under the debugger with ClickOnce security enabled, to ensure you did not miss any required permissions.

If you use the permissions calculator to set the required permissions for your application, your application manifest will likely state that many more permissions are required than really are. This means you are removing some of the protections that running under partial trust brings you. However, running with a set of permissions determined by the permissions calculator under partial trust will still offer more protection to the client machine than running under full trust. So if you are unsure what permissions you need and don't want to jump the security requirements all the way to full trust as a result, go ahead and use the permissions calculator.

Configuring ClickOnce Security Permissions with Mage

It should be a fairly rare thing that you would change the permissions your application requests after you have published from Visual Studio. After all, the permissions required are determined by the code that executes, not based on administrative whims. However, if you find that you need to modify the set of permissions that your application requests without publishing a new version from Visual Studio, you have some ability to do so with the Mage tools.

Using the command line mage.exe tool, you can only set the security to one of the predefined zone levels of Internet, LocalIntranet, or FullTrust. You do this by running mage with a command line switch of –TrustLevel (or –tr for short). Because you are editing the manifest by doing this, you will also need to re-sign the manifest with a certificate. You do this with other command line options. The following example shows how to set the security zone to full trust and re-sign the manifest.

```
mage.exe -Update MyApp.exe.manifest -TrustLevel FullTrust -CertFile
MyCert.pfx -Password SomeSecretPwd
```

You can use the Mage UI tool, mageui.exe, to edit the permission settings in a dialog-based user interface. Start mageui.exe from a Visual Studio command prompt and open the application manifest that you want to edit. Select the Permissions Required category in the list on the left and you will see the view shown in Figure 6.7.

You can drop down the list of permission set types on the right in Figure 6.7 to select one of the predefined zones, including Internet, Local Intranet, and Full Trust. When you select one of these values, the Details pane below it will display the XML `PermissionSet` element that will be placed in the application manifest. Under this element, there will be individual `IPermission` elements for each permission you require, except in the case of Full Trust, which just sets the permission set to unrestricted. You can also select a value of Custom in the permission set type list to manually enter whatever settings you would like. This requires that you understand the full schema of the `PermissionSet` element and its child elements to determine what to put into the Details box. This schema is beyond the scope of this book to describe in detail, but follows a common convention with the way permission sets are defined for security configuration files. Consult the MSDN Library documentation for more information on manually creating XML permission set entries.

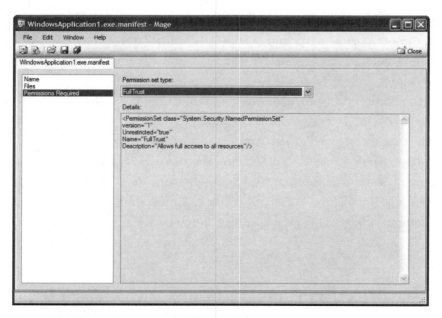

FIGURE 6.7: Setting Permissions with Mage UI

Note that using the Custom permission set type and figuring out the right XML elements and attributes to add is the only way to go beyond the permission sets and options that are exposed to you in Visual Studio. You could also write a custom tool to set these through the APIs exposed in the `Microsoft.Build.Tasks.Deployment` namespace, but that is not a trivial task either.

Understanding and Managing Publisher Certificates

The publisher certificates used to sign ClickOnce manifests are Authenticode Class 3 Code Signing certificates. This is just one form of an Authenticode certificate.[2] There are many different kinds for various forms of authentication and authorization security scenarios.

Publisher certificates are generated with a public-private key pair and additional metadata about the publisher. The organization that creates a certificate is called the **certificate authority** or **certificate issuer.** The organization the certificate represents is the publisher. The Windows operating system has a built-in infrastructure for storing and authenticating certificates. There are a number of built-in certificate stores in the operating system, and you can create additional custom stores as needed.

Certificates are based on the concept of a trust chain. If you are presented with a certificate, you can determine from the certificate who the publisher organization is that the certificate represents, as well as who issued that publisher the certificate. From the issuer's certificate, you can determine the issuer's identity, as well as who issued the issuer their certificate. You can follow this chain of issuers back to what is called a **Trusted Root Certification Authority.** This chain of issuers provides a path of discovery that ensures that if you can verify the identity of all of the issuers in the chain, you have a way to track down and contact the publisher.

This way, if you deploy an application to your machine that is signed with a publisher certificate, and that application does harmful things to your machine, you can track down the publisher through the information in the certificate, or through the information that is retained by the issuer

---

2. For an overview of Authenticode code signing, see http://msdn.microsoft.com/ workshop/security/authcode/intro_authenticode.asp.

when issuing the certificate. Some certificate issuers include liability insurance as part of their certificate issuance services; this guarantees that if you cannot contact a publisher that was issued a certificate by that authority (to pursue a liability claim), the certificate issuer will assume the liability up to some limited degree.

To support this concept, a number of companies are in the business of verifying the identity of other organizations for the purposes of issuing certificates to them. VeriSign and thawte are two well-known companies who perform these services. The issued certificate (whether a code signing or publisher certificate, or one of the many other forms of certificates) becomes a digital representation of the organization's identity. Certificates from well-known and trusted certificate authorities are installed with the operating system or can be added later, which identifies them as a trusted issuer of other certificates. As a result, if you obtain a publisher certificate from an application vendor, and that certificate has been issued by an organization like VeriSign, you can be relatively certain that the company is who they say they are (they are a legal business entity), and that the organizational information contained in the certificate has been verified by the issuer (which includes the location of the organization or where its business license information can be verified).

The verification chain may be deeper than one level, however. A Trusted Root Certification Authority can issue certificates to themselves or other certification authorities to issue specific kinds of certificates. For example, see Figure 6.8 for the trust chain for a code-signing certificate for my company, Software Insight. You will see that the root VeriSign Class 3 Public Primary CA (certificate authority) certificate was used to issue a VeriSign Class 3 Code Signing CA certificate, which was then used to issue my Software Insight Class 3 Code Signing publisher certificate. To issue that certificate, VeriSign had to verify my existence as a legal business entity. They can do this through articles of incorporation or by verifying that a legal business license has been issued by your state or city, for example.

You do not have to purchase a certificate from a third-party certificate issuer to use ClickOnce. In an enterprise environment, your domain administrators can generate a certificate for themselves and configure that

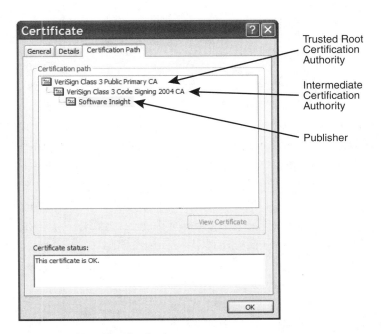

FIGURE 6.8: Certification Path

certificate as a Trusted Root Certification Authority (CA) on all the machines in the enterprise, allowing them to issue publisher certificates to your development organization with a single-level trust chain back to a known CA. Or if you are not concerned with providing any kind of assurances of identity with your ClickOnce publication, you can generate your own publisher certificate with either Visual Studio 2005 or with command line tools.

To make matters even more complicated, there are a number of different file formats that are used for delivering certificates. Third-party certificate issuers usually issue a certificate in the form of a .cer or .spc file. These certificate files usually only contain the public key portion of the certificate, so you can freely distribute them to client machines and install them in those machine's certificate stores. When you purchase a certificate, you also usually receive a separate .pvk file that contains the private key corresponding to that public key. You will need both the public and private key portions of a certificate, in a single .pfx file format, to use it for ClickOnce publishing. You can combine .cer or .spc file portions with the .pvk portion by using the pvkimprt.exe tool that is available from Microsoft downloads.[3]

There are several certificate stores on your Windows machines that you will use with ClickOnce deployment. Any certificate you use for ClickOnce publishing will be added to the Personal certificate store for the logged-in user when you publish the application. Additionally, if you want to avoid user prompting on the client machine, you will want to install your publisher certificate into the Trusted Publishers store on the client machine as discussed in the section Trusted Publishers' Permission Elevation later in this chapter. If you are installing a publisher certificate into the Trusted Publishers store, you will want to make sure the certificate's issuer is in the Trusted Root Certification Authorities store or the Intermediate Certification Authorities store, and that the root issuer of the trust chain is in the Trusted Root Certification Authorities store (see Figure 6.8).

Generating or Configuring a Publisher Certificate with Visual Studio 2005

If you publish a Windows Application project with Visual Studio without configuring a publisher certificate ahead of time, Visual Studio will generate a self-signed publisher certificate for you. In this kind of certificate, the identity of the issuer and the publisher are set to the logged-in Windows identity of the user.

The public and private key portions of the certificate are placed in a file with a .pfx file extension and the file is added to your project. The certificate is then configured as the signing certificate for ClickOnce publication, and is also added to your Personal certificate store on the development machine. When your application is published, the deployment and application manifest files are signed with this certificate. The .pfx file that is generated is a password-protected file, but when Visual Studio automatically generates the file for you the first time you publish, the password of the generated file is set to an empty password.

You can generate your own certificates through Visual Studio (with the option to password-protect the file), or you can select an existing certificate

---

3. Search for *pvkimprt* at www.microsoft.com/downloads.

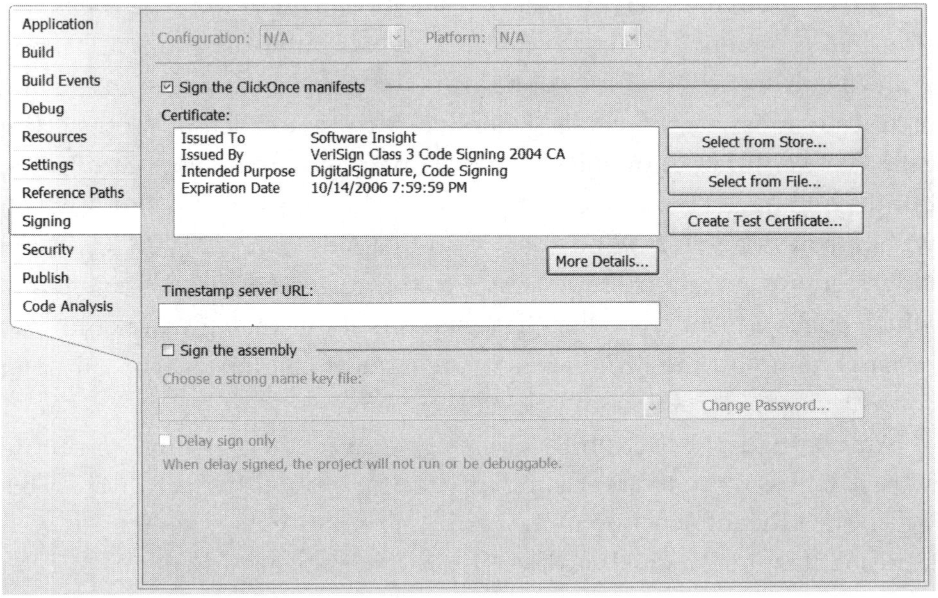

FIGURE 6.9: ClickOnce Signing Settings

to use for signing as well. You do this through the Signing tab of your project properties editor (see Figure 6.9).

After checking the box that is labeled *Sign the ClickOnce manifests,* you can either select a certificate from the logged-in user's Personal certificate store on the development machine, from a .pfx file, or generate a new certificate. If you click the Select from Store button, you will see the dialog shown in Figure 6.10 to select a certificate.

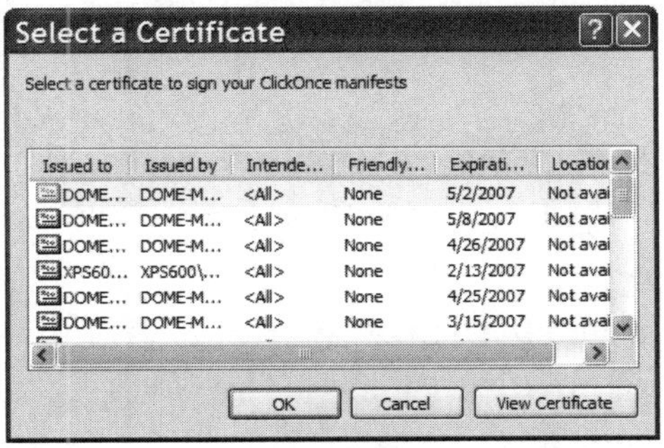

FIGURE 6.10: Select a Certificate Dialog

You can see that there are several small challenges to using the Select from Store option. The first is that if you test publishing an application with ClickOnce without first configuring the Signing tab to use an existing certificate, a new certificate is generated each time. Each of those certificates have a different public-private key pair and are distinct certificates, but they all have the same common name, known as *CN* for short, which will be your logged-in Windows account name (e.g., DOME-M200\Brian Noyes on my current machine). As a result, it is almost impossible to tell which one is which. The other challenge is that this dialog will not let you resize it, and you can see that there are a lot of columns, each with long content, so the usability of the dialog is extremely low.

An alternative to selecting a certificate from the Personal certificate store is to just point to an existing .pfx file for a publisher certificate. This will extract the information in the certificate and use it for signing, as well as install it in the Personal certificate store if it is not already there. You can see an example of this in Figure 6.10 as well—the entry that starts with *XPS600* is from a certificate generated on a different machine of mine (named XPS600), and was automatically imported into my Personal certificate store on the current machine when I selected that .pfx file for my certificate. Clicking the Select from File button on the Signing tab gives you a standard file dialog to navigate to the location of your certificate file.

If you click the Create Test Certificate button on the Signing tab, you will be prompted for a password as shown in Figure 6.11. The dialog does not enforce strong passwords; you can leave it blank if desired.

After you click OK in the Create Test Certificate dialog, the process is similar to what Visual Studio does if you do not configure a certificate and publish the application.

- A test certificate is generated with the issuer and publisher (labeled *Issued By:* and *Issued To:*, respectively, in most places in the UI) set to your logged-in Windows identity.
- The certificate is placed in a .pfx file with the name <appname>_TemporaryKey.pfx with the password you provided set on the file.
- The .pfx file is added to the Visual Studio project files.
- The certificate is imported into your Personal certificate store.

> **■ WARNING** **Selecting a Certificate File Copies It to Your Project Folder**
>
> One important thing to be aware of is that if you point to a certificate file by using the Select from File option on the project properties editor's Signing tab, the file you point to will be copied to your project folder and added to your project. A .pfx file for a publisher certificate includes both public and private keys. If you subsequently zip up your project and send it off to a friend, you will have compromised that certificate because now someone else has physical access to the certificate's private key. If the file is password protected, as it should be, that person will have a very difficult time using the certificate, but the possibility now exists. If it is a self-generated test certificate, then it is no big deal. But if it is a real company certificate, such as one purchased from VeriSign, then you should revoke that certificate. Unfortunately, I mention this from the vantage point of one who has done exactly this. I zipped up the code from a demo I did using my VeriSign company certificate and forgot to remove my certificate file from the project directory first.

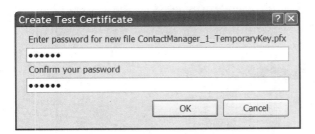

FIGURE 6.11: Create Test Certificate Dialog

Once you have configured a certificate through the Signing tab, that certificate will be used for any subsequent publications of your application to sign the ClickOnce manifests.

Installing a Certificate in a Store with Visual Studio 2005

Visual Studio lets you install a certificate into any certificate stores on your machine if desired. As described earlier, any certificate that you configure to sign your ClickOnce manifests by generating the file or selecting a file will be installed into your Personal certificate store on your development machine. Additionally, if the certificate is password protected, then you can use Visual Studio to manually install that certificate into other stores on your machine.

Do the following if you want to install a signing certificate into a different store on your machine.

1. Click on the More Details button on the Signing tab (see Figure 6.9). This will display the certificate information dialog shown in Figure 6.12.

2. At the bottom of the dialog, click the Install Certificate button.

3. This will bring up the Certificate Import wizard shown in Figure 6.13. (This same wizard can be accessed by running certmgr.exe and clicking the Import button in that tool). Click Next to start the process.

4. The second step in the wizard (see Figure 6.14) lets you select which store the certificate will be placed into. Select the radio button labeled *Place all certificates in the following store* and click the Browse button.

5. The Select Certificate Store dialog shown in Figure 6.15 will display, and you can pick from the available stores on the machine. Select the store you want to place the certificate into, such as the Trusted Publishers store, and click the OK button.

FIGURE 6.12: Certificate Information Dialog

FIGURE 6.13: Certificate Import Wizard

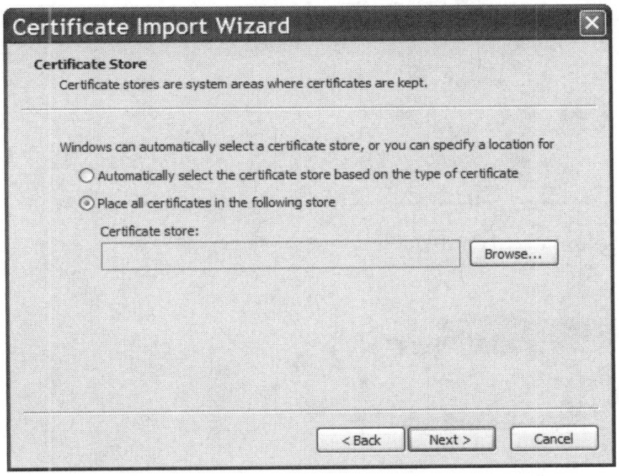

FIGURE 6.14: Certificate Import Wizard – Store Selection

FIGURE 6.15: Select Certificate Store Dialog

6. You will return to the wizard and the selected store will be displayed in the Certificate store field in the middle of the form (see Figure 6.16). Click the Next button to continue.

7. The final step of the wizard (see Figure 6.17) will display, summarizing the import that is about to happen. Click the Finish button to complete the installation of the certificate into the selected store.

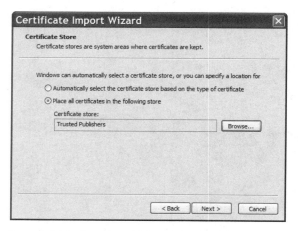

FIGURE 6.16: Completed Store Selection Step

FIGURE 6.17: Certificate Import Wizard Completion

Command Line Certificate Tools

There are several command line tools that come with the .NET Framework SDK or that you can download to assist you in generating, configuring, and managing publisher certificates. To generate a test certificate from the command line, you can use the makecert.exe command line tool. This tool offers more fine-grained options for generating publisher certificates. Run `makecert.exe` from a command line with the `-?` switch for a brief summary of options or with the `-!` command line switch for more detailed options. The makecert.exe tool uses the CryptoAPI under the covers and is available in the .NET Framework SDK binaries (\Bin) folder underneath your Visual Studio 2005 installation (C:\Program Files\Microsoft Visual Studio 8\SDK\v2.0\Bin path with a default installation).

To configure certificates with respect to the machine certificate stores, you can use the certmgr.exe tool. If you run certmgr.exe without any arguments, it launches a UI version of the tool as shown in Figure 6.18.

This tool provides a graphical management console for importing, exporting, and removing certificates from the named stores on your development machine. Clicking the Import button shown in Figure 6.18 launches the same wizard discussed in the previous section for installing certificates in stores.

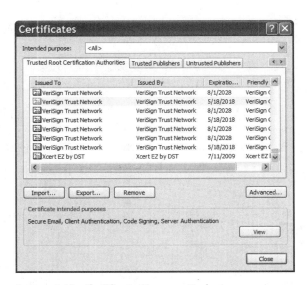

FIGURE 6.18: Certificate Manager Tool

You can also incorporate certmgr.exe in a Windows Installer installation package and use it to configure certificates on a client machine as well using command line options. For example, the following command line will install a certificate in the Trusted Publishers store on a target machine if the certmgr.exe tool is available in the command prompt PATH environment variable.

```
certmgr.exe -add MyCompany.cer -s TrustedPublisher
```

Another command line tool to be aware of that was mentioned earlier is the pvkimprt.exe tool. This tool is available for download from Microsoft (www.microsoft.com/downloads) or through the Platform SDK. Pvkimprt.exe lets you take a .cer or .spc file that just contains the public key portion of a publisher certificate, combine it with a .pvk file that contains the private key portion of the certificate, and generate a .pfx password-protected certificate file that contains the entire certificate. To do this, you run the tool with a −pfx switch, also passing the .spc or .cer file path and the .pvk file path. This will bring up a wizard that will step you through the process of providing a password and then exporting the keys to a .pfx file.

Signing Application Updates

An important security limitation to understand with ClickOnce is that you cannot deploy updates to an application that are signed by a different publisher certificate than the one that was originally used to sign previous deployments of the application. If ClickOnce sees that an update is available, but that the update is signed by a different publisher certificate than the one used to sign the version currently installed on the client machine, ClickOnce will disable the application and present the message box shown in Figure 6.19.

FIGURE 6.19: Changed Publisher Certificate Message

If you click the Details buttons to see the error, it will specify that the problem is, "The deployment identity does not match the subscription." This behavior was designed to protect the tamper assurances that were discussed earlier in the section ClickOnce Tamper Protection. If someone were to gain access to your published application directory on the server, he could introduce a virus or malware into one of the application files, and then just regenerate and re-sign the manifests with his own certificate. Because updates do not typically prompt users (unless elevating the permissions of the application beyond their current trust level), there would be no way for users to realize that they could be introducing the compromised application onto their machines. Disabling the application if the certificate has changed is designed to make it as safe as possible and not allow updates to be signed with a different publisher certificate from the original certificate.

As a result, if you do publish an update to an application from Visual Studio 2005 that is signed with a different certificate than the previous version, you will be prompted as shown in Figure 6.20 to ensure this is your intent.

If you do have a previous version of a ClickOnce application that users have installed and you need to put out a new version signed by a different certificate (perhaps your company changed names or was acquired by a new parent company), you will need to instruct users to launch the new version using the full URL to the deployment manifest on the server. This will force a fresh install of the application, and the new install will not be related to the old version at all. Before users do this, it is recommended that you have them uninstall the previous version first from the Add or Remove Programs item. If they do not, they will end up with two application installations. The old one will have the original program name (e.g., My Application), and the new one will have the old name with a – 1 appended to it (e.g., My Application – 1). This is likely to confuse users when they go to

FIGURE 6.20: Visual Studio Publisher Certificate Change Warning

launch the application from the Start menu. Unfortunately, there is no way to automate this process. For online-only applications this is not a problem because if the certificate has been changed, it will just be treated as a new application being launched, and users will be prompted with the security warning again.

User Prompting

Despite the name *ClickOnce*, often users will need to click twice to get the application deployed and running. The first click is the one that starts the process of deployment and launching of the application. Users click on a URL provided in an e-mail or on a Web site to start the deployment process. If the application is configured to run offline, then users will also be prompted because the application will create a Start menu item and an Add or Remove Programs entry, which causes visible changes on their machines. As a result, users are notified of this change before it occurs and has the opportunity to refuse the application. Additionally, if the application requires elevated permissions to run, users will also be prompted to decide whether they should allow the application's elevated permissions on their machine. The kind of prompt presented to users in both of these cases also gives an indication of whether the publisher is verifiable through a trust chain on the machine.

Table 6.1 summarizes the prompting dialogs users will see and the associated risk levels, and Figures 6.21 through 6.26 show the range of prompting dialogs that users will see, starting from lowest risk to highest risk to the local machine. For any of these prompts, if users click the Install button, the installation will complete and the application will launch. If users click the Don't Install button, no modifications to the client machine will be made. The different levels of prompting are just intended to convey different degrees of risk to users based on how well known the publisher is and whether the application requires elevated permissions on the local machine.

Once users have been prompted and they click the Install button, they will not be prompted again for running that application, even if updates are installed, unless an update requests higher permissions than the currently installed version. In that case, the prompting will follow the same

TABLE 6.1:   Security Dialog Risk Levels

Risk Level	Icon	Cause
Low	Green check mark	Known publisher, no security permission elevation, only adding Start menu shortcut and Add or Remove Programs item.
Medium	Yellow exclamation point	Known publisher, security permissions elevation needed to run, may also be adding Start menu shortcut and Add or Remove Programs item.
Medium	Yellow exclamation point	Unknown publisher, no security permission elevation, but adding Start menu shortcut and Add or Remove Programs item.
High	Red X	Unknown publisher, security permission elevation needed to run, may also be adding Start menu shortcut and Add or Remove Programs item.

logic as an initial install in determining which prompts to provide. This is true for both installed and online-only applications. The following subsections describe those different prompts.

Low-Risk Install

Figure 6.21 shows the install prompt users will see if an application is being launched for the first time where:

* The application is an installed application
* The application is signed by a publisher that was issued its certificate by a Trusted Root Certification Authority known by the client machine
* And the application is not requesting any permissions beyond what it would be granted by default by CAS based on its launch URL

Figure 6.22 shows the More Information dialog for this deployment scenario. You can see that the only thing the dialog is really cautioning users about is that it will add a Start menu item and an Add or Remove Programs item.

FIGURE 6.21: Low-Risk Install Prompt

FIGURE 6.22: Low-Risk Install More Information Dialog

Medium-Risk Install

Figure 6.23 shows the install prompt users will see if an application is being launched for the first time where:

- The application is an installed application
- The application is signed by a publisher that was issued its certificate by a Trusted Root Certification Authority known by the client machine
- And the application is requesting elevated permissions beyond what it would be granted by default by CAS based on its launch URL

Figure 6.24 shows the More Information dialog for this deployment scenario. You can see that in this case users are being warned that the application requires access to "additional resources on your computer," meaning elevated permissions. It also adds the normal caution that it will

FIGURE 6.23: Medium-Risk Install Prompt

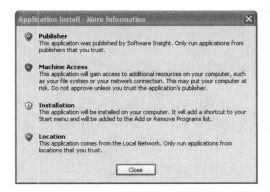

FIGURE 6.24: Medium-Risk Install More Information Dialog

add a Start menu item and an Add or Remove Programs item. However, you can see that this dialog makes it clear that the publisher is considered to be a known entity since its certificate was issued by a known certificate authority (CA).

High-Risk Install

Figure 6.25 shows the install prompt users will see if an application is being launched for the first time where:

- The application is an installed application
- The application is signed by a publisher that is unknown (meaning its certificate was issued by an unknown certificate authority)
- And the application is requesting elevated permissions beyond what it would be granted by default by CAS based on its launch URL

FIGURE 6.25: High-Risk Install Prompt

FIGURE 6.26: High-Risk Install More Information Dialog

Figure 6.26 shows the More Information dialog for this deployment scenario. You can see that in this case users are being warned that the publisher of the application is unknown, and the application requires access to "additional resources on your computer," meaning elevated permissions. It also adds the normal caution that it will add a Start menu item and an Add or Remove Programs item.

The high-risk prompts shown in Figures 6.25 and 6.26 are what users will see if you deploy a ClickOnce application using a self-generated test certificate (created with Visual Studio or the makecert.exe tool).

User Prompting for Online-Only Applications

When users click on a link to an online-only ClickOnce application, they will only be prompted if the application needs to elevate permissions. If

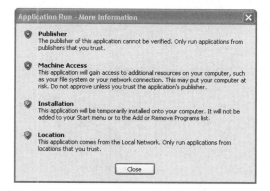

FIGURE 6.27: Online-Only High-Risk Install More Information Dialog

the application does not need to elevate permissions, users will not be prompted at all after they click on the link to the application, even if the publisher is unknown. The application will just download and launch.

If the application does need to elevate permissions, then users will be prompted with a dialog similar to either Figure 6.23 or 6.25, depending on whether the publisher is known (certificate issued by a trusted root CA) or unknown. The only difference in the prompting dialogs in this case is that the buttons will be labeled *Run* and *Don't Run* for the online-only application instead of *Install* and *Don't Install* for the installed application. If users inspect the More Information dialog, they will see the green status for installation, indicating that no modifications to their Start menu or Add or Remove Programs items will be made (see Figure 6.27).

Trusted Applications' User Security Policies

When an application gets installed or run, a user security policy is created to record the set of permissions that have been granted to that application. This policy can be viewed using the Microsoft .NET Framework 2.0 Configuration tool. If you open this tool (from the Administrative Tools menu) and expand the Runtime Security Policy node down to the user level, you will see a child node under User for Trusted Applications. If you select this and click the link in the right pane labeled *View List of trusted applications*, you will see something like Figure 6.28.

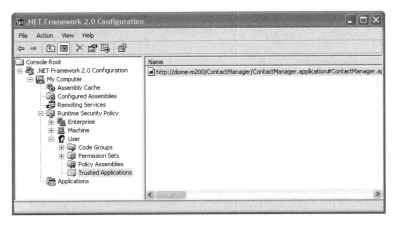

Figure 6.28: Trusted Applications' Security Policies

Depending on how many different ClickOnce applications and how many different versions of those applications have been deployed to your machine, you may see many more entries in the list on the right. You will get one entry in the list for each application version for which a different set of permissions were issued. This always includes the first install or run of a ClickOnce application, and then additional entries will be made for subsequent versions of an application only if they elevate permissions beyond what the previous version required.

You can inspect the permissions set for a given application version by double-clicking on the entry in the list. This displays the Properties dialog shown in Figure 6.29, where you can inspect and browse through the assigned permissions.

Trusted Publishers' Permission Elevation

The problem with the default security model for an enterprise environment is that it puts the trust decision of whether to elevate permissions or not into the users' hands. If an application needs elevated permissions, it prompts the users, and if they click the Install button, the application can elevate its permissions all the way to full trust if it wants to, effectively removing the runtime protections that ClickOnce is capable of providing.

This is often not what the IT administrators for the enterprise want—they want to have explicit control over the machines that they are responsible for.

FIGURE 6.29: Trusted Application Permissions

Many users do not have the experience to discern a true high-risk scenario from one that is acceptable. From an IT administrator's perspective, an application should not run on a user's desktop unless the administrator has configured it to do so, either directly or implicitly through a trust relationship with the publisher of the application.

There is also a downside to the default prompting model from the users' perspective as well. If they are going to be launching various applications from a known and trusted publisher, why should they be repeatedly prompted when those applications launch the first time? It would be good to let end users establish a trust relationship with a publisher as well to avoid unnecessary prompting.

ClickOnce supports giving the administrators more explicit control and avoiding unnecessary prompting through a model known as **trusted publishers.** A trusted publisher is a publisher whose certificate has been installed in the Trusted Publishers certificate store on a client machine. This can be done manually using the techniques discussed early in the chapter in the section Understanding and Managing Publisher Certificates, or it can be done automatically through something like Microsoft Systems Management Server or group policy.

If an application is deployed through ClickOnce to the client machine and that application's manifest has been signed by a trusted publisher's certificate, then the runtime can use that to automatically elevate the permissions for the application rather than prompting the user. As a result, the prompting model is actually even more complex than the different levels of prompting discussed in the User Prompting section.

When the ClickOnce runtime determines that a user prompt is required to elevate permissions, it will also check to determine if it is allowed to prompt the user. The settings that drive this decision are based on the zone that the application is being launched from. For each launch zone (My Computer, Local Intranet, Internet, Trusted Sites, Restricted Sites), there is a default setting that says when the runtime is allowed to prompt the user. This setting can take on one of the following values.

- **Enabled**—The runtime can prompt users if needed to elevate the permissions for the application. However, if the application's publisher is a trusted publisher, then the application will automatically elevate its permissions and users will not be prompted to install the application (i.e., it will be a true Click*Once* application). This is the default value for the My Computer, Local Intranet, Trusted Sites, and Internet zones.

- **Authenticode Required**—The runtime can prompt users if needed to elevate the application's permissions only if the publisher certificate for the application has a trust chain back to a Trusted Root Certification Authority. If the publisher is unknown, the application will be disabled. If the publisher is a trusted publisher, users will not be prompted to install the application and the permissions will be automatically elevated.

- **Disabled**—The application can only run if signed by a trusted publisher, in which case the permissions will automatically elevate. With this setting, users will never be prompted and only applications from trusted publishers will be allowed to launch through ClickOnce. This is the default value for the Restricted Sites zone.

If you want to change the default prompting behavior for a given zone, you will have to add a registry key with values set for the zones for which you want to change the defaults. You will need to create a TrustManager key under the HKLM\Software\Microsoft\.NETFramework\Security key, and another key under that named PromptingLevel. Once you have created those keys, you add named string values under the PromptingLevel key for each zone that you want to modify. The name of the key should match the zone name: MyComputer, LocalIntranet, Internet, TrustedSites, or RestrictedSites. The value for the string value should be set to one of the three levels discussed earlier: Enabled, Authenticode Required, or Disabled.

Using these registry settings, you can achieve a much more secure configuration for client machines in an enterprise environment. If you add the named values just described and set them all to Disabled, it means that the only ClickOnce applications that are allowed to run on users' machines are those that are signed by publisher certificates that have been installed in the Trusted Publishers store on those machines. In other words, the only ClickOnce applications that get to run are those for which the administrator established a trust relationship on the client machine with the publisher of the application. When that is the case, the application will download, automatically elevate its permissions to the level needed, and execute. Any application not coming from a trusted publisher will not be allowed to launch through ClickOnce. Figure 6.30 depicts this configuration in the registry.

Adding Restricted Code Sections

The set of permissions an application has is determined by the permissions its application manifest says it requires to run and the permissions that would be granted to it based on the zone it is launching from. However, if

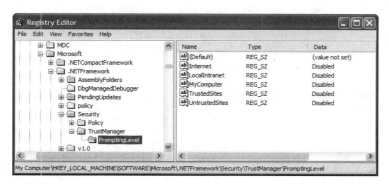

FIGURE 6.30: User Prompting Registry Settings

you need to elevate permissions for certain parts of your application, you may not want to leave your entire application vulnerable because of those elevated permissions. For example, you may have a very limited scope to perform on-demand updates from your application. As discussed in Chapter 4, on-demand updates require full trust. As a result, you will need to configure your application for full-trust permissions as far as ClickOnce deployment is concerned. However, there may be other portions of your code where you are doing things such as calling out to third-party components, and you want to make sure that they cannot perform any operations or access any resources other than what they are supposed to based on their design purpose.

For example, say for a limited scope you were going to call out to a component that is supposed to perform certain kinds of computation for you, and perhaps it may also present a user interface in doing so or to present error messages to users. However, by design, the component should never do anything other than execute and present user interfaces.

You can use the capabilities of Code Access Security to lock down the security context for a given scope of code. Listing 6.1 shows a section of code where a component is going to be used for a limited scope of code, and you want to ensure that the only thing that component does is to present a user interface to users. To do this, you can use a stack walk modifier, based on the IStackWalk interface, to turn on only a particular permission type.

LISTING 6.1: Restricting Permissions for a Code Scope

```
private void OnCallUntrustedCode(object sender, EventArgs e)
{
   IStackWalk stackWalk =
      new UIPermission(PermissionState.Unrestricted);
   stackWalk.PermitOnly();
   UIOnlyComponent uoc = new UIOnlyComponent();
   uoc.DoUIStuff();
   CodeAccessPermission.RevertPermitOnly();
}
```

With the PermitOnly stack walk modifier in place, any code that is called out to in that scope will be restricted based on the specifications that the stack walk modifier puts in place. You can use stack walk modifiers to permit only a specific permission or set of permissions as shown in Listing 6.1, deny a specific permission or set of permissions, or prevent checking for specific permissions beyond the local scope of code. The latter capability is called a *security assertion* and requires elevated permissions to be performed.[4]

Securing the Application Based on User Roles

A ClickOnce deployed application is no different than any other .NET application when it comes to role-based security. If you want to control what users can do with your application based on the roles they are associated with, you can use .NET principal permission demands. .NET principals can be based on a user's logged-in identity, or they can be based on custom authentication credentials and roles.

You can use role-based security in .NET to make security demands through either attributes applied to methods, classes, or assemblies, or you can make them imperatively with code. The following code shows an example of using principal-based security demands to ensure that only users in an appropriate role get to execute certain sections of code.

```
[PrincipalPermission(SecurityAction.Demand, Role = @"Managers")]
private void DoSomethingPrivileged()
{
    // Do manager stuff
    if (Thread.CurrentPrincipal.IsInRole(@"BUILTIN\Administrators"))
    {
        // Do admin stuff
    }
}
```

In the preceding code, only users who are associated with the Managers role will be allowed to execute the DoSomethingPrivileged method. The inline check using the CurrentPrincipal property on the thread lets you check whether the user is in a particular role and execute conditional code based on that.[5]

---

4. For more information on Code Access Security, stack walk modifiers, and permissions control, see *Programming .NET Components*, Second Edition, by Juval Löwy (O'Reilly & Associates, 2005).
5. For more information on role-based security in .NET applications, see *Programming .NET Components*, Second Edition, by Juval Löwy (O'Reilly & Associates, 2005).

Securing Access to ClickOnce Application Files on the Server

ClickOnce does not include any built-in provisions for restricting access to the application files on the deployment server. If you are using ClickOnce to deploy an application to the local Intranet, and the Windows identity of the logged-in user can propagate to the deployment server via Windows networking (i.e., no firewalls between the client and the deployment server), then you can use Windows Access Control Lists (ACLs) to restrict access at the file or folder level on the deployment server to specific users or groups. If you do this and a user attempts to launch an application to which she has not been granted file access rights, one of two things will happen.

If the user has been denied access to the .application file (the deployment manifest) and she tries to launch a ClickOnce application through a link or URL, she will see an HTTP 401 error (access denied) in the browser. If the user is allowed to get to the deployment manifest, but is denied access to the application manifest or any of the application files, she will get a launch error dialog like the one shown in Figure 6.31. The details under this dialog will specify that there was an HTTP 401 access denied error.

If you have an application that you are deploying over the open Internet or a network where you cannot rely on the logged-in identity of the user to get passed to the deployment server, then there is no practical way to secure access to the server files. When you deploy an application with ClickOnce, it is a set of individual file requests from the client machine to the deployment server. There are actually two for the deployment manifest (due to a level of indirection supported by the runtime where one deployment manifest can point to another), one for the application manifest, and then one for each application file. These file requests are not correlated in any way.

FIGURE 6.31: Authentication Error Launch Dialog

You can prevent users from being able to do a normal ClickOnce application launch by using an online-only application that you have to launch from a Web application that requires a login to access, but you can only restrict access to the .application file in that case. The request for the .application file will be made by the browser, but the subsequent file requests are made by the ClickOnce runtime and will not contain any cookies or headers from the previous file requests.[6] Each file request is completely isolated from the others.

Where Are We?

This chapter discussed the complex security mechanisms and options for ClickOnce deployment. You learned about the way ClickOnce applications identify the set of permissions that they require to run, how the .NET runtime determines what permissions they would be granted based on their launch URL, and how permissions can be elevated through user prompting or trusted publishers. You learned about certificates and their role in protecting application files from tampering and in determining trust relationships with application publishers.

The following are some of the key takeaways from this chapter.

- ClickOnce provides both install-time and runtime protections to the client machine.
- ClickOnce checks to see if an application requires more permission than it would be granted by default based on its launch URL. If so, it will elevate permissions based on either user prompting (the default) or trusted publishers.
- Manifests are signed by Class 3 Code Signing Authenticode certificates. Configuring a certificate as a trusted publisher on a client machine will avoid user prompting for most deployment zones.

---

6. For more information on possible strategies to secure deployment server files and to track application usage, see the "Administering ClickOnce Deployments" whitepaper by Brian Noyes at http://msdn.microsoft.com/library/default.asp?url=/library/en-us/dnwinforms/html/admincodep.asp.

- You can restrict access to deployment server application files based on Access Control Lists if all users will come from the local network and their logged-in user identities can be determined based on the individual file requests.

In the next chapter, we will look at how to configure and deploy prerequisites for your ClickOnce applications. Prerequisites include setup steps that require administrative privileges you do not want to require your users to have.

7

Prerequisite Deployment with the Bootstrapper

C LICKONCE IS A LIGHTWEIGHT DEPLOYMENT mechanism for getting rich user interface applications running on the client machine. As discussed in earlier chapters, by design ClickOnce limits your ability to perform any custom installation steps. The intent of this limitation is to provide a trustworthy deployment mechanism that lets administrators be confident that other user data or applications will not be corrupted just through the act of deployment. To deploy your applications as easily as possible with ClickOnce, you should try to minimize the requirements your application has for the client machine as much as possible. This means that to the extent possible, your ClickOnce deployed application should depend only on other assemblies that are deployed along with the application as local assemblies and other local data and resource files. These assemblies and files get deployed with the application through ClickOnce to your application and data folders, and your application accesses the files from those folders.

In the real world, things are never that simple. Your application may be using a third-party component library that can only be deployed to the Global Assembly Cache (GAC). You may have dependencies on other optional operating system components or libraries from Microsoft such as DirectX or Microsoft Data Access Components. If you are migrating an existing application to ClickOnce, it may have requirements to create registry keys, files, databases, or other shared local resources before the application runs the first time. For any ClickOnce application, the .NET Framework 2.0 must be installed on the client before attempting a ClickOnce deployment. All of these kinds of requirements are things that cannot be done directly through a ClickOnce deployment.

For all of these scenarios, and any other form of custom installation requirements where you need to get some additional components installed on the client before the application runs, there is a solution called the **Bootstrapper,** which is a new facility in .NET 2.0 that is not limited to ClickOnce, but is designed to directly support it.

The Bootstrapper is an integrated installer for tying together multiple installer packages, install scripts, or executables into a single setup.exe launch program. This chapter will discuss the capabilities of the Bootstrapper, show how to configure it, and step you through some examples of deploying both predefined packages and custom installers with the Bootstrapper to support your ClickOnce deployments.

Bootstrapper Features

The Bootstrapper generates a single lightweight executable that wraps up one or more separate installers into a single installation process. The Bootstrapper gives you a ClickOnce-like experience for deploying prerequisites to a client machine. You just need to provide users a link to a setup.exe file that you place on your deployment server. That file is a small, unmanaged code executable that will kick off and manage the installation of any number of individual install packages, scripts, and executables. As long as users executing setup.exe have sufficient privileges to run the individual installers that the Bootstrapper calls, they will be able to get all the prerequisites for your application installed on their client machines. Typically this means they must be an administrator on the machine, but that is dependent on what installer packages or scripts the setup.exe calls.

Additionally, by default the Bootstrapper setup.exe is configured to support a ClickOnce deployment. The Bootstrapper will request the ClickOnce application's deployment manifest after it completes installing the prerequisites. This makes it so the one click to launch the setup.exe takes users all the way from installing the prerequisites to running the Click-Once application.

The following subsections highlight some of the additional capabilities and benefits of the Bootstrapper.

Flexible Launch Capabilities

The Bootstrapper can call just about any kind of installation program as one of the steps in the process of deploying prerequisites. This includes Windows Installer .msi files, script files, batch files, any executable designed to run from a command prompt, and even custom installer classes in .NET executables. Visual Studio has a collection of preconfigured common prerequisite installers, and you can include them in your Bootstrapper by simply checking a few boxes (see Figure 7.1). You can add your own custom installers to this list by generating a Bootstrapper manifest file and the associated installer package as described in the later section entitled Adding Items to the Bootstrapper.

Prerequisite Download Options

When you select a prerequisite for inclusion in your Bootstrapper, you also can select where the Bootstrapper will obtain the files for the prerequisite when users run the Bootstrapper on their machines. The options include

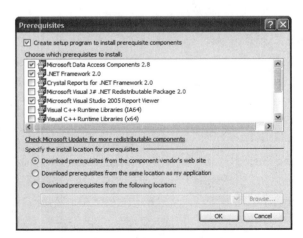

FIGURE 7.1: Visual Studio Prerequisites Dialog

downloading the files from the prerequisite vendor's Web site, downloading them from the same location the Bootstrapper was obtained, or downloading them from a specified URL.

Minimal Dependencies

The Bootstrapper itself is just a lightweight setup.exe file that is downloaded and executed from the client machine. It is an unmanaged executable that has no external dependencies other than libraries that are part of all current versions of the Windows operating system (Windows 98 and later). There is also an implicit dependency between the Bootstrapper and the prerequisite files you configure it to deploy. But other than those, you do not have to make any assumptions about the configuration on the client machine other than that it has Web access to the sites where the prerequisite files reside.

Installer Requirements Detection

For each installer that the Bootstrapper is configured to run, it first detects whether the component is already installed and will skip that installer if that is the case. The Bootstrapper can also be configured to detect platform requirements for each installer, such as the required operating system, and will refuse to run the installer if those requirements are not met.

Reboot Management

If any of the components that the Bootstrapper installs requires a reboot, the Bootstrapper will perform the restart and will resume execution after the restart and login of the user. Components can specify whether a reboot is required immediately or at the end of the installation process to avoid requiring multiple reboots. By default, the Bootstrapper assumes that a prerequisite does not require a reboot.

License Presentation

Some components require that users acknowledge an End User License Agreement (EULA) before proceeding installing the component. If you want to include a component in your Bootstrapper that needs to present a EULA to users, the Bootstrapper supports this. In addition, a single shared presentation of multiple licenses is used to minimize the number of dialogs users have to click through during the installation process. If you need to do any other kind of prompting to let users enter registration or license keys, you can do that from your custom installer, but you should definitely strive to support a silent install other than possibly presenting a EULA for the best Bootstrapper user experience.

Bootstrapper and ClickOnce Sample Deployment

Certainly one of the best ways to understand what the Bootstrapper can do for you is to try it out. One trick for most developers reading this book is that you probably already have all of the common prerequisites installed on your development machine, so you won't see much happen even if you do configure a ClickOnce application to include some prerequisites. To really see the effects of prerequisite deployment with the Bootstrapper, you need to have access to a machine that does not already have the prerequisites installed so that you can observe the full installation process. One of the best ways to do that is to use a virtual machine for the client that just has a baseline Windows XP installation on it. However, if all you have available is your development machine, you will still get a sense of what the Bootstrapper can do for you. However, you will definitely want to have a virtual machine (using Microsoft Virtual Server or VMware Workstation) or a clean test machine available on which you can try out full deployments of prerequisites before you ship.

You configure the Bootstrapper for a Windows Application project through Visual Studio from the project properties editor's Publish tab. On that tab, the button labeled *Prerequisites* brings up the dialog shown in Figure 7.1. Because you are configuring the Bootstrapper as part of a Visual Studio project, the Bootstrapper setup.exe that is generated will automatically launch the ClickOnce deployment when you finish installing the prerequisites.

To create a sample Bootstrapper deployed application, do the following.

1. Create a new Windows Application project in Visual Studio and name it **BootstrapperTest.**

2. Go to the project properties editor and select the Publish tab.

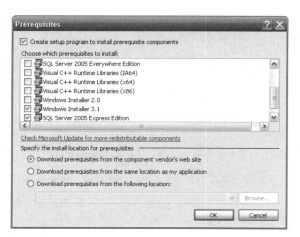

FIGURE 7.2: Prerequisites Dialog

3. Click the Prerequisites button to bring up the Prerequisites dialog.

4. Select the following items in the list (as shown in Figure 7.2).
   - .NET Framework 2.0
   - Windows Installer 3.1
   - SQL Server 2005 Express Edition

5. Select the option near the bottom of the dialog to download prerequisites from the same location as the application. This will copy all of the prerequisite installer files out to the publish directory, as well as the application itself when you publish the application.

6. Click OK to accept the configuration for the prerequisites.

This completes defining what install steps the Bootstrapper will perform when called by the client. Next, you will publish and install the application prerequisites and launch the application.

1. Publish the application by selecting Build > Publish BootstrapperTest from the main menu in Visual Studio. The normal publishing process will occur, but in addition to copying the ClickOnce application files and manifests, subfolders will be created under the publish directory to contain each of the prerequisites you configured (see Figure 7.3). The Bootstrapper setup.exe file will also be signed using the same publisher certificate used to sign the ClickOnce manifests.

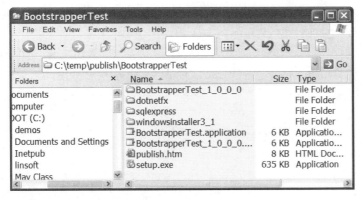

FIGURE 7.3: Bootstrapper Package Subfolders

2. At the completion of the publishing process, the publish.htm test page will be displayed (see Figure 7.4). It will show what prerequisites the application requires. The Install button on the page will no longer point directly to the deployment manifest as described in Chapter 2, but will instead point at the setup.exe Bootstrapper file (see the address bar at the bottom of Figure 7.4).

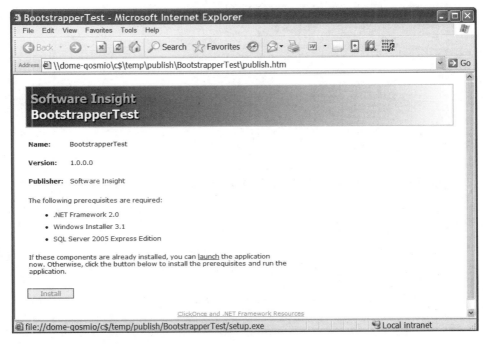

FIGURE 7.4: Publish.htm Test Page

3. From a computer or virtual machine that does not have the prerequisites installed and on which you are an administrator, go to the publish.htm page in a browser. Click on the Install button. The first thing you will see is the File Download – Security Warning dialog shown in Figure 7.5. The browser displays this dialog because you clicked a link to an unmanaged executable—the setup.exe Bootstrapper file.

4. Click on the Run button, and you will then be prompted with the security warning shown in Figure 7.6, which warns that setup.exe is not signed by a known publisher. This dialog will not be displayed if the Bootstrapper file is signed with a known publisher certificate, meaning its issuer is a Trusted Root Certification Authority.

5. Click Run in the second security warning dialog, and finally the Bootstrapper will run. It prompts you with the EULA for each of the packages included in the Bootstrapper that has one. You will get a separate pop-up dialog like the one shown in Figure 7.7 for each product that needs to present a EULA.

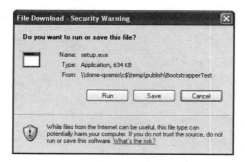

FIGURE 7.5: File Download – Security Warning Dialog

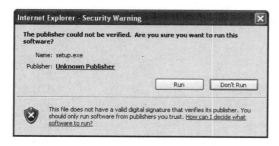

FIGURE 7.6: Unknown Publisher Security Warning

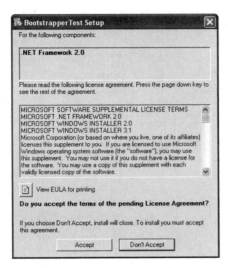

FIGURE 7.7: Product EULA Dialog

6. Click the Accept button for all of the EULA dialogs that display. After you have done this, the Bootstrapper will get down to the business of installing all those prerequisites. You will see a progress dialog like the one shown in Figure 7.8 for each prerequisite as it does its individual install.

7. Once all of the prerequisites have completed their install, the last step the Bootstrapper performs by default is to do a Web request for the deployment manifest of the ClickOnce application that it was published with. This will result in the normal security prompt for a ClickOnce application shown in Figure 7.9, assuming that you have not configured the client machine with the publisher certificate as a trusted publisher (as discussed in Chapter 6).

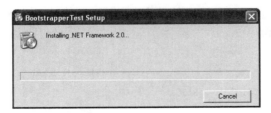

FIGURE 7.8: Bootstrapper Progress Dialog

FIGURE 7.9: ClickOnce Security Dialog

8. Click the Install button and the ClickOnce deployment will occur, and the application will be up and running on the client machine with all of the prerequisites installed.

A lot of variations could happen for this simple example. The Bootstrapper checks to see if each prerequisite is already installed on the target machine before attempting to install it, so if any of the prerequisites are already on the machine, you won't see any prompting or install activity for those. If you do not have administrative privileges on the machine where you are trying to run the Bootstrapper, installation packages like the .NET Framework will not let you run them, so you will get an error message in that case and you will be prevented from completing the prerequisite deployment. But the normal processing for a machine that has none of the prerequisites will be like that shown in the figures in this section.

Adding Items to the Bootstrapper

If you want to add additional items to the Bootstrapper besides the ones that are there by default, there are a few nontrivial, but not particularly difficult, steps you have to go through.

1. Build or obtain the installer package (.msi) or executable that you want to execute as part of the Bootstrapper install.

2. Generate or obtain Package and Product manifest files that describe the installer package to the Bootstrapper.

3. Deploy the manifests and installer package to the appropriate Bootstrapper folder.

Depending on what you are trying to add, the installer package may already be available to you. Any Windows Installer .msi package, script file, executable, batch file, command file, and so on—any executable file—can be added as a Bootstrapper package that will be run from the setup.exe Bootstrapper file. If the package is a Windows Installer package that supports silent (no wizard) installation, then it will be run without the usual prompting. The Bootstrapper does support identifying a separate EULA file so that you can do a minimal prompt upfront presenting the EULA and requiring users to accept it before doing the installation, but from there it will be a silent install with only a progress bar displayed.

Depending on what you are trying to add to the Bootstrapper, you may also be provided with the manifest files needed for the Bootstrapper. An example is the SQL Server 2005 Compact Edition Community Technical Preview (CTP) that is available at the time of this writing. You can download the .msi file to do an install of SQL Compact, and you can also download the Bootstrapper manifests needed to add SQL Compact to your Bootstrapper. If you are provided the Bootstrapper files, all you need to do is place those files in the right location.

Let's walk through a step-by-step example to make all this concrete. Visual Studio Setup and Deployment projects make it easy to create a simple Windows Installer package for an existing Visual Studio project. Full coverage of the capabilities of these projects and creating installers is beyond the scope of this book, but this section will step through the process for a common scenario: creating an installer for deploying an assembly to the GAC.

Creating a Shared Assembly Project

The first thing you need to do is create an assembly that you want to deploy to the GAC. Perform the following steps to do so.

1. Create a new Class Library project in Visual Studio named
   MySharedAssembly.

FIGURE 7.10: Renaming Dialog

2. Rename the Class1.cs file in Solution Explorer to **MyComponent.cs.** Visual Studio will prompt you to do a rename with the dialog shown in Figure 7.10. Click Yes.

3. Add a method to the component that returns a string like the following.

```
public class MyComponent
{
   public string SayHello()
   {
      return "Hello";
   }
}
```

4. Go to the project properties editor (Project > MySharedAssembly Properties in the main menu) and select the Signing tab.

5. Check the box near the bottom that's labeled *Sign the assembly.*

6. From the combo box just below that, select New.

7. The dialog shown in Figure 7.11 will appear. Enter any name you like for the key file, and uncheck the box to password protect the key file for demo purposes. Click OK.

8. Build your project to make sure all is well. You should see a Build Succeeded notification in the status bar and no build errors.

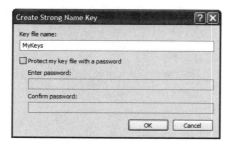

FIGURE 7.11: Creating a New Key File

Creating a Windows Installer Package

The next step is to create a Windows Installer .msi package that will deploy your shared assembly to the GAC on the target client machine. Creating a Visual Studio Setup project will make this very easy.

1. Add a new project to the solution by right-clicking on the Solution root node in Solution Explorer, and selecting Add > New Project from the context menu.

2. In the Add New Project dialog (see Figure 7.12), expand the tree of project types in the left side and select Setup and Deployment as the project type. In the pane on the right, select Setup Wizard as the template. Enter the project name **MySharedAssemblySetup** and click OK.

3. Step 1 in the Setup wizard displays, which describes what the wizard is for. Click Next.

4. Step 2 in the wizard lets you pick the kind of setup project you want to create. Leave the default of Windows application selected (see Figure 7.13) and click Next.

5. Step 3 in the wizard lets you pick which project outputs in the solution you want to include in the setup project. Select the Primary output from MySharedAssembly checkbox as shown in Figure 7.14 and click Next.

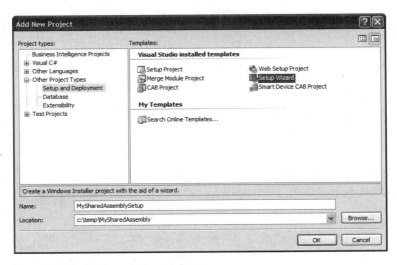

FIGURE 7.12: Adding a Setup Project

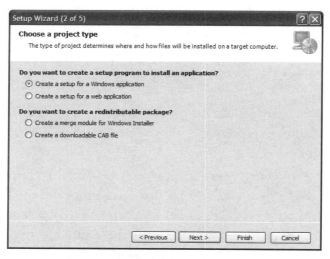

FIGURE 7.13: Selecting the Setup Project Type

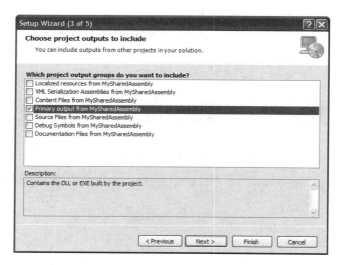

FIGURE 7.14: Selecting Project Outputs

6. In Step 4 of the wizard you can select any additional files you want to add into the installer that are not project outputs. In this case, don't select any and just click Next.

7. The final step of the wizard summarizes what the wizard will do upon completion. Click the Finish button and a setup project will be added to the solution. You should see the File System View of the setup project as shown in Figure 7.15.

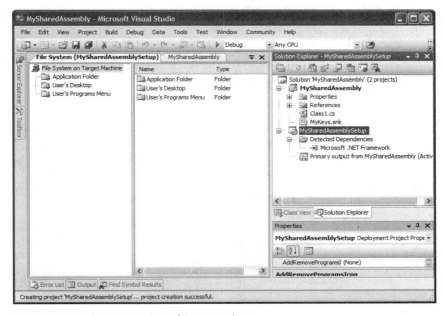

FIGURE 7.15: File System View of Setup Project

8. Right-click on the File System on Target Machine node at the top of the tree in the left pane. Select Add Special Folder from the pop-up menu, and select Global Assembly Cache Folder near the bottom of the list (see Figure 7.16).

9. Select the Application Folder in the tree view in the left pane so that you can see the Primary Output from MySharedAssembly in the right pane. Drag and drop Primary Output from MySharedAssembly onto the Global Assembly Cache Folder to move it there (see Figure 7.17).

10. Right-click on the MySharedAssemblySetup project in Solution Explorer and select Build from the context menu. This will build the project and create the .msi file output.

Creating the Bootstrapper Manifests

Once you have a deployment package that you want to add to the Bootstrapper, the next step is to create the manifests that the Bootstrapper requires to attach your installer package to the Bootstrapper. There are two manifests required: a product manifest and a package manifest. The product manifest describes the product to be deployed in a language-neutral

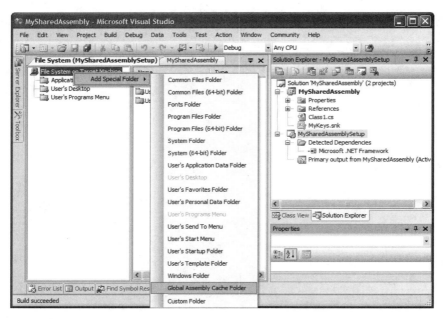

FIGURE 7.16: Adding the GAC Special Folder

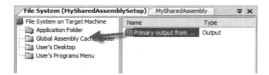

FIGURE 7.17: Moving the Primary Project Output to the GAC Folder

way. The package manifest describes the language-specific aspects of the package, including things such as localized strings for the prompting presented by the Bootstrapper. You can also deploy language-specific versions of your installer package, each of which might be localized itself for a particular culture. The contents of each of these manifests are defined by the same schema, identified by the namespace http://schemas.microsoft.com/developer/2004/01/bootstrapper. The full schema, allowable elements, and attributes and their values can be explored by searching for "Product and Package Schema Reference" in the MSDN Library.

The manifests you create will need to go in a particular location on the development machine on which you will be creating the Bootstrapper. The folder where Bootstrapper packages reside is:

```
C:\Program Files\Microsoft Visual Studio 8\SDK\v2.0\BootStrapper\Packages
```

To create the manifests, do the following.

1. Go to the Bootstrapper packages folder just described. You will need to create a subfolder in that location to contain your product, preferably naming it to match the name of your product. Add a subfolder named **\MySharedAssembly** and open that folder.

2. Using Visual Studio or your text editor of choice, create a new XML file named **Product.xml** and place it in that folder.

3. Enter the following XML as the contents of the Product.xml file:

```xml
<?xml version="1.0" encoding="utf-8"?>
<Product ProductCode="MySharedAssembly"
xmlns="http://schemas.microsoft.com/developer/2004/01/bootstrapper"
/>
```

The Product element is the root element for your product manifest, and it should always contain a ProductCode attribute that identifies the product name. If you are not deploying language-neutral packages, the Product element can be empty. If you are deploying language-neutral packages, the schema for the elements describing those language-neutral packages is the same as the schema for language-specific packages that you put in the package manifest, described shortly.

4. Create a subfolder under the MySharedAssembly folder named **\EN.** This stands for the English culture code. Open that folder.

5. Copy the build output (MySharedAssemblySetup.msi) from the setup project (in the \Debug subfolder under that project) into the \EN folder.

6. Create a new XML file named **Package.xml** in the \EN subfolder.

7. Enter the following for the contents of the Package.xml file.

```xml
<?xml version="1.0" encoding="utf-8"?>
<Package Name="MySharedAssembly"
 Culture="en"
 xmlns="http://schemas.microsoft.com/developer/2004/01/bootstrapper">
  <PackageFiles CopyAllPackageFiles="false">
    <PackageFile Name="mysharedassemblysetup.msi" />
  </PackageFiles>
```

```xml
<Commands Reboot="Defer">
  <Command PackageFile="mysharedassemblysetup.msi" Arguments="">
   <ExitCodes>
      <DefaultExitCode Result="Success"
       FormatMessageFromSystem="true" />
    </ExitCodes>
  </Command>
 </Commands>
</Package>
```

The Package.xml file includes elements describing the package name, culture, what files it is composed of, and what commands to run as part of the package's execution. The `Package` root element should always contain a `Name` attribute, which identifies the name that will appear in the Bootstrapper dialog in Visual Studio when selecting your prerequisites. Under that, the `PackageFiles` element contains individual `PackageFile` elements, each of which has a `Name` attribute at a minimum that specifies the package file's name. The Bootstrapper expects to find these files in the same folder as the package manifest file.

The Commands section lets you specify individual commands to execute for each package as the Bootstrapper runs. At a minimum you will want to have a command for the installer package itself, with a `Default-ExitCode` inside the `ExitCodes` collection to specify that the result of the operation should be a `Success` if a specific system error does not occur. You can add additional `ExitCode` elements to that collection to capture specific return codes from the installer package. By doing this you can map specific error messages to those errors in a language-specific way by adding a `Strings` element to the root `Package` element, containing a collection of string elements for specific prompts.

Deploying the Shared Assembly with the Bootstrapper

Once you have the Bootstrapper manifests defined and in the right location under the SDK subfolders, your installer package is ready to be used in a ClickOnce application as a Bootstrapper setup step. Start by creating an application with a dependency on the shared assembly as a prerequisite.

1. Create a new Windows Application project named **Custom-PrereqTest.**

2. Add a reference to the MySharedAssembly.dll file in the build output directory (\bin\Debug) under that project.

3. Add a button to the form and double-click on it.

4. Add the following code to the button event handler:

```
MyComponent comp = new MyComponent();
MessageBox.Show(comp.SayHello());
```

5. Add a using statement to the top of the file:

```
using MySharedAssembly;
```

6. Select the MySharedAssembly reference in the References node in Solution Explorer.

7. Set the Copy Local property to False in the Properties window (see Figure 7.18).

Now set the publishing prerequisites and test the deployment.

1. Go to the project properties editor's Publish tab.

2. Click the Prerequisites button.

3. You should see MySharedAssembly toward the bottom of the list as shown in Figure 7.19. Check the box next to that prerequisite, select the option near the bottom to download the prerequisites from the same location as the application, and click OK.

4. Publish the application (Project > Publish CustomPrereqTest).

5. When the publish.htm test page appears, click the Install button.

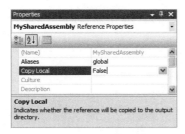

FIGURE 7.18: Setting Copy Local to False

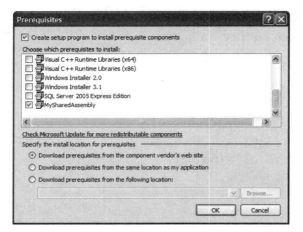

FIGURE 7.19: Selecting a Custom Prerequisite

6. When the first File Download – Security Warning dialog appears, click Run.

7. When the Internet Explorer – Security Warning dialog appears, click Run.

8. When the Bootstrapper dialog appears (see Figure 7.20), click Install. Notice that this dialog is different than the one shown in Figure 7.7 because you did not configure an End User License Agreement for the application.

9. A progress dialog should appear briefly, then the ClickOnce launch dialog, followed by the application downloading and launching.

10. Click on the button on the form to confirm that you are able to call the MySharedAssembly component, which was deployed to the GAC by the Bootstrapper.

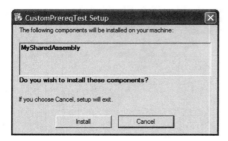

FIGURE 7.20: Bootstrapper Component Summary

You can see from this walkthrough that the only real complexity in adding custom installer packages to the Bootstrapper comes from the knowledge required to put together the manifests correctly. In the next section, you'll see that this task is made much easier with the help of a free tool from one of the developers at Microsoft.

Generating Bootstrapper Manifests

You probably don't want to have to hand-code the XML for the manifests every time you need to add a custom installer package to the Bootstrapper. Luckily, there is a tool that makes it so that you do not have to. David Guyer, a Test Lead on the Visual Basic team at Microsoft, put together a nice little tool called the *Bootstrapper Manifest Generator* (BMG) that gives you a dialog-driven way of creating Bootstrapper manifest files. The BMG has a workspace on GotDotNet.com (www.gotdotnet.com/workspaces/workspace.aspx?id=ddb4f08c-7d7c-4f44-a009-ea19fc812545) that you can go to for information and to download the tool. The BMG itself is a Click-Once deployed application, so you just have to go to the site, follow the links to the deployment page, click on the link, click on the Install button in the ClickOnce Security Warning dialog, and you will have the application deployed to your machine.

As its name implies, the BMG lets you generate the Bootstrapper manifest through a fairly straightforward user interface. To create the manifests from the previous sections using the BMG, you could do the following.

1. Find the folder you created earlier for the MySharedAssembly manifests under the folder C:\Program Files\Microsoft Visual Studio 8\SDK\v2.0\BootStrapper\Packages and move it somewhere else on your machine (remove the MySharedAssembly folder from under the Packages folder).
2. Launch the BMG application.
3. In the BMG main window, click on the New Project button in the toolbar (first button from the left).
4. Select Package Manifest as the type of project to create (see Figure 7.21) and click OK.

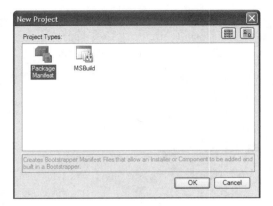

FIGURE 7.21: Selecting Project Type

5. Type in **MySharedAssembly** for the Project Name and tab to the next control. MySharedAssembly will fill in for the Product Code as well (see Figure 7.22).

6. Click the Add Install File button in the toolbar of that window (first button on the left). This will bring up the dialog shown in Figure 7.23. Select English as the target language and browse to the location of the MySharedAssemblySetup.msi file. Click OK.

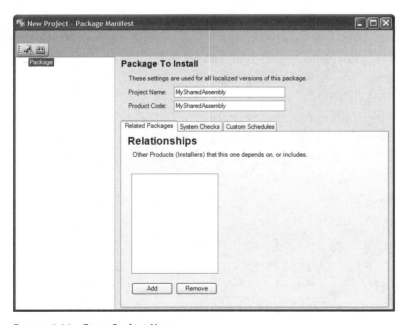

FIGURE 7.22: Enter Project Name

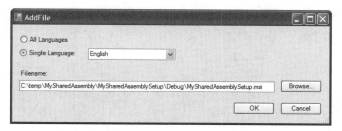

FIGURE 7.23: Add Install File Dialog

7. The Package Manifest window shown in Figure 7.24 will appear. Enter a display name of **MySharedAssembly,** then click the Build button in the toolbar (second button from left).

8. You should see a scrolling status window that shows progress as the build occurs, with an end status of 0 Warnings and 0 Errors. Once this is complete, your manifests have been generated and placed in the appropriate folder. You can save the BMG project at this point if you expect to do updates to the installer package and will need to regenerate.

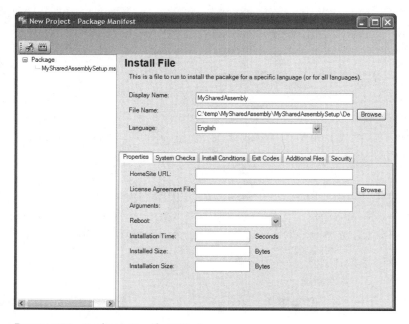

FIGURE 7.24: Package Manifest Window

As you can see, this tool lets you generate manifests quickly and easily without needing to know the manifest schema and what elements to put where.

Where Are We?

In this chapter you learned how to deploy prerequisite components for your ClickOnce application using the Bootstrapper. You learned how to select existing Bootstrapper packages through the Prerequisites dialog in the Publish settings of a Visual Studio project, and how to create and add custom installers to the Bootstrapper by creating the product and package manifests required. Finally, you learned how to generate those manifests easily using the Bootstrapper Manifest Generator.

The following are some of the key takeaways from this chapter.

- The Bootstrapper lets you run a set of individual installer packages or executables through a single setup.exe application that can be easily deployed over the Web.
- You configure which packages are included in your application Bootstrapper through the Prerequisites dialog from the Visual Studio project properties editor's Publish tab.
- You can add additional packages to the Bootstrapper by adding the appropriate Product.xml and Package.xml manifest files under the SDK Bootstrapper packages folder.
- You can generate the manifest using the Bootstrapper Manifest Generator tool available on GotDotNet.com.

The next chapter tackles the few remaining concepts you might need to add to your ClickOnce tool belt to address a variety of advanced scenarios that sometimes come up when deploying applications with ClickOnce.

■ 8 ■
Advanced ClickOnce Topics

THE OTHER CHAPTERS in this book have focused on the key capabilities of ClickOnce: automatic installation and update, on-demand updates, working with application files, security, and the Bootstrapper. This chapter is an attempt to address the loose ends—a variety of capabilities and situations that have come up frequently regarding ClickOnce as advanced scenarios that you might need to address.

Using URL Query String Parameters

It has been a common approach in the past to let your application modify its behavior based on command line parameters passed to it when it is launched. In a .NET application, you can capture any command line parameters passed to your application with a `Main` method as your entry point, which does something like the following.

```
static void Main(string[] args)
{
    if (args.Length > 0)
    {
        if (args[0] == "TodayIsFriday")
        {
            // Party on!
        }
    }
}
```

ClickOnce still supports this same notion, although it manifests itself a little differently since you do not launch ClickOnce applications from the command line; you always launch them either through a URL or a Start menu shortcut. To pass arguments into a ClickOnce application when you launch it, you have to do so through URL query string parameters instead of command line arguments. So instead of launching an application that is designed to look at the arguments to the `Main` method with a command line like one of the following:

```
C:\>MySpecialApp.exe TodayIsFriday
C:\>MySpecialApp.exe /Param1:TestValue /Param2:AnotherVal
```

you instead launch it with a query string that looks like one of the following:

```
http://myappserver/MySpecialApp.application?TodayIsFriday
http://myappserver/MySpecialApp.application?Param1=TestValue&Param2=
AnotherVal
```

You also do not get to the query string parameters through the `Main` method arguments. Instead, you use part of the ClickOnce API to obtain the command line parameters.

There are also some important limitations to using query string parameters in ClickOnce applications to be aware of before you decide you want to try to employ this approach.

- Your application can only receive query string parameters if it is launched through a full URL to the deployment manifest on the server. The locally cached manifest for an installed (available offline) application will not contain any query string parameters, even if the server-side manifest included query string parameters in the deployment manifest's deployment provider URL. So when the installed application is launched through the Start menu shortcut, no parameters will be passed to it, and there is no way to introduce parameters through that launch mechanism.

- You need to be very careful what you do with any parameters passed to the application. Startup parameters are often used as an attack vector by hackers to try to compromise an application. You need to do good validation on any input parameters and ensure that there is no combination of inputs that someone could enter that would result in unexpected behavior.

Because online-only applications are always launched through a full URL to the deployment manifest on the server, you can easily embed query string parameters in that URL, and after the application is launched, those parameters will be available to the running application. In an installed (available offline) application, the application is typically launched through the Start menu shortcut after the initial install, and the URL passed to the ClickOnce runtime will not contain query string parameters even if they exist in the deployment manifest.

Because the URL parameters will not be passed when an application is launched from the Start menu, the only way to get consistent application behavior based on URL parameters is to design it to be an online-only application. You could perhaps support special diagnostic options such as enabling tracing log output based on a query string parameter for an installed application, or setting initialization parameters through the initial launch URL, but you would not want to design any key application features around the parameters that are needed for every launch, since the user will most likely launch the application from the Start menu if it is installed.

For an online-only ClickOnce deployed application, if you have the user launch it through a link in a portal Web site, you could dynamically generate the link based on the logged in user to provide user-based context-sensitive application behavior (e.g., passing a license key to enable or disable application features).

Enabling URL Parameters

To pass URL query string parameters to an application, you first have to enable the ClickOnce option that allows URL parameters to be passed to the application. You do this in Visual Studio through the project properties editor's Publish tab. On that tab, you click the Options button and you get the dialog shown in Figure 8.1. You need to check the option to allow URL parameters before you publish. If you do not, it does not matter if URL query string parameters are included in the launch URL or not—they will not be passed to the application even if they are included.

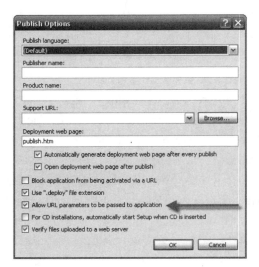

FIGURE 8.1: Allow URL Parameters Option

This option can also be set when editing the deployment manifest using the mageui.exe program as shown in Figure 8.2. This option is not exposed through the mage.exe command line tool.

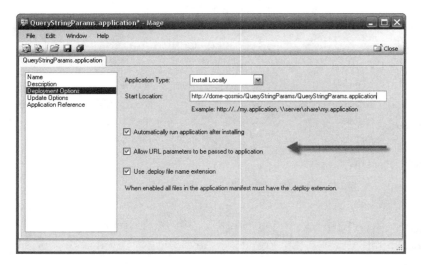

FIGURE 8.2: Allow URL Parameters Option in MageUI

Using URL Parameters

The download code for this chapter contains a sample called QueryString-Params that lets you experiment with intercepting and using query string parameters. It is a simple form application that lets you press a button to see any query string parameters that were passed to the application when it was launched (see Figure 8.3).

The form code for the QueryStringParams sample uses a helper class included in the download code named `QueryStringHelper`. This class has a couple of static helper methods on it. The top-level method called by the form is named `GetQueryStringParams` and is shown in Listing 8.1.

LISTING 8.1: GetQueryStringParams Helper Method

```
public static Dictionary<string, string> GetQueryStringParams()
{
   Dictionary<string, string> queryStringParams =
      new Dictionary<string, string>();
   if (ApplicationDeployment.IsNetworkDeployed)
   {
      Uri uri =
ApplicationDeployment.CurrentDeployment.ActivationUri;
      if (uri != null && uri.Query.Length > 0)
      {
         queryStringParams = ParseQueryString(uri.Query);
      }
   }
   return queryStringParams;
}
```

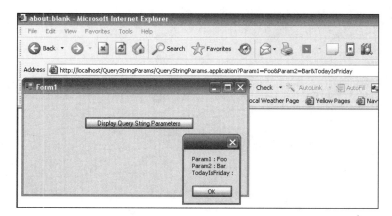

FIGURE 8.3: QueryStringParams Sample

GetQueryStringParams first checks to see if the application was launched through ClickOnce using the ApplicationDeployment.IsNet-workDeployed property. If it was, then the ActivationUri property is checked. This property will be set to null if the publisher of the application did not explicitly set the Allow URL parameters property. After the method has verified that the ActivationUri property contains something to parse, another helper method, ParseQueryString, is called. The return value from these methods is a Dictionary<K,T> generic collection of key/value pairs. The way ParseQueryString is designed, it will return one entry in the dictionary for each parameter found in the query string (separated by & characters). If the parameter includes both a name and a value (separated by an = character), then the name and value will be set as the key and value, respectively, in the dictionary item. If the parameter is just a value (no = character), then that value will be set as the dictionary entry's key with a null value. The reason for this is that dictionary items must always have a unique key. ParseQueryString is shown in Listing 8.2. This method uses the HttpUtility class from the System.Web namespace to convert any URL-encoded values back to their normal characters, and takes care of stripping off the ? character if present, then splits out all the parameters and their name/value pairs, adding each to the dictionary that is returned. I chose not to use the ParseQueryString method of the HttpUtility class directly because of the way it groups all parameters that are not in name/value format into a single string.

LISTING 8.2: ParseQueryString Method

```
public static Dictionary<string, string> ParseQueryString(
    string queryString)
{
    Dictionary<string, string> queryStringParams =
        new Dictionary<string, string>();
    if (string.IsNullOrEmpty(queryString))
        return queryStringParams;
    queryString = HttpUtility.UrlDecode(queryString);

    if (queryString[0] == '?') // strip ?
    {
        queryString = queryString.Substring(1);
    }
    string[] parts = queryString.Split('&');
    foreach (string part in parts)
```

```
    {
        string trimmedPart = part.Trim();
        if (!string.IsNullOrEmpty(trimmedPart))
        {
            string[] pieces = trimmedPart.Split('=');
            if (pieces.Length == 1)
            {
                queryStringParams.Add(pieces[0], null);
            }
            if (pieces.Length == 2)
            {
                queryStringParams.Add(pieces[0], pieces[1]);
            }
        }
    }
    return queryStringParams;
}
```

Executing Custom Install/Initialization Code

As discussed in Chapter 7, the best way to take care of custom installation steps is to create a custom installer package that you deploy through the Bootstrapper to provision the client machine before doing a ClickOnce installation. However, since most Bootstrapper installers will require administrative privileges, the Bootstrapper may not be the best option in every case.

Ultimately, once your application is launched through ClickOnce, your application code can do whatever the combination of ClickOnce security permissions and user privileges the machine allows the application to do. So you can embed custom startup code in your application to perform custom installation steps if needed. You will want to be very careful about not overusing this capability. You might be tempted to use this to do something like create registry keys or install assemblies in the GAC as custom startup actions in your application. But just realize that doing these things may start making assumptions about user privileges that may not be valid for all users.

If you need to embed custom startup install or initialization code in your application, the best thing to do is combine it with the `Application-Deployment.IsFirstRun` property to detect whether this is the first time a given version of your application has run. Be aware that using this property requires full-trust permissions for the application, which is another down-side to this approach.

The download code for this chapter includes a sample named Custom-InitSample that demonstrates this concept. The code that does the checking looks like the following.

```
public static void InitUser()
{
    if (ApplicationDeployment.IsNetworkDeployed)
    {
        if (ApplicationDeployment.CurrentDeployment.IsFirstRun)
        {
            if (string.IsNullOrEmpty(Settings.Default.UserName))
            {
                SetUserForm form = new SetUserForm();
                form.ShowDialog();
            }
        }
    }
}
```

As with other parts of the ClickOnce API discussed in Chapters 4 and 5, you will always need to first check the `ApplicationDeployment.IsNet-workDeployed` property before using other parts of the `Application-Deployment` class. If this property is true, then you know the application has been launched by ClickOnce. You can then check the `IsFirstRun` property, which will be true the first time each version of an application is launched through ClickOnce. So at initial install, it will be true for the first launch. Then when an update is downloaded and launched, it will be true again for the first run of that version, and so on.

Debugging ClickOnce Applications

When you intend to deploy your application via ClickOnce, in addition to all your usual debugging techniques, there are several special techniques for debugging ClickOnce deployed applications.

Debug in Zone

Once your application is running correctly as a normal Windows Forms application in the debugger, you should enable ClickOnce security through the project properties editor's Security tab. If you are going to publish your application with full trust as its security permission requirements, then this will not really have any significant effect. But if you are going to deploy your application as a partial-trust application as discussed in Chapter 6, then you will want to do some thorough debug runs with ClickOnce security enabled and the planned partial-trust permissions selected so that you can detect and debug any security exceptions that result in the debugger.

With ClickOnce security enabled and your application set to request partial-trust permissions, then if you run in the debugger and your code violates the requested permissions, you will get a `SecurityException` thrown and caught by the debugger as shown in Figure 8.4. This capability is often called *Debug in Zone*, because the debugger runs your code in the selected security zone and permissions context like it will run in the target environment.

Attaching the Debugger to a ClickOnce Application

Using Debug in Zone will only help you to discover any security exceptions that might be thrown when you run in the ClickOnce security sandbox. It will not help you when it comes to debugging code that uses the ClickOnce API, because you are still not being launched by ClickOnce the

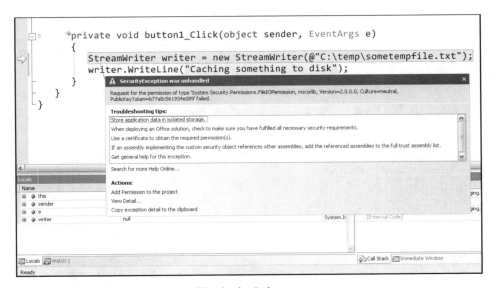

FIGURE 8.4: SecurityException Handling in the Debugger

> **⸙ TIP   VSHost.exe Enables Debug in Zone**
>
> The Debug in Zone capability is enabled by the fact that Visual Studio 2005 runs an executable named <appname>.vshost.exe for debug sessions by default and attaches the debugger to that shim application. It then creates an AppDomain in that process each time you start a debug session, restricts the security policy for that AppDomain based on the selected security settings, and then loads your application-executable assembly into that AppDomain and calls the `Main` method to start it running. You can do a similar thing in your own applications if you want to restrict the security context for executing code.[1]

way your application will be launched on the client machine. To debug any ClickOnce API code, the application will need to have been launched by ClickOnce. If the code you are trying to debug executes sometime after the startup of the application, such as an update on-demand feature, you can debug this using the Attach to Process feature of the Visual Studio debugger to attach to a process after it is running.

To use this for a ClickOnce application, do the following.

1. Design, build, and publish a ClickOnce application as a Debug build that has some code you want to debug after a ClickOnce launch. The download code has a copy of the SynchronousOnDemandUpdates sample from Chapter 4 in this chapter's sample code that you can use.

2. Make sure the project is open in Visual Studio and that you have any breakpoints set in the code that you want to hit after the ClickOnce launch. In order to hit the breakpoints, there will have to be sufficient time between when the application launches and when the code in question is executed for you to attach the debugger. If the code is invoked by a user action, this is easy to achieve. If the code is called

---

1. "Do You Trust It? Discover Techniques for Safely Hosting Untrusted Add-Ins with the .NET Framework 2.0," Shawn Farkas, *MSDN Magazine,* November 2005. http://msdn.microsoft.com/msdnmag/issues/05/11/HostingAddIns/default.aspx.

automatically when the application is starting up, you may need to insert a time delay or a blocking operation to give you time to attach the debugger. You can also use the `Debugger.Break` technique described in the next subsection instead.

3. Launch the application through the URL to the deployment manifest like a user would. The publish.htm page generated by Visual Studio is a good way to do this.

4. Once the application is up and running, go to the Debug menu in Visual Studio and select Attach to Process. You will see the window in Figure 8.5. Note that you can select other machines on your network, but usually it is best to do this on the local machine unless you have something that you cannot duplicate locally that you are trying to debug.

5. Find your application process in the list, select it, and click the Attach button. It will have the full executable name if you are running as full trust. Note that if you are running on the local machine, you may also see an <appname>.vshost.exe process running from previous debug sessions in Visual Studio. If you are running a partial-trust application, the process name will be AppLaunch.exe instead. However, you

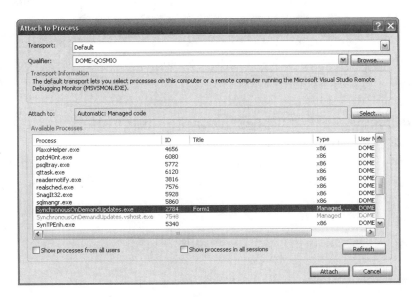

FIGURE 8.5: Attach to Process Window

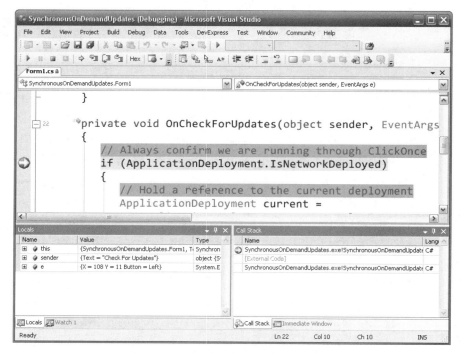

FIGURE 8.6: Hitting a Breakpoint after Attaching the Debugger

cannot use the ClickOnce API in partial trust anyway, so it should be fairly rare that you would need to attach to AppLaunch.exe.

6. Invoke a function that hits a breakpoint, such as the Update button in the synchronous updates sample. You should hit your breakpoint in the debugger as shown in Figure 8.6.

Using Debugger.Break to Debug ClickOnce Startup Code

If the code you need to debug in a ClickOnce application is invoked as the application starts up, it can be difficult to get the debugger attached in time using the Attach to Process method described in the previous subsection. One straightforward solution is to embed a call to the `Debugger` class' `Break` method.

To see this in action, you can do the following.

1. Modify the `InitUser` method presented earlier for the CustomInit-Sample to include a call to `Debugger.Break`. This method gets called in the sample as the main form is being constructed.

```
public static void InitUser()
{
    Debugger.Break();
    if (ApplicationDeployment.IsNetworkDeployed)
    {
        if (ApplicationDeployment.CurrentDeployment.IsFirstRun)
        {
            if (string.IsNullOrEmpty(Settings.Default.UserName))
            {
                SetUserForm form = new SetUserForm();
                form.ShowDialog();
            }
        }
    }
}
```

2. Publish and launch the application. As the application is launching, you will see a dialog like the one shown in Figure 8.7. Click on the Debug button.

3. The Just-in-Time Debugger selection dialog will pop up (see Figure 8.8). Find the item in the list that represents the open solution for your application in Visual Studio and click the Yes button to debug.

4. Control will be transferred to the bugger as shown in Figure 8.9. Press F10 to start stepping through the code.

Deploying Unmanaged Applications with ClickOnce

A .NET 2.0 compiled executable is required as the entry point to launch an application through ClickOnce. But you can actually use ClickOnce to launch any application with a small degree of trickery. By creating a thin .NET 2.0 shim executable whose only purpose is to launch another executable, you can use ClickOnce to launch anything, such as a legacy Visual Basic 6 application.

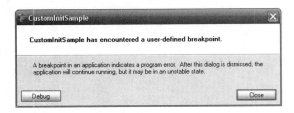

FIGURE 8.7: User-Defined Breakpoint Dialog

FIGURE 8.8: Just-In-Time Debugger Dialog

```
{
    public partial class SetUserForm : Form
    {
        public static void InitUser()
        {
            Debugger.Break();
            if (ApplicationDeployment.IsNetworkDeployed)
            {
                if (ApplicationDeployment.CurrentDeployment.IsFir
```

FIGURE 8.9: Stepping Through the Code

To do this, you will need to create a Windows Application project, but then you will remove the main form and just call `Process.Start` from the `Main` method. The sample code for this chapter has a reusable application project named COAppLauncher that you can use to launch any application. The `Program` class in COAppLauncher looks like this:

```
static class Program
{
    [STAThread]
    static void Main()
    {
        Process.Start(Settings.Default.ExeName);
    }
}
```

The project uses an application-scoped Visual Studio setting to store the application's executable file name in the config file, so that you could just use this project over and over again with any executable. The config file contains the setting value that gets read in from the call to Settings.Default.ExeName in the preceding code.

```xml
<?xml version="1.0" encoding="utf-8" ?>
<configuration>
    <configSections>
        <sectionGroup name="applicationSettings" ... />
    </configSections>
    <applicationSettings>
        <COAppLauncher.Properties.Settings>
            <setting name="ExeName" serializeAs="String">
                <value>SomeExecutable.exe</value>
            </setting>
        </COAppLauncher.Properties.Settings>
    </applicationSettings>
</configuration>
```

To use this sample to launch other executables, you would just do the following.

1. Remove SomeExecutable.exe from the Visual Studio project.
2. Add the .exe file that you want to launch to the project.
3. Edit the app.config file to contain the name of the executable file.
4. Publish the application.

You will probably also want to configure the project's Publish options to set the appropriate publisher and product name as you want them to display in the user's Start menu.

Note that this will only work if you configure the launching application for full trust in ClickOnce security settings. This is because Process .Start requires unmanaged code security permissions, and also because the runtime directory of partial-trust applications is not the application folder where the application files get deployed to, so there is no way to access the unmanaged executable you deploy via ClickOnce with a partial-trust application.

When you combine this approach with Reg-Free COM, discussed in the next section, you will have a very powerful combination for deploying legacy VB6 and other applications that use ActiveX and COM controls with ClickOnce, greatly simplifying the client application deployment picture even for non-.NET applications.

Reg-Free COM

There was a little-publicized yet very powerful capability introduced with Windows XP and later operating systems called **Reg-Free COM** (also known as *native component isolation*). Anyone who has done or dealt with COM components and ActiveX controls in the past knows that one of the banes of COM deployment was the need to register the components on the target machine. That meant you had to have a deployment mechanism that allowed you to run, with administrative privileges, a script or installer that could call the RegSvr32.exe command line utility to add the COM library CLSIDs, IIDs, and various other registration entries into the registry.

In Windows XP, the capability was introduced to instead deploy a manifest file along with your COM library, and Windows XP would automatically register the components contained in the library the first time an application in the same executable directory tried to access a COM component. Unless you jumped straight to this chapter, you have already gotten a good sense of what the concept of a manifest file is and how it is used by both ClickOnce and the Bootstrapper. Well, the fact is that the ClickOnce product team did not invent the concept; Windows XP introduced manifests for Reg-Free COM, and both ClickOnce and the Bootstrapper are just expanding the capabilities and usage scenarios that XP manifest files can be used with.

If you are also familiar with the way that the .NET runtime probes for assemblies when it needs to load them, the way Reg-Free COM works should also sound familiar as well. Normally COM looks in the registry for the appropriate unique identifiers for the components that are being called to determine where those components live (the path to their libraries), and then the components are loaded from there. This is similar to the fact that the .NET runtime first looks in the Global Assembly Cache for an assembly that it needs to load to see if it exists there. The next step for the .NET run-time is to look in the local executable directory for the application making the call. Reg-Free COM brings this same kind of logic to the registration of COM components. If Windows XP, Windows Server 2003, or Windows Vista does not find the appropriate registry entries for a component that COM is trying to load, it will then look in the local executable directory for a manifest file that contains the needed information for the COM compo-nent. If the manifest is found there, Windows will dynamically register the COM component so that it can then be found by COM's normal type dis-covery process.

The steps to do this are quite simple using Visual Studio 2005. If you need to use a COM component or ActiveX control from a ClickOnce deployed application (even if it is a shim application as discussed in the previous section), you just need to set a reference to the COM component from the ClickOnce application project (by selecting the COM tab in the Add References dialog and selecting the COM/ActiveX component name from the list). After you have added the reference, you select the reference in the Solution Explorer References node and go to the Properties window. From there, you set the Isolated property to *True* (see Figure 8.10).

By setting the Isolated property to *True*, the COM library will be pub-lished along with the other application files, and the appropriate entries will be added to the ClickOnce manifests when you publish the applica-tion, and the COM component library will be deployed with the application

FIGURE 8.10: Setting COM Component Isolation

and will be automatically registered on the client machine when the application is launched. A file element that is added to the application manifest for each COM library you set as *Isolated* looks like the following.

```
<file name="SomeLegacyControl.ocx" asmv2:size="20480"
  xmlns="urn:schemas-microsoft-com:asm.v1">
  <hash ... />
  <typelib tlbid="{366e2e56-f675-4ee4-a1ce-38190ddbcc94}"
    version="1.0" helpdir="" resourceid="0"
    flags="CONTROL,HASDISKIMAGE" />
  <comClass clsid="{a681de5d-eaa8-4a02-9df0-63bbe577a92e}"
    threadingModel="Apartment"
    tlbid="{366e2e56-f675-4ee4-a1ce-38190ddbcc94}"
    progid="Project1.UserControl1" />
</file>
```

If you have any experience working with COM controls, you will see that this element contains all of the usual information that is associated with a registered COM component.

Deploying ClickOnce Applications with Firefox

When you launch a ClickOnce application through a URL to the deployment manifest on the server (such as an initial deployment of a ClickOnce application to the client machine), a Web browser on the client machine will be used to request and download the deployment manifest (.application file). After the .application file has been downloaded, the ClickOnce launcher (fdsvc.exe) takes over and downloads the application manifest and the rest of the application files. However, at the time of this writing, only Internet Explorer will be configured properly after .NET 2.0 is installed on the client machine to properly handle a ClickOnce deployment. If you have a machine that has a different default browser, such as Firefox, then ClickOnce applications will not launch properly on the client machine by default.

There are a couple ways to solve this problem. The simplest is that if Internet Explorer is still installed on the client machine, but is not the default browser, users can open Internet Explorer and enter the URL to the deployment manifest in Internet Explorer's address bar. Or if you expose the link to the manifest on a Web page, you just need to give users instructions to make sure that they click on that link from inside Internet Explorer instead of their alternate browser.

Firefox in particular is a popular browser with developers, so efforts are underway in the Firefox community to solve this problem. At the time of this writing, there is one add-on for Firefox that fixes this problem so Firefox will launch ClickOnce applications properly. This add-on can be found on the Firefox add-ons site at https://addons.mozilla.org/firefox/1608/.

Launching a ClickOnce Application Programmatically

Another thing you might need to do sometimes is to automate the launching of a ClickOnce application. For example, you might have one ClickOnce application that needs to launch another ClickOnce application. You might need to do this if you are deploying a "suite" of applications through individual ClickOnce deployments, and you want those applications to be able to "activate" one another from a user's perspective. The only way to get ClickOnce to run an application is through the Start menu or a link to the deployment manifest on the server. You could launch a ClickOnce application programmatically using either one of these.

To launch a new application from another in .NET, you can use the `Process` class from the `System.Diagnostics` namespace. This class has a method on it named `Start` that has a couple of overloads. The main one you will use for this scenario is the overload of the `Start` method that simply takes a string parameter for the path to the executable you want to run.

In the case of a ClickOnce application, the path you will want to pass to the `Process.Start` method is either the URL to the deployment manifest on the server or the path to the Start menu shortcut that is created when an application is installed. If you pass the URL to the deployment manifest, `Process.Start` will fire up Internet Explorer (or the default browser) briefly and will request the deployment manifest through the browser. The browser window will then go away automatically after the deployment manifest is downloaded and the ClickOnce runtime takes over with the launch process. If you pass the path to the Start menu shortcut, then the application will launch the same way as if the user had clicked on the shortcut in the Start menu and no browser window will appear (or be involved in the launch).

The Start menu shortcuts are installed under the user's profile and have a file extension of .appref-ms (which does not show up in Windows Explorer when viewing the folder or shortcut properties). An example of the path to an installed ClickOnce application shortcut on my machine is

```
C:\Documents and Settings\Brian Noyes\Start Menu\Programs\Software
Insight\CustomInitSample.appref-ms
```

The following sample console application shows examples of using both launch approaches.

```
static void Main(string[] args)
{
    // Start through Start menu shortcut
    string path =
      @"C:\Documents and Settings\Brian Noyes\Start Menu
        \Programs\Software Insight\CustomInitSample.appref-ms";
    Process.Start(path);

    // Start through deployment manifest URL
    path =
      @"http://localhost/CustomInitSample/CustomInitSample.application";
    Process.Start(path);
}
```

Credit for this clever approach of launching the application through the Start menu shortcut goes to Shawn Weisfield from Orlando, Florida.[2]

Pushing ClickOnce Installations to the Client Machine

There is no prebuilt, centrally managed way to install ClickOnce deployed applications on a bunch of machines in an enterprise. However, there is Framework support for developing a tool to do so. The `System.Deployment` namespace has a class named `InPlaceHostingManager` that will let you programmatically perform a ClickOnce installation from another program. Using this class, you can write a little ClickOnce helper application

2. "Launching a ClickOnce Application from another ClickOnce Application," Shawn Weisfield, CodeProject.com, May 2006. www.codeproject.com/useritems/ClickOnce-Launcher.asp.

that an administrator could run on all the client machines in an enterprise (possibly in an automated way through something like Systems Management Server or Microsoft Operations Manager). This helper application would use the API exposed by the `InPlaceHostingManager` to point to the deployment URL of the ClickOnce application and get it preinstalled on each user's machine. Once that is done, then users could just find the application in their Start menu and would not have to go through the initial installation process of clicking on a link to the deployment manifest on the server themselves.

The `InPlaceHostingManager` class implements an asynchronous API to perform the install in three steps.

1. Download the manifests.
2. Check that application requirements are met.
3. Download the application files.

In order to use this class, there are a couple of prerequisites.

* The application that is being installed must be designed to run with full trust.
* The certificate with which the application manifests are signed must be configured as a trusted publisher on the client machine already (see Chapter 6).

Listing 8.3 shows a utility application contained in this chapter's download code named ClickOncePushInstall that lets you pass the URL of a ClickOnce deployment manifest to the application on the command line. When you do, the application will get installed silently on the client and will be ready to run from the Start menu the next time the user logs in from whose account this was run.

The code in Listing 8.3 first constructs an instance of the `InPlaceHostingManager` class in the `PushInstallApp` method. It then hooks up an event handler for the `GetManifestCompleted` event and invokes `GetManifestAsync` to start the download of the manifest. Once the download is complete and the event handler is called, the `AssertApplicationRequirements` method is called to ensure that the application's prerequisites and security requirements are met. There is some minimal error checking in the event handler, but that could be expanded to check for other kinds of exceptions if you want to do specific error messages for different exception types.

After the manifest is downloaded and checked, the next stage is to hook up an event handler for the `DownloadApplicationCompleted` event. After hooking up the handler, the `DownloadApplicationAsync` method is invoked to start the download process for the application files asynchronously. As long as that succeeds, you are done.

The code in Listing 8.3 uses an `AutoResetEvent` to keep the console process alive until the download process exits, either normally or abnormally. The call to `WaitOne` is a blocking call until some other thread calls `Set` on the event. Since all of the work of doing the downloads is done asynchronously using the `XXXAsync` methods in the `InPlaceHosting-Manager` class, the various error handlers or completion events `Set` the event at the appropriate time to unblock the main thread and let the process exit.

LISTING 8.3: Using the InPlaceHostingManager Class

```
class Program
{
    static InPlaceHostingManager m_Mgr = null;
    static AutoResetEvent m_Event = new AutoResetEvent(false);
    static void Main(string[] args)
    {
        if (args.Length != 1)
        {
            Console.WriteLine(
              @"You must pass the URL for the ClickOnce application
                you want to install");
            return;
        }
        string deploymentUrl = args[0];
        // Validate URL...
        PushInstallApp(deploymentUrl);
        m_Event.WaitOne(); // Blocks until download process complete
    }

    private static void PushInstallApp(string deploymentUrl)
    {
        try
        {
```

```
      m_Mgr = new InPlaceHostingManager(new Uri(deploymentUrl),
       false);
      m_Mgr.GetManifestCompleted += OnManifestDownloadDone;
      m_Mgr.GetManifestAsync();
   }
   catch (Exception ex)
   {
      Console.WriteLine("Error initiating manifest download: "
         + ex.GetType().ToString() + " - " + ex.Message);
      m_Event.Set();
   }

}

static void OnManifestDownloadDone(object sender,
   GetManifestCompletedEventArgs e)
{
   try
   {
      if (e.Error != null)
      {
         Console.WriteLine("Error downloading manifest: " +
            e.Error.GetType().ToString()
            + " - " + e.Error.Message);
         m_Event.Set();
         return;
      }

      try
      {
         m_Mgr.AssertApplicationRequirements();
      }
      catch (Exception ex)
      {
         Console.WriteLine(
           "Error verifying application requirements: " +
             ex.GetType().ToString() + " - " + ex.Message);
         m_Event.Set();
         return;
      }

      // Do the rest of the download
      m_Mgr.DownloadApplicationCompleted +=
         OnAppDownloadCompleted;
      m_Mgr.DownloadApplicationAsync();

   }
   catch (Exception ex)
   {
      Console.WriteLine("Error initiating application download: "
```

```
            + ex.GetType().ToString() + " - " + ex.Message);
        m_Event.Set();
    }
}

static void OnAppDownloadCompleted(object sender,
    DownloadApplicationCompletedEventArgs e)
{
    if (e.Error != null)
    {
        Console.WriteLine("Error installing application: " +
            e.Error.GetType().ToString() + " - " + e.Error.Message);
        m_Event.Set();
        return;
    }
    else
    {
        Console.WriteLine(
            "Application installed and ready to run.");
        m_Event.Set();
    }
}
}
```

Web Server ClickOnce Configuration

As mentioned in Chapter 2, ClickOnce supports deployment from any server that can serve up files via HTTP or a UNC file path. If your server is not running Windows 2000 Server with .NET 2.0 installed, or if you are having trouble getting ClickOnce applications to deploy correctly, one of the first things to check is that your server has the appropriate MIME file type mappings set up. Windows Server 2003 locks down most file content types by default, so you need to configure any Windows Server 2003 machine to allow ClickOnce deployments.[3]

ClickOnce deployments consist of a set of file requests: deployment manifest, application manifest, then each application file listed in the application manifest. The application files are usually renamed on the server to always end with the .deploy file extension. With that configuration, you just need to have the three file type mappings shown in Table 8.1.

---

3. For step-by-step instructions on configuring a Windows Server 2003 machine for ClickOnce deployments, see Knowledge Base Article Q326965 at http://support.microsoft.com/default.aspx?scid=kb;en-us;326965.

TABLE 8.1: MIME File Type Mappings

File Extension	MIME Content Type Mapping
.application	application/x-ms-application
.manifest	application/x-ms-application
.deploy	application/octet-stream

MSBuild ClickOnce Publishing

If you have not already been exposed to it, the build system used by Visual Studio 2005 is called MSBuild. This command line exposed system can be used to develop automated build scripts so that you don't always have to have a developer running builds from Visual Studio. If you are doing automated builds and also want to automatically generate the ClickOnce manifests and folder structure for a deployment using MSBuild, it is quite easy if the project is already configured for ClickOnce deployment from Visual Studio.

For the MSBuild publishing to work, you will need

- A Windows Application project that builds clean from a compilation perspective
- A ClickOnce signing certificate configured for the application

If these conditions are met, the only thing needed to generate the Click-Once manifests as part of an MSBuild build is to use the `/target:publish` command. For example, by running the following command line in the folder where the Visual Studio project file resides, you will get a build output folder under the \bin\Debug folder that contains the published ClickOnce manifests and application files.

```
msbuild /target:publish
```

You can also override project properties that are set in the project file using the `/property` switch. For example, to set the Publisher as part of the build, you can use

```
msbuild /target:publish /property:PublisherName=IDesign
```

Note that publishing from MSBuild just generates the publishing outputs—the deployment manifest, application manifest, and application files renamed with the .deploy extension. It does not copy the files to a publishing location the way that Visual Studio does, although that would be fairly easy to handle with a couple of other MSBuild tasks as part of your automated build.

For more in-depth examples, the best thing is to just dive into the MSBuild documentation and see what other task types there are, how to configure them, what options they accept, and so on.

Where Are We?

Well, done actually, other than a short appendix on ClickOnce differences in Windows Presentation Foundation. This chapter has covered a collection of assorted advanced topics that you can add to your toolbox of ClickOnce knowledge to help you tackle more complicated scenarios when needed. If you have absorbed the lessons from the rest of the chapters in this book, you can now consider yourself a ClickOnce expert!

The following are some of the key takeaways from this chapter.

- Startup parameters can be passed to a ClickOnce application via query string parameters only when the application is launched through a full URL to the deployment manifest on the server. You harvest the query string parameters by enabling the application to pass URL parameters when you publish it, and by including code that strips off the query string parameters from the `ActivationUri` property of the `ApplicationDeployment` instance when launched through ClickOnce.

- You can use the `IsFirstRun` flag on the `ApplicationDeployment` class to determine whether you need to run any custom initialization code in your application when it first installs.

- There are several ways to debug ClickOnce-related code in an application, including using the Debug in Zone features in Visual Studio, attaching the debugger to the ClickOnce launched application after it is already running, or by using the `Debugger.Break` statement to invoke the debugger when needed.

- You can deploy just about any executable using ClickOnce, or any file that can be run from the command line, by deploying a lightweight shim application that simply calls `Process.Start`, calling the additional file that you deploy as an application file along with the shim application.

- You can easily deploy COM and ActiveX components along with your ClickOnce application by using Reg-Free COM, which adds appropriate entries to your ClickOnce manifests when you publish so that the components will self-register on the client machine.

- You can configure any Web server to host ClickOnce published applications as long as you set up the right MIME type mappings for the .application, .manifest, and .deploy files.

■ A ■
ClickOnce Deployment of WPF Applications

W INDOWS PRESENTATION FOUNDATION (WPF) is the new vector-based rich graphics model for developing Graphical User Interface (GUI) applications in .NET 3.0.[1] WPF lets you write Windows applications that can present rich media, 3D models, animation, and other advanced rendering approaches with much less code than preceding technologies. WPF fundamentally changes the way you develop Windows applications. With WPF, you will program against a whole new API that is based around a rich composition model of elements, and you will do a lot of that programming in a new XML-based programming language: eXtensible Application Markup Language (XAML).

WPF can also present traditional Windows application user interface elements such as buttons, text boxes, list boxes, and so on. However, for the current time and at least until the next version of Visual Studio (code-named "Orcas") releases, there is not a fully functional designer for laying out and coding interactive data applications. There are Beta versions of the new design tools for WPF, but in my opinion they are not ready for production coding at this time. So for the near future, Windows Forms is still

---

1. For detailed information on WPF development, see *Essential Windows Presentation Foundation* by Chris Anderson (Addison-Wesley, 2006).

going to be the technology of choice for designing most business applications, or at least the lion's share of functionality in them. For those applications that need to do things like present rich image processing, 3D models, or animation as a portion of their UI, you can embed WPF controls in Windows Forms. You can also embed Windows Forms controls in WPF applications as well.

Let's take a look at how you can use ClickOnce and WPF applications, keeping in mind that WPF is a new technology initiative and the features and APIs will continue to evolve over the next couple years.

This appendix was written against the June 2006 Community Technical Preview (CTP) of .NET 3.0. The landscape is constantly changing with the .NET (previously WinFx) Betas and CTPs. Expected release for this technology is around the timeframe that this book will be coming out in print, so you should at least have a released .NET 3.0 Framework by that time with WPF in it. However, the Visual Studio designer will still be in Beta or CTP form at that point, so it is unclear whether you will be able to follow along with the step-by-step instructions later in this appendix by that time or not. The top-level concepts and approach described in this appendix should not change, but some of the Visual Studio labeling and features most likely will.

WPF Anatomy 101

The way a WPF application "look and feels" to end users fits the normal paradigm of a Windows Forms-based application: you launch it, it runs, you interact with it in its windows. Under the hood, on the most general level of abstraction—its code, its controls, its components, its interactive facilities—end users may never realize (or care) that parts of it are being rendered in a graphics card with processing horsepower undreamed of even five years ago.

But development of WPF applications and controls or components requires new techniques for developers. WPF uses a number of new design strategies that you have to get used to in order to write WPF applications. For some of you, the new design strategies may mirror and fit in nicely with your current design practices. For others, particularly if you are "rooted" in Windows Forms development where code is tightly coupled to controls, you may have some stretching of your "mental models" ahead of you.

WPF separates layout and appearance from behavior and logic to a much greater degree than Windows Forms does. Windows and controls in WPF are composed of **elements,** the lowest-level construct for the chunks of code that a UI is composed of. Elements can contain other elements. Controls are themselves elements, as are windows. The way that elements present themselves on the screen can be specified separately from the way they behave through styles and themes. WPF supports themed user interfaces, animation, 3D rendering, and presentation of rich media (images, video, and audio) as part of its core capabilities.

WPF uses DirectX under the covers to offload as much of the graphics rendering to the video card as possible. The net result is that WPF takes greater advantage of the full capabilities of the latest platforms available today and in the future, and will get the bits rendered on your display as quickly as possible.

WPF applications can be composed of code only, code plus eXtensible Application Markup Language, or even just XAML for simple applications. Normally the static layout will be specified through XAML, and the dynamic aspects hooked up to the XAML through code. XAML is a markup language for describing the visual state of user interfaces, controls, components, and their links to the compiled code that gets executed at runtime. The end result of building a WPF application is just compiled, managed code that runs using the .NET Framework and common language runtime.

WPF supports two major styles of applications: normal Windows applications and WPF applications that run in browsers. Normal WPF Windows applications are directly analogous to Windows Forms applications. A WPF Web Browser Application is a hybrid somewhere between a traditional ASP.NET-based Web page-oriented application and a Windows Forms application. If you have been exposed to running Windows Forms controls in a Web page, the model is somewhat similar to that. It is much like running ActiveX controls in a Web page, but without all the negative security and system stability impacts that ActiveX controls can cause.

ClickOnce Deployment of WPF Applications

There are two different modes of ClickOnce deployment for WPF applications. If you've read this book, you have already thoroughly explored the capabilities of ClickOnce with Windows Forms applications. WPF Windows applications deploy with ClickOnce in exactly the same way that Windows Forms applications deploy with ClickOnce if you choose the installed mode (available offline and online). You design and build your application in Visual Studio; set its publishing, signing, and security properties; and publish the application just like you have done with many other examples in this book. You can apply what you have learned about ClickOnce to WPF immediately by choosing the installed mode (available offline and online).

What's new with WPF and ClickOnce is the new application style of a "Web Browser Application." These applications have the full capabilities of WPF available like a locally installed WPF application. However, they run in a Web browser and are launched by addressing the application through the address bar or a link. This should sound familiar—online-only ClickOnce applications are launched by addressing the application through the browser as well. But online-only ClickOnce Windows Forms applications don't run in the browser once they have launched, whereas WPF Web Browser Applications do.

As a result, you will only use the selection for online-only ClickOnce with WPF Web Browser Applications. You cannot deploy a normal WPF application as online only; you can only deploy them as installed applications.

One big difference between WPF Web Browser Applications and Windows Forms online-only ClickOnce applications has to do with the security model. With Windows Forms applications, even online-only applications can elevate their permissions through either user prompting or the Trusted Publishers' mechanism. Web Browser Applications can only perform actions that are allowed in the Internet security zone, and there is no way to elevate their permissions. If you set higher permissions on the project properties editor's Security tab, the application will be blocked from launching in the browser.

Another difference with WPF Web Browser Applications is that the deployment manifest that gets generated and to which you point your users no longer has an .application file extension; it has an .xbap extension instead. It basically works the same way and contains the same information as any other ClickOnce deployment manifest, but the different file extension lets the ClickOnce runtime for WPF recognize the application as a browser application and launch it in the browser instead.

Sample Web Browser Application Walkthrough

To give you a quick sense of what the differences are in the deployment and runtime experience when deploying WPF Web Browser Applications, this section will quickly put together a WPF application and deploy it as a Web Browser Application. This example will not illustrate any deep WPF concepts. It is a simple "Hello WPF" application to demonstrate the online deployment of the application with ClickOnce.

This section assumes you have the June CTP of .NET 3.0 installed. That includes the runtime components, the Windows Vista SDK, and the Visual Studio "Orcas" Development Tools. By the time you read this, this release will be out of date, the names of the pieces you need to download will likely have changed, and the experience in Visual Studio might be slightly different, so you may have to do some modifications to follow along with whatever bits you are using.

Creating the Application

You first need an application to deploy. To quickly create a simple application to deploy, do the following.

1. Open Visual Studio and select File > New > Project from the menu.
2. Select the appropriate project type for WPF (Windows (WinFx) in the June CTP), and select the Web Browser Application type from the templates on the right (see Figure A.1).
3. Name the project **HelloWPFApp** and click OK.
4. Your project should look something like Figure A.2 in Solution Explorer. You will have two XAML files—one for the Application class itself and one for the first page in the application. There will also be a publisher certificate file (.pfx file) in the solution already that will be used to sign the manifests when you publish the application.

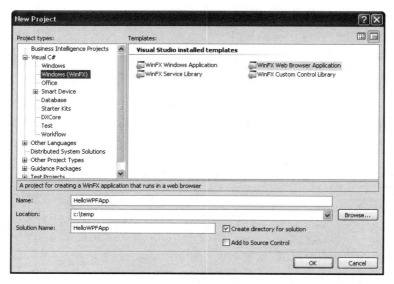

FIGURE A.1: Selecting the Web Browser Application Project Type

FIGURE A.2: Project in Solution Explorer

5. Double-click on the Page1.xaml file to open the form in the designer. You will see that there is no window border for the form because it will run in the browser. Drag and drop a Label control from the toolbox onto the form (see Figure A.3).

6. Click and drag the bottom right selector (small round dot in Figure A.3) to expand the size of the label.

7. Select the Content property in the Properties window and replace "Label" with **Hello from WPF**.

8. Build the application to make sure all is well.

9. Run a debug session and the browser will start up and load the application. Visual Studio automatically attaches the debugger to the browser

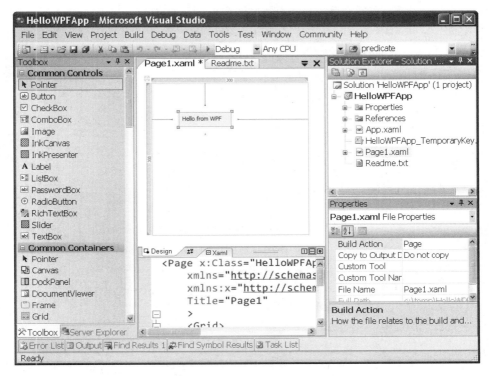

FIGURE A.3: Adding a Label Control to the Form

process so you can debug the application through Visual Studio while it is running in the browser. You will see something like Figure A.4. Notice that the address loaded into the browser is an .xbap file, which is the WPF file extension for the deployment manifest. The application was compiled, published to the debug output folder, loaded into the browser, and the debugger attached to the browser for you.

Publishing the Application

You already published the application when you did your debug run. When the application is built, the deployment and application manifest files are generated and signed in the build output folder so that you can run a debug session using the local file path to the .xbap file. But if you want to test it the way it will be run more directly, you will want to publish the application to IIS or another remote server and test it from there the same way that you do with other ClickOnce applications.

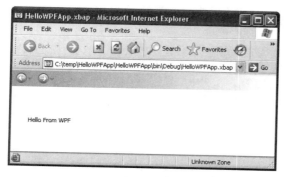

FIGURE A.4: Debugging in the Browser

To publish the application, you use the Publish command from the Build menu as you do for Windows Forms applications. In the June CTP, the Publish Location property in the Publish settings is just set to a sub-folder of the build output folder, so you will need to change that to an HTTP path to get it to publish to IIS.

To try this out, do the following.

1. Go to project properties editor (from the Project menu, choose Hel-loWPFApp Properties).
2. Select the Publish tab.
3. Enter **http://localhost/HelloWPFApp** for the Publish Location.
4. Click the Publish Now button.
5. After publishing, open a browser and type in the address to the .xbap file (e.g., http://localhost/HelloWPFApp/HelloWPFApp.xbap). You will see an embedded download progress dialog in the browser (see Figure A.5).
6. The application will be running in the browser as before.

Where Are We?

This appendix gave you a quick preview of how you use ClickOnce to deploy WPF applications and the special considerations that come into play when you use the new Web Browser Application model. The offline/installed application ClickOnce deployment works exactly the same for

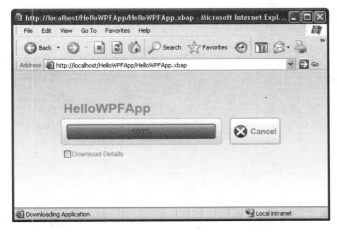

FIGURE A.5: Launching the Published Application

WPF applications as it does for Windows Forms applications. The process of publishing and launching the application is the same.

The other option is to deploy browser applications, which are WPF forms that run inside the Web browser. WPF Web Browser Applications require a different project type and a different approach to coding the application to account for the different execution environment, but they can still be published via ClickOnce. After publishing, you launch them by entering a URL to the deployment manifest (.xbap in the case of WPF Web Browser Applications).

The following are some of the key takeaways from this appendix.

- Installed/offline ClickOnce WPF applications publish and deploy in exactly the same way as Windows Forms applications.
- Online-only WPF Web Browser Applications run in a browser.
- Web Browser Applications rely on ClickOnce to publish and deploy them. They require a deployment manifest and application manifest, along with all the application files, to be published to the deployment server like any other ClickOnce application.
- The file extension for a WPF Web Browser Application deployment manifest is .xbap instead of .application.
- The specifics of WPF development will likely change some by the time this book is published.

Index

Microsoft .NET Development Series

.NET Framework Standard Library Annotated Reference
Volume 1: Base Class Library and Extended Numerics Library

Brad Abrams

0321154894

.NET Framework Standard Library Annotated Reference
Volume 2: Networking Library, Reflection Library and XML Library

Brad Abrams
Tamara Abrams

0321194454

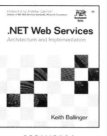

.NET Web Services
Architecture and Implementation

Keith Ballinger

0321113594

A Developer's Guide to SQL Server 2005

Bob Beauchemin
Dan Sullivan

0321382188

Visual Studio Tools for Office
Using C# with Excel, Word, Outlook, and InfoPath

Eric Carter
Eric Lippert

0321334884

Visual Studio Tools for Office
Using Visual Basic 2005 with Excel, Word, Outlook, and InfoPath

Eric Carter
Eric Lippert

0321411757

Graphics Programming with GDI+

Mahesh Chand

0321160770

Framework Design Guidelines
Conventions, Idioms, and Patterns for Reusable .NET Libraries

Krzysztof Cwalina
Brad Abrams

0321246756

ASP.NET 2.0 Illustrated

Alex Homer
Dave Sussman

0321418344

The .NET Developer's Guide to Directory Services Programming

Joe Kaplan
Ryan Dunn

0321350170

Essential C# 2.0

Mark Michaelis

0321150775

The Common Language Infrastructure Annotated Standard

James S. Miller
Susann Ragsdale

0321154932

Essential ASP.NET
with Examples in C#

Fritz Onion

0201760401

Essential ASP.NET
with Examples in Visual Basic .NET

Fritz Onion

0201760398

Building Applications and Components with Visual Basic .NET

Ted Pattison
with Dr. Joe Hummel

0201734958

.NET Internationalization
The Developer's Guide to Building Global Windows and Web Applications

Guy Smith-Ferrier

0321341384

The Visual Basic .NET Programming Language

Paul Vick

0321169514

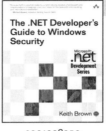

THIS BOOK IS SAFARI ENABLED

INCLUDES FREE 45-DAY ACCESS TO THE ONLINE EDITION

The Safari® Enabled icon on the cover of your favorite technology book means the book is available through Safari Bookshelf. When you buy this book, you get free access to the online edition for 45 days.

Safari Bookshelf is an electronic reference library that lets you easily search thousands of technical books, find code samples, download chapters, and access technical information whenever and wherever you need it.

TO GAIN 45-DAY SAFARI ENABLED ACCESS TO THIS BOOK:

- Go to **http://www.awprofessional.com/safarienabled**

- Complete the brief registration form

- Enter the coupon code found in the front of this book on the "Copyright" page

Addison
Wesley

If you have difficulty registering on Safari Bookshelf or accessing the online edition, please e-mail customer-service@safaribooksonline.com.